# ICE Cream

Hilary Walden

CLB

Colour Library Books

CLB 4419
This edition published 1995 by Colour Library Books
© 1994 Colour Library Books Ltd, Godalming, Surrey
All rights reserved
Printed and bound in China
ISBN 1-85833-370-9

# Contents

# Flavours

| | | | |
|---|---|---|---|
| 18<br>*Almond* | 32<br>*Blackcurrant* | 44<br>*Chocolate* | 62<br>*Gooseberry* |
| 20<br>*Apple* | 34<br>*Blueberry* | 48<br>*Coconut* | 64<br>*Grape* |
| 22<br>*Apricot* | 36<br>*Brown Bread, Cereals* | 50<br>*Coffee* | 66<br>*Grapefruit* |
| 26<br>*Avocado* | 38<br>*Butterscotch, Caramel, Fudge* | 54<br>*Cranberry* | 68<br>*Hazelnut* |
| 28<br>*Banana* | 40<br>*Cherry* | 56<br>*Dried, Candied & Glacé Fruits* | 70<br>*Herbs, Flowers, Leaves* |
| 30<br>*Blackberry, Loganberry* | 42<br>*Chestnut* | 60<br>*Ginger* | 72<br>*Honey* |

# Introduction

Home-made ices and ice creams have a subtlety, purity and intense flavour that just don't exist in commercial products. And, thanks to modern refrigeration techniques, the whole range of iced desserts from refreshing, palette-cleansing sorbets to rich, foaming mousses, from light-as-air soufflés to crystal-clear water ices can be prepared at home by any cook who is capable of whipping cream or making an egg custard.

This had been a virtual impossibility until recently. Although the Romans are known to have cooled their wines with snow and ice, it was the mid-16th century before their freezing technique was improved upon – by a Sicilian who discovered that adding saltpetre to ice would speed up the process and produce a smoother, less crystalline iced mixture. The next development was in the second half of the 18th century when egg yolks and sugar syrups were used as the basis for ices and ice creams. Iced desserts became more elaborate, and bombes and other spectacular creations were served at banquets and fashionable dinner parties.

However, the majority of cooks still did not make their own ices. Although ice cream churns were comparatively early inventions (and have their devotees to this day), they required a supply of ice and were laborious to use – the mixture had to be churned by hand for almost an hour. As a result, most people had to be content with what saloons and ice cream parlours could supply.

Making ice creams and ices at home only became really practical during this century. Today ice creams can be frozen quickly and easily in a freezer or in the ice-making compartment of a refrigerator – all that is necessary is to whisk the mixture occasionally while it freezes. Electric machines, the latest development in ice cream making, even do away with this chore.

Food processors, blenders and electric hand whisks are useful additional aids. However, there are so many kinds of ice that special equipment is not essential. Iced mousses, iced soufflés and very rich mixtures can be left to freeze undisturbed with no risk that ice crystals will form and make the mixture hard. Freezing an ice in individual containers speeds up the process and also ensures a smooth texture.

One of the delights of making your own iced desserts is the opportunity it gives to experiment with your favourite ingredients, alone or combined with contrasting or complementary flavours. Try fresh-tasting yogurt to add a tang and only a few calories, low-fat cottage or curd cheese (or tofu, its vegetarian equivalent) for lightness, egg yolks for richness and a golden glow, cream – single, soured, whipping, double or crème fraîche – for creaminess, or full-fat cheese for smoothness.

Home-made ices can also be made from the most basic of store cupboard ingredients – canned milk, for example – and are perfect for using up gluts of cheap, or even free, fruit. On the other hand, the flavour and texture of the finest, most luxurious and exotic ingredients are emphasized to delicious effect.

# Author's Notes

The main part of the book consists of recipes for ices and ice creams grouped by flavour, in alphabetical order. These are followed by a selection of popular, old-fashioned recipes and finally a section on iced desserts for special occasions.

Many of the recipes include dessert or serving suggestions, varying from easy combinations of different-flavoured ices to more complicated creations and simple ideas in which presentation is all-important. Cakes, biscuits, decorations, etc. called for in these suggestions are highlighted with an asterisk, and recipes for these are in the final part of the book (pages 145 to 152). Here you will also find instructions for the various techniques (pages 152 to 155) involved in some of the more complicated desserts. Check with the index for exact page numbers, if necessary. I have deliberately not given quantities in these suggestions as they can be varied in order to use up leftover ices.

The book starts with information on making ice creams and ices, using an old-fashioned ice cream churn as well as refrigerators, freezers and electric machines. This is followed by a section on ingredients and where and how you can make substitutions. Then there are definitions of the various kinds of iced mixtures and, finally, recipes for traditional ice cream bases.

Many recipe groupings start with a simple idea for combining the main flavour with these basic recipes or, provided they mix well, with a good-quality commercial vanilla ice cream.

I have included a selection of recipes for low-fat and other dietary needs. These are all highlighted in the index.

As all products labelled 'yogurt' must, by law, be natural and 'live' (unless described as U.H.T.), I prefer to call unflavoured, unsweetened yogurts 'plain' rather than the quite frequently used 'natural' which I feel is confusing (it refers to the flavour rather than the product).

Measurements for honey and syrups are given by weight as I find this the most accurate way of measuring larger quantities. Line the scale pan with cling film or greaseproof paper and slightly warm the honey or syrup before weighing it – nearly every trace will go into the mixture.

I have given both imperial and metric measurements throughout. They are not interchangeable, so remember to use either one or the other.

I would like to thank everyone who has contributed towards making this book possible – too many to mention individually. My very real gratitude goes to the friends and colleagues who made and tested different versions of the recipes, and to the many people who designed and organized the project from the beginning, who typed and edited, corrected and photographed, who answered endless queries and generously offered advice.

I'd also like to give a special vote of thanks to ICTC and Sheila Fitzjones, their representative in Britain, who lent us the miraculous Gelato-Chef which made our work so much easier. Ice cream making machines are still relatively new. As most people use either the freezing compartment of a refrigerator or a freezer, the recipes in this book have been written with them in mind.

Finally, I would like to dedicate this book to ice cream fanatics everywhere – a largely anonymous group of people whose enthusiasm in searching out (and often creating) the perfect parfait, the fruitiest sorbet, the finest frozen mousse and the simplest, most subtle of flavours has made this book possible.

# Making Ice Creams and Ices

Refrigerators, freezers and electric ice cream makers have revolutionized ice cream making at home. Instead of relying on time-consuming techniques using ice cream churns or even ice blocks, it has now become a practical proposition to make the most delicious of all ice creams – home-made ones.

## Ice Cream Churns

The introduction of ice cream churns was an important development. They are, however, tedious and laborious to operate.

Ice cream churns consist of two containers. One fits inside the other and the space between is packed with chipped ice and rock salt in the proportion of three parts ice to one part salt. (The salt lowers the temperature at which the iced mixture freezes and so produces a smoother result.)

The procedure is as follows: first fit the inner metal container into position in the bucket. Pack in the ice and salt tightly in layers. Leave for a few minutes until the metal container is well chilled. Pour the chilled ice cream mixture into the container, filling it not more than three-quarters full. The ice and salt must be well above the level of the ice cream mixture. Fit in the paddle or 'dasher'. Line the lid with greaseproof paper and put it in place. Start turning the handle, slowly at first and then at a steady pace until turning becomes difficult. This will take about 30 to 45 minutes. At this point remove the paddle and scrape it down. This is when nuts, candied fruits, etc, are added. Wipe the lid, put it back on and plug the hole with a cork.

Pour away the melted ice from the bucket and replace it with more ice and salt. Cover the bucket with newspaper or a rug and leave for at least an hour for the ice cream to mature.

## Refrigerators and Freezers

Making ices in the ice-making compartment of a refrigerator or in a freezer calls for a certain amount of attention but is not time-consuming or complicated. It is a good idea to use maximum freezing power because ice cream has a smoother texture if it is frozen quickly. Also, chill all the equipment and ingredients such as yogurt, fruit juices and purées before starting.

### Freezers

After the mixture has been made, pour it into a suitable freezing container – a shallow metal tray is best – and cover it with its own lid or with foil. Freeze rich aerated mixtures immediately, but if the mixture is not rich or aerated, chill it for 30 minutes or so in the refrigerator, then place it in the freezer.

When there is a border of hardening mixture about an inch (2.5 cm) deep round the container, beat the mixture thoroughly, preferably with a hand-held electric beater or in a food processor or blender, to prevent the formation of ice crystals and to incorporate air into the mixture. But try not to let it melt. Return the mixture to the freezing container, and put it back in the freezer compartment. Leave for 20 to 60 minutes, depending on the ingredients in the mixture and the temperature of the freezer, before beating again. If necessary beat a third or even a fourth time during the freezing process to ensure the end result is really smooth. If the mixture freezes too hard between beatings, place it in the refrigerator until it is soft enough to whisk.

If the mixture is frozen in a shallow container, transfer it to a chilled bowl each time it is beaten. This is unnecessary if you have used a larger container – but remember to scrape the ice crystals that have formed on the sides and base towards the centre.

Freeze until firm. Freezing times will vary according to the recipe and the amount to be frozen. A 2 pint (1.1 litre) mixture will take from two to three hours to set depending on the recipe. When it is ready reset the dial to its normal setting.

### Refrigerators

Recipes in this book refer to making ice creams in freezers, but they can just as easily be made in the ice-making compartment of a refrigerator.

Set the refrigerator dial at the coldest setting (usually the highest number on the dial) at least an hour before making the iced mixture, and remember to remove items that might freeze, such as eggs, from the main compartment.

Freeze the mixture until firm. Freezing times vary. A general guide is that a 1 pint (600 ml) mixture for four people will take up to four hours to freeze completely, and a 2 pint (1.1 litre) mixture for six to eight people will take up to five hours. Once the ice is made, return the refrigerator to its normal setting.

Whether using a freezer or the ice-making compartment of a refrigerator, it is almost always necessary to allow the ice to soften slightly in a refrigerator.

The more airy and rich a mixture, the less attention it will require. The time spent whisking can be reduced by using a food processor or by making a rich mixture, and can even be eliminated entirely by making very rich ice creams, iced mousses or soufflés, or by freezing the mixture in individual dishes (this speeds up the freezing process). As a general rule, add flavourings before folding in the whisked egg whites and whipped cream.

## Electric Ice Cream Makers

Electrically driven ice cream makers or sorbetières take the effort out of making ice creams.

There are two types of machine: free-standing ones and those that are placed in a freezer or in the ice-making compartment of a refrigerator. Both types have an electrically driven paddle that slowly and rhythmically turns the mixture to prevent the formation of ice crystals. In most models these will lift up automatically when the mixture reaches a consistency that can be safely left undisturbed, on average after about 10 to 15 minutes for a sorbet, and 20 to 30 minutes for an ice cream, depending on the recipe and machine. This is the time to add nuts, dried, crystallized and glacé fruits, etc., and to fold in whisked egg whites and whipped cream. Sorbets should just about be ready for serving at this point, but ice creams will need another one to two hours before they are completely frozen. They can be left *in situ* during this time, provided the paddles are removed, or the mixture can be turned out into a container, covered and returned to the freezer.

The free-standing ice cream makers produce very good results and allow you to use less rich ingredients and still get smooth, soft ices. Although they are fairly large – and fairly expensive – they are the ultimate labour-saving device for ice cream enthusiasts.

'Freezer' machines are less expensive but the results are not as good, often no better than if the ice had been made by hand. Also, they take up room in a freezer and must be placed on a flat surface to work efficiently, which can be a problem if you are using a chest freezer or the ice-making compartment of a refrigerator. The interiors of some of these machines are in the shape of a decorative mould so that the ice is ready for serving.

A modern, electrical (and reasonably priced) version of the old-fashioned ice churn is also available. A free-standing model, it has an outer, plastic container that is packed with a mixture of iced water, ice cubes and salt and an inner, metal container for the ice cream ingredients. The iced mixture will freeze after about 25 to 50 minutes, depending on the richness of the ingredients; it is ready when the ice cream seems to wrap itself around the paddle. It is generally necessary to top up the level of the iced water/ice/salt mixture after about 15 to 20 minutes and the ice cream must be removed once it has reached the correct consistency.

As the recipes in this book describe ices made in a freezer, follow the manufacturer's instructions if you are using an ice cream machine.

## Serving

Before serving, most machine or hand-made ices should be transferred to the main part of the refrigerator, unless a recipe specifically states otherwise. Allow the ice to 'come to' and soften slightly; if it is too cold it will be hard and will not taste as good as it should. The actual time needed in the refrigerator depends on the richness of the mixture, whether it has been kept in a freezer or the ice-making compartment of a refrigerator, how long it has been kept, the size of the container, the temperature in the refrigerator and how soon after serving it will be eaten.

On average, allow about 30 to 40 minutes for sorbets and simple ice creams, and 20 to 30 minutes for rich ice creams, iced mousses and soufflés; add a little extra time if the ice has been kept for a while in the freezer. Mixtures frozen in small moulds should be left in the refrigerator for only five to ten minutes and can be served immediately if they are rich or aerated or if the surroundings in which they will be eaten are warm.

For special occasions, ices can be frozen in all kinds of decorative moulds; for suggestions, see page 155.

## Storage

Because home-made ices do not contain all the additives found in most commercial products, they cannot be kept for the same length of time. Water ices and sorbets, especially fruit ones, are at their best if eaten within a day of being made. Light mixtures such as yogurt ices should, preferably, be eaten after a couple of days, while rich ices may benefit from two or three days' 'ripening' in a freezer. At the most, they should not be kept for longer than a few weeks if their full glory is to be savoured. Granitas, of course, should be eaten at once.

# Ingredients

Part of the fun of making ice creams at home is choosing the ingredients and deciding whether or not you want to improve on classical flavours or to try out new combinations to create an exotic or unusual taste.

## Cream

Cream is synonymous with ice cream, even though it is not used in all ices. Originally double cream was used, but nowadays we use the whole spectrum of creams. In ascending order of richness, these are: soured, single, whipping cream, crème fraîche and, of course, double cream. The different fat contents of these creams influence the texture as well as the flavour of the finished dish. The higher the fat content, the smoother and richer the ice cream; soured cream and crème fraîche will vary the flavour.

In recipes where no particular type of cream is specified, you can use whichever you prefer, depending on the style of ice you want to make and what is available. Even when a particular type of cream is specified, another can usually be substituted, although there will be a change in the texture and flavour. As fat masks other flavours it may be necessary to adjust other ingredients accordingly.

**Single cream** has a lower fat content than double cream and cannot be whipped on its own.

**Double cream** is thick textured, mild tasting and ideal for whipping.

**Soured cream** is made from single cream with the addition of bacterial culture; its hint of acidity adds sharpness to flavouring.

**Whipping cream** has a fat content in between single and double cream, and can of course be whipped. Make a home-made version by mixing equal quantities of single and double cream.

**Crème fraîche** is becoming increasingly available. However, if it is not obtainable an acceptable imitation can be made. Stir some soured cream with double the quantity of whipping cream (or double cream for a richer version). Heat the cream slowly to 194°F (90°C), pour it into a jar and leave overnight in a warm place, about 167°F (75°C). Next day, stir the cream and keep in the refrigerator. Crème fraîche tends to thicken on standing so it may be necessary to add a little milk when whipping it.

## Milk

As fat is a determining factor in the smoothness of an ice, it follows that recipes made with milk will become harder and more crystalline than those made with cream. Milk ices should therefore be whisked more frequently and more vigorously during freezing to prevent the build-up of ice crystals. Additional fat, in the form of unsalted butter or egg yolks, will soften the ice, as will the inclusion of almost calorie-free whisked egg white and dissolved gelatine.

**Evaporated milk and sweetened condensed milk** are sometimes recommended as 'everyday' alternatives to cream. However, because they taste of caramel (and the condensed version is very sweet), they are best used in ices with a complementary flavour – butterscotch or caramel – or when making ices for children.

If you are substituting evaporated or condensed milk for ordinary milk or cream, reduce the amount of sugar and taste the prepared mixture to see whether other flavourings need to be increased.

**Skimmed milk and buttermilk** contain even less fat than ordinary milk and must be thoroughly whisked during freezing. 'Cultured' buttermilk is more widely available than the uncultured variety. It is slightly thicker and adds a refreshing acidity that blends particularly well with fruit ices.

**Soya milk** is a vegetarian, lower calorie, no cholesterol version of milk and can easily be substituted for cow's milk. It produces softer, more 'creamy' ices as it has more body. Commercial soya milks are often, though not always, sweetened and nearly all are mild flavoured. (They remind me of milk that has been very thoroughly blended with ground almonds.)

Soya milk ices can be made almost as creamy as cream ices by the inclusion of 2 tablespoons (2 × 15 ml spoons) oil (such as sunflower oil) to a ½ pint (300 ml) soya milk.

## Yogurt

Ices made with yogurt have a fresh, light flavour. Most are low in calories, with the exception of those using yogurt made from full-cream milk or with added cream. These full-fat yogurts add smoothness and richness to ices, and retain their characteristic fresh flavour when frozen; use them if calorific value is of no consequence. Add gelatine or whisked egg white to mixtures with low-fat yogurt to soften an ice which would otherwise be hard.

Yogurt can be used on its own or blended with milk, creams or soft cheeses.

## Soft Cheeses

Although soft cheeses are not traditionally used, I find them extremely useful for their versatility and for the variety and interest they add.

**Cream cheese** has a fat content ranging from 45 to 65 per cent, and is made from drained set cream. Other soft cheeses are made from drained milk curds and their fat content ranges from almost nothing to 45 per cent. They can be used on their own, in combination with each other, or with milk, cream or yogurt, to vary flavour and texture. Beat high-fat soft cheeses until they are smooth before use.

**Cottage and curd cheese** should be sieved to ease blending and for a smooth iced mixture.

**Ricotta** is a soft, mild Italian cheese traditionally made from sheep's milk and now also made in other countries and from cow's milk. It has a low fat content.

**Quark** is a fresh cheese with a low fat content.

**Tofu** is a vegetarian cheese. Made from soya milk, it does not contain any cholesterol and is low in calories and fat. Its protein content is high. It can be used in any recipe to replace soft cheese. Beat tofu with other ingredients until smooth.

**Fromage frais** is a French cheese with a lighter texture and sharper flavour than British or American soft cheeses. It can have a high or low fat content. Fromage frais with a high fat content can be used as a rich alternative to yogurt.

**Fromage blanc** is also from France and has a very low fat content.

## Sugar

As well as its obvious sweetening effect, sugar also affects the hardness of an ice. Too much will make the ice sickly and will also hamper freezing. But bear in mind that freezing takes the edge off sweetness, and if too little sugar is used the ice will not be as soft and will be lacking in flavour.

It is important to dissolve sugar completely by stirring over direct heat, or by whisking either over heat or vigorously with an electric beater. Undissolved crystals give a grainy texture to the frozen mixture.

**Granulated sugar** can be used if the mixture is heated directly.

**Caster sugar** can be used when the mixture is unheated because its small crystals dissolve comparatively easily.

**Icing sugar** is excellent in fresh fruit sorbets.

**Brown sugar** affects both the colour and taste. Although its crystals are slow to dissolve, it adds a new character and dimension to flavours such as rhubarb, apple, butterscotch and brown bread.

**Sugar syrup** is the foundation of water ices and of most sorbets, iced mousses and soufflés.

Put the sugar and water in a heavy-based pan and heat gently. Stir until the sugar has dissolved then bring to the boil. Allow to boil for the length of time specified or until the required temperature is reached. The best way to test this is to use a special thermometer. The proportion of sugar to water will vary according to the sweetness and richness of the other ingredients and the type of ice being made.

**Fructose** is the sweetest of the natural sugars. It cannot be used to make a sugar syrup, but can otherwise be substituted for sugar. You need about half as much fructose as other sugars, unless the mixture is particularly acidic, and it is therefore useful if you want to reduce your sugar intake. Fructose is suitable for diabetics, who should take medical advice on exact amounts.

## Liquid Sweeteners

These give a smooth texture and add individuality and character to ices.

**Honey** has a distinctive flavour. Use a mild-tasting one that will not dominate the ice, unless it is being used as a flavour in its own right.

**Maple syrup** is very popular both as a flavour and as a sauce. It has a smooth, rich, sweet taste. The best grades are pale in colour.

**Corn syrup** may be light or dark, the former being the more refined and less strongly flavoured. Twice as much syrup as sugar is needed to obtain the equivalent degree of sweetness.

**Molasses** is a dark, thick, sticky syrup that combines acidity with sweetness.

## Artificial Sweeteners

Many artificial sweeteners and very low-calorie sweeteners lose their sweetness when heated above a certain temperature or beyond a certain time, and can only be used in recipes that do not require sugar syrup. When making a custard-based ice cream, add the sweetener to the custard after it has cooled.

Normally, 3–4 artificial sweeteners are the equivalent of 1 ounce (25 g) sugar, but some sweeteners react differently with different flavours and ingredients; they are enhanced by fruits, for example, and diminished by fats. Tasting and personal experience with a particular sweetener are the best guides to the amounts to use. Remember, though, that the mixture should taste a little over-sweet before it is put into the freezer.

## Eggs

The more yolks there are in a recipe, the richer and smoother the frozen mixture will be. When making custard-based mixtures the number of egg yolks used is generally in inverse proportion to the amount and richness of the cream – in other words, the creamier the custard, the fewer the egg yolks. Whisked yolks will add lightness to a mixture. If you are following a recipe that only requires egg yolks, save the whites and use them to make an iced soufflé.

Egg whites also add lightness, and in addition they prevent the formation of ice crystals, and make a mixture go further. They are usually whisked to maximize their effectiveness.

# Definitions

The definitions that follow are based on classical sources such as Larousse and Escoffier, combined with accepted modern usage. However, most of them are frequently misused or very loosely applied.

## Ice Cream

This is a generic name for a frozen mixture, always containing milk or cream, based on egg custards, cream or mousse. It is often used to describe a variety of desserts, including iced mousses, iced soufflés and parfaits.

## Water Ice

A water ice is a simple frozen dessert containing a basic sugar syrup, and flavouring such as fruit juice or puréed fruit. It may also be flavoured with wine, spirit, liqueur, coffee or an infusion of tea, spices, blackcurrant leaves, and so on.

## Granita

A granita is made from a light sugar syrup and flavouring. Ice crystals are allowed to form during freezing, giving the ice a grainy, granular texture. It should be served when it is still at the slushy, semi-frozen stage.

## Sorbet, Sherbet

Smoother than a granita, a sorbet is made from a more concentrated sugar syrup and is beaten several times during the freezing process to break up the ice crystals and create a smooth texture. It should be served when it is one stage harder than being slushy, and just capable of being moulded.

A sherbet is a sorbet that has egg white or cream or milk added. (In the latter two cases, the dishes could also be referred to as cream ices or milk ices respectively.)

There is a great deal of confusion about the terms sorbet and sherbet. The traditionalists, Larousse and Escoffier, always added egg white to the mixture in the form of Italian meringue, which is made by whisking boiling sugar syrup into the egg whites, then cooking the mixture over a pan of hot water. They called this a sorbet. They also called the mixture a sorbet when they added cream to it as it was just beginning to freeze. But nowadays a sorbet need not contain egg white or cream, and many of today's top chefs claim that these ingredients mask the clarity and purity of both the flavour and appearance of a sorbet. In fact modern fruit sorbets are the simplest and freshest tasting of all ices, as they often contain no more than fruit and neat sugar – not even syrup.

To add to the confusion, the English translation of sorbet from French cookbooks is sherbet. Yet the term sherbet is more frequently used in the United States than in England, which usually uses the term sorbet whether or not egg white, cream or milk is added.

## Spoom, Spumone

A spoom is a very light, frothy water ice made from fruit juice or wine. It is based on a more highly concentrated sugar syrup than a sorbet, and includes twice the amount of Italian meringue.

## Iced Mousse

An iced mousse is a light-textured but fairly rich dessert based on well-whisked egg yolks, often with the addition of whipped cream and sometimes with egg whites. It is often frozen in the dish in which it will be served with a deep collar of greaseproof paper supporting the mousse as it stands above the rim. The collar is removed when the mousse is served and the exposed sides can be decorated with, for example, finely chopped nuts or macaroons.

## Iced Soufflé, Soufflé Glacé

An iced soufflé is a very light, airy dessert made from whisked egg whites and whipped cream. Like iced mousses, a soufflé is often frozen in the container in which it is to be served.

## Parfait

The term parfait originally referred to a coffee-flavoured dessert made from whisked egg yolks and sugar syrup, but today it is used much more widely, and encompasses all manner of other flavours.

## Bombe

A bombe is a shaped and layered moulded iced dessert. It is composed of two or more flavours or textures, with the harder ice forming an outer case – the jacket – and the softer ice the inner layer. The name comes from the mould that is traditionally used. It is dome shaped and made of copper, which, being a good conductor of heat or cold, not only accelerates the freezing but also makes unmoulding easier. It has a tight-fitting lid, and should have small feet or a screw-on pedestal so that it stands upright during freezing. This facilitates turning out the dessert because the hole left when the pedestal or feet are removed releases any air lock that may have formed.

There are over 50 classical combinations, most of which are named after people, many of them women. They include Coppelia (coffee jacket with a praline centre), Marie-Louise (chocolate jacket with a vanilla centre), Josephine (pistachio inside a coffee jacket).

Whenever I see these names I wonder who inspired them and whether there was any particular reason for the choice of ingredients. What qualities did Miss Heylett have that brought forth vanilla surrounded by raspberry to create the Miss Heylett bombe? And what of the portentous Gladstone bombe with its outer jacket of ginger and interior mixture flavoured with gin, diced ginger and angelica?

## Cream ice

A cream ice is a sorbet mixture enriched with whipped cream.

# Basic Mixtures

These are the foundations on which iced mixtures are created.

## Whipped Cream

The simplest base for an ice cream is whipped cream with sweetening and flavouring folded in. You can use double or whipping cream, a combination of the two, or a combination of single and double creams.

Folded-in whisked egg white makes for a less rich ice cream and increases the number of portions that can be served. A cream base is particularly good with fruits, especially berries such as raspberries, loganberries, blueberries and cranberries.

### Basic Whipped Cream Ice Cream

*½ pint (300 ml) cream (double, whipping or crème fraîche; double and single; double and whipping; double and soured cream)*
*Approximately 4 ounces (100 g) caster sugar*
*Flavouring: about ¾–1 pound (350–450 g)/8 fluid ounces–½ pint (225–300 ml) fruit, puréed and sieved; 4 ounces (100 g) whole or segmented fruit; approximately 4 ounces (100 g) chopped nuts; other flavourings to taste*
*1 teaspoon (5 ml spoon) genuine vanilla essence (see method)*
*1–2 egg whites, optional*

In a cold bowl, whisk the cream until soft peaks are formed. Fold in the sugar and flavouring; only add the vanilla if it will blend with, or complement, the main flavouring. If egg white is used, whisk in a clean bowl until stiff but not dry, then fold into the cream. No beating is necessary during freezing, and 'softening' will take 15–35 minutes depending on the flavouring used. Allow the longer time for ice creams flavoured with fruit.

Serves 4 (without egg whites), 5 (1 egg white), 6 (2 egg whites)

## Custard

An egg custard base produces very smooth, velvety ice creams and is the foundation most frequently used in professional kitchens. The custard can be made with milk or single, whipping or double cream or a mixture of any of these. The richness of the custard will determine the smoothness of the ice cream. For a lighter result, fold whipped cream or whisked egg whites into the custard when it is cold. Yolks or whole eggs can be used to thicken the custard. The richer creams normally require fewer egg yolks, although some very luxurious recipes call for a high proportion of both cream and egg yolks.

A custard base can be made from a number of different ingredients combined in all sorts of different ways, but this is the recipe I find most useful.

### Basic Custard Ice Cream

*½ pint (300 ml) single cream*
*Vanilla pod*
*3 egg yolks*
*Approximately 3–4 ounces (75 g–100 g) caster sugar*
*Flavouring: ¾–1 pound (350–450 g)/8 fluid ounces–½ pint (225–300 ml) fruit, puréed and sieved; 3–4 ounces (75–100 g) chopped nuts; other flavourings to taste. See note below*
*¼ pint (150 ml) whipped cream*

In a heavy-based saucepan gently heat the single cream with the vanilla pod to just on simmering point. Remove from the heat, cover and leave to infuse for 15–30 minutes, depending on the strength of vanilla flavour required.

In a bowl, whisk the egg yolks with the sugar until thick and light, then strain in the warm cream. Return the mixture to the rinsed pan and cook over a very low heat, stirring constantly, until the custard thickens, but do not allow it to boil as it will curdle.

As this stage of making the ice cream is very critical and a little tricky, until you are experienced you may prefer to use a longer but safer method for cooking the custard. Place the bowl containing the egg yolks and milk over a pan of hot, not boiling, water. Put the pan over low heat and whisk constantly until the sauce thickens and coats the back of a spoon.

Whether cooking the custard in a saucepan or in a bowl, plunge the base immediately into cold water to prevent further cooking, or pour the custard into a cold bowl.

Straining the custard will give a smoother-textured ice cream. Leave the custard to cool. To prevent a skin forming, cover the surface closely with cling film or greaseproof paper, or stir the sauce occasionally.

Pour the mixture into a shallow metal container, cover and chill for 30 minutes before freezing. Beat twice if making the ice cream by hand. Fold in the whipped cream after the last beating, if making by hand, or when the machine has stopped working if using an electric ice cream maker. 'Soften' for 15–35 minutes, depending on the richness of the custard and the flavouring used. Allow the longer time if a fruit flavouring is used.

Serves 4–6

**Note:** Acidic fruits such as puréed rhubarb and plums and most other flavourings are usually added when the custard is cold (acidic fruits must never be mixed into a hot custard otherwise it will curdle). The exceptions are ingredients such as vanilla essence, coffee and spices, which impart extra flavour if they are added to the custard while it thickens.

# Iced Mousse

As with the custard base, ingredients and the proportions in which they are used can vary. The following is a good, basic recipe.

**Basic Iced Mousse**

*3 egg yolks*
*Approximately 3 ounces (75 g) sugar*
*Flavouring: ¾–1 pound (350–450 g)/8 fluid*
*    ounces–½ pint (225–300 ml) fruit, puréed and*
*    sieved; 3–4 ounces (75–100 g) chopped nuts; other*
*    flavourings to taste*
*1 teaspoon (5 ml spoon) vanilla essence (see method)*
*½ pint (300 ml) cream, whipped*
*2 egg whites*

In a large bowl placed over a pan of hot, not boiling, water whisk the egg yolks with the sugar until well increased in volume, thick and light in colour.

Remove the bowl from the heat, and continue to whisk the mixture until it is cool, then fold in the flavourings and whipped cream with a metal spoon. Only add the vanilla if it will blend with, or complement, the main flavouring. Whisk the egg whites until stiff, then lightly fold them into the mixture until the ingredients are evenly blended.

Spoon the mixture into a shallow metal container, mould or cake tin. Cover and freeze until firm. No beating is necessary and 'softening' will take 15–35 minutes depending on the type of flavouring and size of the container.

Serves 4–6

# Iced Soufflé, Soufflé Glacé

The following is a good, all-round base.

**Basic Iced Soufflé**

*4 egg whites*
*4 ounces (100 g) caster sugar*
*Flavouring: ¾–1 pound (350–450 g)/8 fluid*
*    ounces–½ pint (225–300 ml) fruit, puréed and*
*    sieved; 4 ounces (100 g) whole or segmented fruit;*
*    3–4 ounces (75–100 g) chopped nuts; other*
*    flavourings to taste*
*1 teaspoon (5 ml spoon) vanilla essence (see method)*
*½ pint (300 ml) cream, whipped*

Place a large bowl over a pan of hot, not boiling, water. Put in the egg whites and whisk with the sugar to a stiff meringue. The heat improves the stability of the meringue.

Remove the bowl from the heat, and continue whisking until the meringue is cold. Lightly fold in the flavouring and whipped cream. Only add vanilla if it will blend with, or complement, the main flavouring. Spoon into a shallow metal container, mould, cake or loaf tin or prepared soufflé dish. Cover.

If the surface of the mixture is above the level of the dish, place the dish in a rigid container with a lid. Alternatively, leave the soufflé to freeze until firm, then protect the top with a dome of foil.

Serves 4–6

# Sorbet

I have not included a basic sorbet recipe, as the proportions of sugar to water for the sugar syrup will vary according to the recipe – fruits differ in the amount of sugar and water they contain. Quantities are given in individual recipes.

Adding Italian meringue, as in the classic sorbets of Escoffier and Larousse, is a comparatively lengthy process that few domestic cooks, and certainly not all professional ones, feel inclined to undertake when making a sorbet.

The easier alternative is simply to whisk a couple of egg whites as normal then fold or whisk them into the mixture when it is halfway through the freezing process. Egg whites will prevent hard ice crystals from forming, a function that dissolved gelatine will also perform.

The more water there is in a recipe, the more vital egg whites are for its success. They are also more necessary if a sorbet is prepared by hand rather than with the assistance of an electric ice cream maker or sorbetière. The more watery mixtures also require more frequent and more vigorous beating during freezing.

Chilling the mixture before freezing it, and using shallow metal trays, will help to make the mixture freeze smoothly.

# Almond

Almonds can be used in all their different forms to make a wide range of ices, each with very different characteristics. They can be flaked or finely or coarsely chopped for different degrees of crunchiness, or ground for smoothness. Plain nuts add a delicate flavour, or they can be toasted for a more nutty taste – bake peeled almonds in a moderate oven (350°F, 180°C, gas mark 4) for about 8–10 minutes. Almonds can also be made into praline, which can be crushed to a fine powder or broken into pieces to add crackle.

**Simple Almond Ice Cream**
Add 4 ounces (100 g) finely chopped toasted almonds to any of the Basic Recipes*, or to a good-quality bought vanilla ice cream.

## Biscuit Tortoni

*½ pint (300 ml) single cream*
*½ pint (300 ml) double cream*
*2 ounces (50 g) icing sugar, sifted*
*4 ounces (100 g) ratafias, crushed*
*¼ pint (150 ml) sweet sherry*
*Crushed ratifias, for decoration*

Put the creams in a bowl and whisk until soft peaks form then whisk in the sugar lightly. Fold in the ratafias and sherry.

Pour the mixture into a 2 pound (900 g) loaf tin, cover and freeze until firm.

About 30 minutes before serving, turn the tortoni out on to a cold plate and leave in the refrigerator. Sprinkle the crushed ratafias over the top just before serving.

Serves 4–6

**Serving suggestions**
*Serve with Chunky Marmalade Sauce* or a Compote* of fresh apricots or oranges.*

## Kulfi (Indian almond ice cream)

*1 pint (600 ml) milk*
*2 eggs*
*2 egg yolks*
*4 ounces (100 g) caster sugar*
*2 ounces (50 g) ground almonds*
*¼ teaspoon (1.25 ml spoon) almond essence*
*1 tablespoon (15 ml spoon) rose water*
*½ pint (300 ml) double or whipping cream*
*Finely chopped pistachio nuts, for decoration*

In a heavy-based pan, bring the milk slowly to boiling point. Whisk the eggs, egg yolks and sugar together in a bowl until evenly blended then gradually stir in the hot milk. Pour the mixture back into the pan and cook gently, stirring constantly, until the custard thickens – do not let it boil. Leave to cool.

Stir in the ground almonds, almond essence and rose water. Pour the mixture into a container, cover and chill for at least 30 minutes. Freeze until slushy. Beat well in a bowl.

Whip the cream in a bowl until soft peaks form and fold into the custard. Spoon back into the container, cover and freeze until firm. Leave for at least 12 hours.

About 30 minutes before serving, transfer to the refrigerator. Serve decorated with the nuts.

Serves 8

**Flavour variations**
*Add 2 ounces (50 g) chopped pistachio nuts.*

*Use half milk and half cream instead of all milk for the custard.*

## Praline Ice Cream

*8 fluid ounces (225 ml) milk*
*3 egg yolks*
*8 ounces (225 g) caster sugar*
*½ pint (300 ml) cream, whipped*
*4 ounces (100 g) shelled, unpeeled almonds*

In a heavy-based pan, gently bring the milk to simmering point. Whisk the egg yolks and half the sugar together in a bowl until thick and light then gradually stir in the milk. Pour the mixture back into the rinsed pan and cook gently, stirring constantly, until the custard thickens but do not allow it to boil. Leave to cool. Fold in the cream, spoon into a container, cover and freeze until just firm.

To make the praline, dissolve the remaining sugar in 3 fluid ounces (75 ml) water in another heavy-based pan. Add the almonds and boil for about 10 minutes until golden brown. Pour on to a cold, oiled surface and leave to set. Place the praline in a thick polythene bag or clean cloth and hit with a rolling pin to break it into small pieces.

Beat the ice cream in a bowl, and fold in all but 1 tablespoon (15 ml spoon) of the praline. Spoon the mixture back into the container, cover and freeze until firm.

About 20 minutes before serving, transfer the ice cream to the refrigerator. Serve decorated with the reserved praline.

Serves 4–5

**Serving suggestion**
*Serve with Cigars Russe*.*

**Dessert suggestion**
*Make into a bombe with Traditional Coffee Parfait (page 50) or Fresh Coffee Ice Cream (page 53) in the centre. Decorate the outside of the turned-out bombe with whipped cream flavoured with coffee liqueur, coffee dragées or sugar-coated coffee beans and crushed praline.*

## Toasted Almond
## Ice Cream

*4 ounces (100 g) full fat soft cheese, beaten*
*8 ounces (225 g) cottage or curd cheese, sieved*
*1 ounce (25 g) ground almonds*
*2 tablespoons (2 × 15 ml spoons) orange or lemon*
  *juice*
*4 ounces (100 g) icing sugar*
*3 ounces (75 g) toasted almonds, finely chopped*
*1 egg white*

*For decoration*
*Toasted flaked almonds*
*Coffee sugar crystals*

Put the soft cheese and the cottage cheese into a bowl and beat until smooth. Beat in the ground almonds and orange or lemon juice and sugar. Stir in the toasted almonds. Whisk the egg white until stiff and fold into the mixture.

Spoon the mixture into individual dishes. Cover and freeze until firm.

About 30 minutes before serving, transfer the ice cream to the refrigerator and decorate with the flaked almonds and sugar crystals.

Serves 4

### Serving suggestion
*Pile scoops into individual glass dishes and decorate with whipped cream and toasted, flaked almonds. Top with a wafer biscuit.*

**Additional recipes using almonds:** Iced Orange and Almond Mousse (page 85), Coffee Almond Ice Cream (page 52).

Both eating and cooking apples are suitable for ices, but it is important to use only well-flavoured varieties like Cox's Orange Pippins, the French Reinettes and Bramley's Seedlings. To add colour and texture to the ice, leave the skin on the apples when you purée them in a blender or through a *mouli legume*. Alternatively, if the fruit is peeled, or the skin is not in good condition, add a few drops of green colouring to the mixture. You can use bought apple purée or thick apple sauce – canned, frozen or bottled – if fresh fruit is not available.

**Simple Apple Ice Cream**
Add ½ pint (300 ml) apple sauce, bought or home-made, to any of the Basic Recipes*.

## Apple and Walnut Ice Cream

*1 pound (450 g) dessert apples, peeled, cored and*
 *sliced*
*2 ounces (50 g) unsalted butter*
*2 tablespoons (2 × 15 ml spoons) orange juice*
*1 ounce (25 g) caster sugar*
*2 eggs, separated*
*¼ pint (150 ml) double cream*
*¼ pint (150 ml) single cream*
*2 ounces (50 g) walnuts, chopped*
*1 red-skinned apple, thickly sliced and dipped in*
 *lemon juice, for decoration*

Cook the apples gently in a covered saucepan with the butter and orange juice until soft. Add the sugar and reduce to a purée. Whisk the egg yolks until light and frothy and stir into the purée. Return the mixture to the pan and cook over a low heat, stirring, until the mixture thickens slightly. Pour into a bowl and leave to cool.

Whisk the creams together in a bowl until thick and fold into the purée with the nuts. Turn into a 2 pound (900 g) loaf tin, cover and freeze for about 1–1½ hours until half frozen.

Turn the ice cream into a bowl. Whisk the egg whites until stiff but not dry and carefully fold into the ice cream. Return the ice cream to the loaf tin, cover and freeze until firm.

About 30–40 minutes before serving, turn out on to a cold plate, decorate with the apple slices and leave in the refrigerator.

Serves 5–6

### Serving suggestion
*Spoon into the centre of small, hollowed-out brioche, sprinkle with chopped stem ginger and serve with a sauce of cream whipped with ginger wine.*

## Apple and Elderflower Ice Cream

*12 ounces (350 g) cooking apples, peeled, cored and*
 *chopped*
*1 ounce (25 g) butter*
*2 ounces (50 g) sugar*
*2 sprigs of elderflowers*
*Finely grated zest of 1 orange*
*¼ pint (150 ml) plain yogurt*
*2 egg whites*
*6 small elderflower sprigs for decoration*

Gently cook the apples, butter, sugar, elderflowers and orange zest in a covered saucepan until the apples are very soft. Leave to become cold. Remove the elderflowers and purée the apple mixture. Chill the mixture then fold in the yogurt. Spoon into a container, cover and freeze to the slushy stage.

Whisk the egg whites in a bowl until stiff but not dry. Beat the apple mixture in a bowl and fold in the egg whites.

Spoon into a 1 pound (450 g) loaf tin, cover and freeze until firm.

About 30 minutes before serving, unmould the ice cream on to a cold plate and leave in the refrigerator. Decorate with elderflowers just before serving.

Serves 6

## Apple and Apricot Ice Cream

*8 ounces (225 g) good-quality dried apricots, soaked*
 *overnight in the minimum of water*
*1 pound (450 g) cooking apples, peeled, cored and*
 *coarsely chopped*
*Finely grated zest and juice of 1 lemon or orange*
*4 ounces (100 g) light muscovado sugar*
*2 large eggs, separated*
*¼ pint (150 ml) cream, whipped*

Drain the apricots and measure ½ pint (300 ml) of the soaking liquor. Put this with the apricots and apples and the zest and juice into a saucepan and simmer gently, covered, until the apricots are tender. Purée the fruit with the liquor and return to the rinsed pan. Add the sugar and egg yolks and cook over a low heat, stirring constantly, until the mixture thickens. Leave to cool, stirring occasionally. Pour into a container, cover and freeze until just becoming firm. Turn into a bowl and beat well.

Fold in the cream. Whisk the egg whites until stiff but not dry and fold into the fruit cream.

Spoon the mixture back into the container, cover and freeze until firm.

About 30 minutes before serving, transfer the ice cream to the refrigerator.

# Apple and Raisin Ice Cream

*2 ounces (50 g) raisins*
*3 fluid ounces (75 ml) calvados or cider, warmed*
*1¹/₂ pounds (700 g) Bramley apples, peeled, cored and roughly chopped*
*Juice and grated zest of 1 orange*
*4 ounces (100 g) caster sugar*
*4 egg yolks*
*¹/₂ pint (300 ml) single cream*

*For decoration*
*Slices of apple, preferably of a red-skinned variety, dipped in lemon juice*
*Small mint leaves*

Soak the raisins in the calvados or cider. In a covered saucepan cook the apples with the orange juice and zest and half the sugar over a low heat until a dryish purée is formed. Leave to become cold.

Put the egg yolks and remaining sugar in a bowl and whisk together until thick and light. In a heavy-based pan, heat the cream to simmering point then gradually whisk into the egg yolks. Pour the mixture back into the pan and cook over low heat, stirring constantly until the custard thickens – do not allow it to boil. Leave to cool then mix with the apples. Pour into a container, cover and freeze until just becoming firm. Transfer to a bowl, beat well and fold in the raisins, calvados or cider. Spoon the mixture into a 2¹/₂ pound (1.25 kg) loaf tin, cover and freeze until firm.

About 20 minutes before serving, turn the ice cream out on to a cold plate and leave in the refrigerator. Decorate with the apple slices and mint leaves just before serving.

Serves 6–8

### Serving suggestions
*Serve as a sundae with Toasted Oat and Nut Ice Cream (page 36), poached apricots and Chunky Marmalade Sauce\*.*

*Spoon into the centre of a ring doughnut soaked in calvados or whisky and studded with hazelnuts. Just before serving spoon over a little cider sauce: use the Wine Sauce\* substituting medium dry cider for the wine. Decorate with fine strips of orange peel.*

---

### To reduce your sugar intake
Replace the sugar with half the quantity of **fructose** or with an **artificial sweetener**, provided the recipe does not call for a sugar syrup. Normally, 3–4 artificial sweeteners are the equivalent of 1 ounce (25 g) sugar but always check that you have the right degree of sweetness. Artificial sweeteners must be added to custard-based ice creams after the custard has cooled.

---

# Apple Cream Ice

*1¹/₂ pounds (700 g) cooking apples (preferably Bramley's) peeled, cored and sliced*
*6 ounces (175 g) sugar*
*Thinly grated zest of 1 lemon*
*Juice of 2 lemons*
*1¹/₂ inch (4 cm) cinnamon stick*
*Green colouring, optional*
*2 fluid ounces (50 ml) brandy, optional*
*¹/₄ pint (150 ml) cream, whipped*

Poach the apples with the sugar, lemon zest and juice, cinnamon and 1 pint (600 ml) water until tender. Remove the cinnamon stick and reduce the mixture to a purée. Leave to cool.

Add the colouring and brandy, if you are using them, and freeze until just becoming firm around the edges. Beat the mixture in a bowl, fold in the cream and pour back into the container. Cover and freeze until firm.

About 30 minutes before serving, transfer the cream ice to the refrigerator.

Serves 4

### Serving suggestion
*Serve with Burnt Honey Sauce\*.*

### Dessert suggestion
*Line a loaf tin with the cream ice. Fill the centre with Blackberry Sorbet (page 30) or Cider Sorbet (page 134).*

# Apple Sauce Yogurt Ice

*¹/₂ pint (300 ml) very thick apple sauce, chilled*
*Large pinch of grated nutmeg*
*Large pinch of ground cinnamon*
*2 ounces (50 g) icing sugar*
*Finely grated zest and juice of 1 orange*
*¹/₂ pint (300 ml) thick plain yogurt, whipped*

Put the apple sauce in a bowl with the nutmeg, cinnamon and icing sugar and whisk until light. Fold in the orange zest and juice and then the yogurt. Pour into individual containers, cover and freeze until firm.

About 25 minutes before serving, transfer the ice cream to the refrigerator.

Serves 4

**Additional recipe using apples:** Chestnut and Apple Meringue Mousse (page 42).

# Apricot

All the forms in which apricots are available – fresh, dried, canned and even good-quality apricot jam – are suitable for making ices. Each imparts its own character – dried apricots give a deep richness, fresh fruit the taste of sun and summer and canned apricots a sweeter, less pronounced (but very smooth) fruit flavour. About 1¼ pounds (550 g) fresh apricots will yield ½ pint (300 ml) purée.

**Simple Apricot Ice Cream**
Add 8 ounces (225 g) canned fruit, drained and chopped, to any of the Basic Recipes*.

## Dried Apricot Ice Cream

*4 ounces (100 g) dried apricots, soaked overnight in*
  *cold, strained tea*
*Long strip of lemon peel*
*3 egg yolks*
*3 ounces caster sugar*
*½ pint (300 ml) cream, whipped*
*2 egg whites*

Cook the apricots and lemon peel in just enough soaking liquid to cover until the fruit is soft. Remove the peel and purée the apricots with the soaking liquid. Boil to reduce, if necessary, until you have ¼ pint (150 ml) purée. Set aside to cool.

Whisk the egg yolks with the sugar in a bowl placed over hot water until they are thick and light. Remove the bowl from the heat and continue whisking until the mixture is cool. Fold in the apricot purée and the cream.

Whisk the egg whites until stiff, then lightly fold them into the apricot mixture. Spoon into a container, cover and freeze until firm.

About 30 minutes before serving, transfer the ice cream to the refrigerator.

Serves 4–6

## Apricot Sorbet

*12 ounces (350 g) very ripe apricots, stoned*
*Juice of 1 large lemon*
*4 ounces (100 g) icing or caster sugar*

Purée the apricots into a bowl. Add the lemon juice and whisk in the sugar with a wire whisk. Pour into a container, cover and freeze until firm, beating 3 times at 45-minute intervals. About 30 minutes before serving, transfer the sorbet to the refrigerator.

Serves 4

**Serving suggestion**
*Place small spoonfuls in the centres of cold ripe apricots from which the stones have been removed. For an extra special touch sprinkle the apricots with a little cognac.*

## Apricot and Wine Ice Cream

*12 large, plump dried apricots*
*Approximately 8 fluid ounces (225 ml) dry white wine*
*1 ounce (25 g) honey*
*Approximately 2 ounces (50 g) sugar*
*Long strip of lemon peel*
*4 ounces (100 g) full fat soft cheese*
*8 ounces (225 g) cottage cheese, sieved*
*2 egg whites*
*Crushed Gingersnaps*, for decoration*

Put the apricots in a bowl and pour in the wine, there should be sufficient to cover the fruit, and soak for 8 hours or overnight.

Put the apricots and the soaking wine in a saucepan. Add the honey, sugar and lemon peel and simmer gently for about 20 minutes until tender. Remove the lemon peel and purée the fruit and liquor – if there is a lot of excess liquor reduce it by boiling rapidly.

Beat the cheeses together in a bowl until very smooth then beat in the apricot purée. Taste and adjust the sweetness if necessary. Spoon into a container, cover and freeze to the slushy stage. Beat well in a bowl. In another bowl, whisk the egg whites until stiff but not dry and fold into the apricot mixture. Return to the container, cover and leave until firm.

About 35–40 minutes before serving, transfer the ice cream to the refrigerator. Serve each portion with some crushed gingersnaps sprinkled over.

Serves 4

## Apricot Ice Cream (with pie filling)

*½ pint (300 ml) cream, whipped*
*Approximately 14 ounce (400 g) can apricot pie*
  *filling*
*1 egg white*

Whisk the cream until soft peaks are formed, then fold in the pie filling. In a clean bowl whisk the egg white until stiff but not dry and fold into the cream and apricot mixture. Pour into a container, cover and freeze until firm.

About 20 minutes before serving, transfer the ice cream to the refrigerator.

Serves 4–5

---

**To reduce your calorie intake**
**Tofu** can be substituted for soft cheese; beat with the other ingredients until smooth. It has no cholesterol and is low in fat.

# Iced Apricot Mousse

3 ounces (75 g) sugar
3 egg yolks
1½ pounds (700 g) fresh apricots, stoned, puréed and
   sieved
3–4 ounces (75–100 g) icing sugar
Juice of 1 lemon
½ pint (300 ml) crème fraîche
3 tablespoons (3 × 15 ml spoons) brandy, optional

Put the sugar and 4 fluid ounces (100 ml) water in a
heavy-based saucepan and stir to dissolve. Bring to the
boil and boil until the temperature reaches 234°F
(112°C).

Meanwhile, whisk the egg yolks until thick in a bowl.
Slowly pour in the syrup, whisking constantly.
Continue whisking until the mixture is very thick and
light.

Flavour the apricot purée with icing sugar and
lemon juice and fold into the egg yolks.

In another bowl, whip the crème fraîche with the
brandy, if you are using it, until thick, and fold into the
apricot mixture. Pour the mixture into a container,
cover and freeze until firm.

About 30 minutes before serving transfer the
mousse to the refrigerator.

Serves 5–6

### Dessert suggestion
*Make into a bombe or freeze in a can or loaf tin, with
a jacket of Champagne Ice Cream (page 132).
Decorate with Benedictine-flavoured whipped cream
and Chocolate Shapes\*.*

# Iced Apricot Soufflé

2 egg whites
4 ounces (100 g) icing sugar
½ pint (300 ml) cream, whipped
8 fluid ounces (225 ml) apricot purée

Put the egg whites in a bowl and whisk until stiff.
Gradually add the sugar, whisking well after each
addition, and continue whisking until a thick meringue
is formed. Fold in the cream and apricot purée until
just evenly blended. Pour into a container, cover and
freeze until firm.

About 20 minutes before serving transfer the soufflé
to the main part of the refrigerator.

Serves 4

### Serving suggestion
*Serve in Coupelles\* to which 1 ounce (50 g) finely
chopped flaked almonds have been added.*

# Apricot Ice Cream

½ pint (300 ml) fresh apricot purée
Squeeze of lemon juice
Approximately 3 ounces (75 g) icing sugar
½ pint (300 ml) cream, whipped

Flavour and sweeten the purée with lemon juice and
sugar, adjusting the amounts of each to give a good
balance. Fold the cream into the purée and pour into a
container. Cover and freeze until firm, beating twice at
hourly intervals.

About 30 minutes before serving transfer the ice
cream to the refrigerator.

Serves 4–5

### Serving suggestion
*After the second beating, pour the mixture into a
sandwich or flan tin with a removable rim, lined with
crushed hazelnut Macaroons\*. Just before serving,
remove the rim and surround with poached, halved
apricots, their centres filled with a swirl of brandy-
flavoured whipped cream and topped by half a
hazelnut.*

# Apricot Yogurt Ice

4 ounces (100 g) dried apricots
2 ounces (50 g) clear honey
½ pint (300 ml) plain yogurt
2 egg whites, whisked until stiff
Fine strips of twisted lemon peel, for decoration

Soak the apricots in ½ pint (300 ml) hot water for at
least 4 hours or overnight.

In a saucepan cook the apricots gently in the soaking
liquor with the honey for about 20 minutes until soft.
Purée the apricots with the liquor and the yogurt.
Leave to cool completely. Fold in the egg whites and
pour into individual containers. Cover and freeze until
firm.

About 20 minutes before serving transfer the ice to
the refrigerator. Decorate each portion with a twist of
lemon peel as it is served.

Serves 4

### Low calorie version
*Substitute fructose, or a low calorie or artificial
sweetener for the honey, adding it to the cold purée.*

### Dessert suggestion
*Swirl with an equal quantity of Banana Custard Ice
Cream (page 28), Butterscotch Ice Cream (page 39) or
Maple Mousse (page 81). Freeze in a can or in an ice-
cube tray with the ice-cube divider in place.*

# Apricot Jam Water Ice

*1 pound (450 g) good-quality apricot jam*
*2 fluid ounces (50 ml) brandy or whisky*
*2–3 tablespoons (2–3 × 15 ml spoons) lemon juice*

Mix the jam with the brandy and ½ pint (300 ml) water in a blender or food processor. Pass through a sieve and add lemon juice to taste. Spoon the mixture into a container, cover and freeze until firm, beating twice at hourly intervals.

About 30 minutes before serving, transfer the water ice to the refrigerator.

Serves 4

### Dessert suggestion
*Remove the stones of fresh apricots, enlarge the cavities, and fill with the water ice. Sandwich the apricot halves together, brush with beaten egg white then roll in desiccated coconut. Place in the freezer for about 45 minutes. Transfer to the refrigerator about 5 minutes before serving.*

# Quick Apricot Ice Cream

*Approximately 14 ounce (400 g) can apricots*
*Approximately 14 ounce (400 g) can condensed milk*
*Juice and finely grated zest of 1 large, juicy lemon*
*¼ pint (150 ml) cream, whipped*

Drain the apricots, purée the flesh and make up to 12 fluid ounces (350 ml) with some of the juice. Whisk the purée with the condensed milk and lemon juice and zest in a bowl or mix in a food processor or a blender. Fold in the cream. Pour the mixture into a container cover and freeze until firm, beating well after about 1½ hours.

About 30 minutes before serving transfer the ice cream to the refrigerator.

Serves 4–6

### Serving suggestion
*Serve with a Compote\* of lemons and Gingersnaps\*.*

# Apricot and Ratafia Ice Cream Dessert

*15 ounce (425 g) can apricots*
*2 ounces (50 g) caster sugar*
*2 eggs, separated*
*2 teaspoons (2 × 5 ml spoons) gelatine*
*½ pint (300 ml) double cream*
*1 ounce (25 g) dark ratafia biscuits*
*2–3 tablespoons (2–3 × 15 ml spoons) Amaretto liqueur*

*For decoration*
*Whipped cream*
*Ratafias*

Purée the apricots with their syrup. Put the purée in a small saucepan with half the sugar and bring to the boil. Beat the egg yolks and gradually whisk in the purée. Return the mixture to the pan and heat gently, stirring and taking care not to let it boil, until it thickens slightly. Pour into a bowl, sprinkle the gelatine over the surface and stir it in so that it dissolves. Leave in a cool place until beginning to set.

Put the egg white in a bowl and whisk to a stiff foam. Gradually whisk in the remaining sugar to make a soft meringue. In another bowl, whip the cream to a similar consistency and fold it into the purée followed by the meringue.

Lightly stir the ratafias and Amaretto together and leave until the liqueur is just absorbed. Fold into the apricot-cream mixture and spoon into a polythene bowl. Cover and freeze until firm.

To serve, turn out the ice cream by gently pulling the sides of the bowl away from it so that it loosens then invert it on to a cold plate and shake. Decorate with whipped cream and ratafias. Leave in the refrigerator for about 15–20 minutes.

Serves 8–10

**Additional recipes using apricots:** Apple and Apricot Ice Cream (page 20), Apricot and Hazelnut Meringue Cake (page 140)

---

### To reduce your sugar intake
Replace the sugar with half the quantity of **fructose** or with an **artificial sweetener**, provided the recipe does not call for a sugar syrup. Normally, 3–4 artificial sweeteners are the equivalent of 1 ounce (25 g) sugar but always check that you have the right degree of sweetness. Artificial sweeteners must be added to custard-based ice creams after the custard has cooled.

# Avocado

With their smooth, rich flavour and texture, and delicate green colour, avocados are ideal ingredients for both sweet and savoury ices. They soon lose their colour once they have been peeled and cut, so wait until the last moment before preparing them. It is also important to freeze the mixture as soon as it is ready – citrus juices will delay discoloration but will not stop it altogether – in order to preserve its attractive appearance.

## Iced Avocado Mousse

*1 large ripe avocado*
*Juice of ½ lemon*
*4 ounces (100 g) full fat soft cheese, softened*
*¼ pint (150 ml) soured cream*
*Finely grated rind of 1 orange*
*2 ounces (50 g) icing sugar*
*½ ounce (15 g) gelatine dissolved in 2 tablespoons*
    *(2 × 15 ml spoons) water*
*1 egg white*

Purée the avocado flesh with the lemon juice. Put the cheese in a bowl and beat until smooth. Gradually beat in the soured cream and the avocado purée. Add the orange rind and sugar. Taste and add more sugar, if necessary. Blend in the dissolved gelatine. In another bowl, whisk the egg white until stiff but not dry and fold into the mixture.

Pour the mixture into a container. Cover and freeze until firm.

About 10 minutes before serving, transfer the mousse to the refrigerator.

Serves 4

### Dessert suggestion
*Layer with Coconut Cake\* sprinkled with lime juice. Spread advocaat-flavoured whipped cream over the turned-out dessert and decorate with shapes cut from lime peel, and Chocolate Shapes\* or Curls\*.*

## Savoury Avocado Ice Cream

*2 ripe avocados*
*2 tablespoons (2 × 15 ml spoons) lemon juice*
*¼ pint (150 ml) soured cream*
*½ teaspoon (2.5 ml spoon) French mustard*
*1 tablespoon (15 ml spoon) chopped chives*
*Salt and freshly ground black pepper*

*For garnish*
*Lemon twists*
*Parsley sprigs*

Cut the avocados in half, remove the stones and scoop out the flesh into a bowl. Rub the inside of the shells with some of the lemon juice and reserve. Mash the avocado flesh with the soured cream, remaining lemon juice, mustard, chives and seasoning.

Spoon the mixture into a container. Cover and freeze until firm, beating the mixture twice at 45-minute intervals. Freeze the avocado shells separately.

About 30 minutes before serving, transfer the avocado ice cream and shells to the refrigerator. Just before serving scoop the ice cream into the shells. Garnish with the lemon twists and parsley sprigs.

Serves 4

### Serving suggestion
*Serve as a starter for a light summer lunch with finely sliced raw courgettes sprinkled with a light lemon vinaigrette; or with poached fresh salmon steaks.*

# Avocado Ice Cream

*2 eggs, separated*
*3 ounces (75 g) sugar*
*1/2 pint (300 ml) single cream*
*2 avocados*
*Finely grated zest and juice of 1 large orange*
*1/2 pint (300 ml) double cream, whipped*

Put the egg yolks with the sugar in a bowl and beat until thick. Put the single cream in a heavy-based saucepan, and heat to just below simmering point then whisk into the egg yolks. Return to the rinsed pan and cook over low heat, stirring constantly, until thickened. Set aside to cool, stirring occasionally.

Remove the flesh from the avocados and purée with the orange zest and juice and put in a bowl. Beat in the cooled custard and fold in the cream. Spoon into a container, cover and freeze until just becoming firm. Beat well in a bowl. Whisk the egg whites until stiff but not dry and fold into the avocado mixture.

Spoon the mixture back into the container. Cover and freeze until firm.

About 30 minutes before serving, transfer the ice cream to the refrigerator.

Serves 6–8

### Serving suggestion
*Fill chilled avocado shells with scoops of Avocado Ice Cream intermingled with scoops of Lemon Sorbet (page 74). Serve with Cigars Russe\*.*

# Avocado Sorbet

*2 large ripe avocados*
*Juice of 2–3 limes or lemons*
*3–4 tablespoons (3–4 × 15 ml spoons) caster sugar*

*For decoration*
*Thick plain yogurt*
*Shapes cut from lime peel*

Peel the avocados, put the flesh in a blender and immediately add the lime or lemon juice. Add the sugar and blend until smooth. Taste and add more lime or lemon juice or sugar if required. Pour the mixture into a container. Cover and freeze until firm, beating 3 times at 30-minute intervals.

About 30 minutes before serving, transfer the ice cream to the refrigerator.

Top each portion with 1–2 teaspoons (1–2 × 15 ml spoons) yogurt and decorate with lime peel shapes.

Serves 4

### Serving suggestion
*Spoon the sorbet into chilled avocado shells and decorate with lemon slices.*

**Additional recipe using avocados:** Lime and Avocado Ice Cream (page 75).

# Banana

Bananas make delicious ices – and have the additional advantage that they are available all the year round. They start turning brown as soon as they have been peeled, so don't prepare bananas until you are ready to add them to the mixture – and blend them immediately with lemon, lime or orange juice. This will protect them against discoloration and also help to 'lift' the flavour.

**Simple Banana Ice Cream**
Mash enough bananas to make about ½ pint (300 ml) purée, blend with citrus juice and add to any of the Basic Recipes* or to a good-quality bought vanilla ice cream.

## 'Irish Coffee' Banana Ice Cream

*½ pint (300 ml) cream, whipped*
*3 bananas, sliced*
*3 ounces (75 g) walnuts, chopped*
*2 ounces (50 g) caster sugar*
*5 tablespoons (5 × 15 ml spoons) Irish Velvet liqueur*
*3 egg whites*

Put the cream in a bowl and fold in the bananas, walnuts, sugar and 2 tablespoons (30 ml) of the liqueur. Whisk the egg whites until stiff but not dry and fold into the cream mixture. Spoon the mixture into a container. Cover and freeze until firm.

About 15 minutes before serving transfer the ice cream to the refrigerator. Spoon a little of the remaining liqueur over each portion of ice cream as it is served.

Serves 6

### Serving suggestion
*Serve in Ice Cream Cones* coated in desiccated coconut, with a little Jamesons Irish Velvet Irish Coffee liqueur spooned over each portion.*

## Banana Ice Cream

*1 vanilla pod*
*½ pint (300 ml) milk*
*3 egg yolks*
*2 ounces (50 g) sugar*
*1 ounce (25 g) plain flour*
*3 ripe bananas*
*Finely grated zest and juice of 1 orange*
*½ pint (300 ml) cream, whipped*

In a heavy-based saucepan, heat the vanilla pod in the milk just to simmering point. Remove from the heat, cover and leave to infuse for 45 minutes.

Put the egg yolks, sugar and flour in a bowl and blend together until smooth.

Remove the vanilla pod and bring the milk to simmering point. Stir the milk into the egg yolk mixture. Return the mixture to the rinsed pan and bring to the boil, stirring constantly. Then simmer gently until the mixture thickens. Remove from the heat and leave to cool, stirring frequently to prevent a skin forming.

In another bowl, mash the bananas with the orange zest and juice. Beat in the custard. Spoon the mixture into a container. Cover and freeze, beating twice at hourly intervals in a bowl. Fold in the cream and spoon the mixture back into the container. Cover and freeze until firm.

About 30 minutes before serving transfer the ice cream to the refrigerator.

Serves 4

### Serving suggestion
*Serve with Bitter Chocolate Sauce*, Burnt Honey Sauce*, Hot Fudge Sauce*, Marshmallow Sauce*, Caramel Sauce* or Mars Bar Sauce*.*

## Banana Custard Ice Cream

*Approximately 14 ounce (400 g) can sweetened condensed milk*
*2 tablespoons (2 × 15 ml spoons) custard powder*
*3 eggs, separated*
*4 bananas*
*Juice of 1 lime or lemon*

Make up the condensed milk to 1½ pints (850 ml) with water. Put the custard powder in a cup and stir in a little milk until smooth. In a heavy-based saucepan, bring the remaining milk to the boil. Pour it on to the blended custard powder, stirring. Return the mixture to the pan and bring to the boil again, stirring constantly, and continue to cook until the mixture thickens.

Beat the egg yolks in a bowl and stir in the hot custard. Mash the bananas with the lime or lemon juice and beat into the custard. Leave to cool, stirring occasionally. Pour the mixture into a container, cover and freeze until just becoming firm. Beat well in a bowl. Whisk the egg whites until stiff but not dry and fold into the custard. Spoon the mixture back into the container. Cover and freeze until firm.

About 30 minutes before serving transfer the ice cream to the refrigerator.

Serves 6–8

### Dessert suggestions
*Ripple with Apricot Yogurt Ice (page 24), or freeze in a ring mould and fill the centre with Orange Water Ice (page 84).*

# Banana Yogurt Ice

*1 pound (450 g) bananas*
*1 tablespoon (15 ml spoon) lime or lemon juice*
*2 ounces (50 g) soft brown sugar*
*1/2 pint (300 ml) thick plain yogurt*
*Praline\* broken into small pieces, for decoration*

Put the bananas in a bowl and mash with the lime or lemon juice and the sugar. Whisk in the yogurt. Spoon the mixture into a container. Cover and freeze until firm, beating 3 times at 45-minute intervals.

About 30 minutes before serving transfer the ice cream to the refrigerator. Serve decorated with the praline.

Serves 4

### Serving suggestion
*Serve with crème fraîche decorated with strips of lemon or lime peel.*

### Low calorie version
*Replace the brown sugar with fructose, or a low calorie or artificial sweetener. Serve with Low Calorie Topping\*.*

# Banana and Honey Ice Cream

*1 pound (450 g) ripe bananas*
*1/4 pint (150 ml) double cream*
*1/4 pint (150 ml) plain yogurt*
*2 tablespoons (2 × 15 ml spoons) lemon juice*
*5 tablespoons (5 × 15 ml spoons) thick honey*
*2 egg whites*
*Toasted flaked almonds, for decoration*

Mash the bananas in a bowl. Blend in the cream, yogurt, lemon juice and honey until smooth. Pour the mixture into a container, cover and freeze, beating twice at 45-minute intervals. Whisk the egg whites until stiff but not dry then carefully fold into the banana cream after the second beating. Pour the mixture into a container. Cover and freeze until firm.

About 30 minutes before serving, transfer the ice cream to the refrigerator. Serve each portion decorated with toasted flaked almonds.

Serves 6

### Serving suggestion
*Pile into sundae glasses with black grapes and Ginger Wine Sorbet (page 60). Top with warm Orange Flower Sauce\* just before serving and sprinkle with chopped hazelnuts.*

# Banana and Chocolate Fudge Ripple Ice Cream

*1 pint (600 ml) milk*
*4 egg yolks*
*4 ounces (100 g) sugar*
*1/4 pint (150 ml) double cream*
*4 bananas*

*For the chocolate fudge*
*2 ounces (50 g) bitter chocolate, chopped*
*1 ounce (25 g) golden syrup*
*4 ounces (100 g) sugar*
*1 tablespoon (15 ml spoon) cocoa powder*
*1 ounce (25 g) unsalted butter*

In a heavy-based saucepan, gently heat the milk to simmering point. Put the egg yolks and sugar into a bowl and beat together then whisk in the hot milk. Return the mixture to the rinsed pan and cook over a low heat, stirring constantly, until the mixture thickens. Leave to cool, stirring occasionally.

Strain the custard into a shallow metal container, cover and chill for 30 minutes before freezing until just becoming firm.

Meanwhile, make the chocolate fudge: put the chocolate, syrup, sugar, cocoa powder and 3 fluid ounces (75 ml) water in a heavy-based saucepan over a low heat. Stir until the chocolate and syrup have melted then bring to the boil and simmer for 5 minutes, stirring. Remove from the heat and beat in the butter. Leave to cool, stirring occasionally.

Remove the semi-frozen custard from the freezer, tip into a bowl and beat well. Whip the cream in another bowl until soft peaks are formed. Purée the bananas and fold into the custard with the cream. Lightly fold in the chocolate fudge to give a rippled effect, spoon back into the container, cover and freeze until firm.

About 35 minutes before serving, transfer the ice cream to the refrigerator.

Serves 6

Recipes for cakes, sauces, etc., asterisked in the dessert and serving suggestions, are given on pages 145 to 152. For instructions on layering, lining and other techniques involved in creating desserts, see pages 152 to 155. Basic recipes are on pages 16 and 17.

# Blackberry, Loganberry

There are two kinds of blackberries – plump, juicy ones with a delicate, slightly perfumed flavour, and hard, less juicy berries that are almost bitter. The first make beautiful ices, the second may need some help from rose water, blackberry liqueur or eau-de-vie (and give out less juice). One recipe specifically calls for loganberries but they can be used in any blackberry recipe.

**Simple Blackberry Ice Cream**
Lightly crush 4 ounces (100 g) blackberries, sweetening them with icing sugar if necessary, and add to any of the Basic Recipes*.

## Blackberry Snow Cream

*12 ounces (350 g) blackberries*
*Blackberry eau-de-vie, optional*
*2 ounces (50 g) sugar*
*6 ounces (175 g) full fat soft cheese*
*2 egg whites*

In a saucepan, gently cook the blackberries in 4 fluid ounces (100 ml) water until they 'fall'. Purée the fruit then pass through a sieve. Measure the purée and make up to ½ pint (300 ml), if necessary, with water or, preferably, blackberry eau-de-vie. Pour the mixture into a container and leave to cool. Cover and freeze to the slushy stage.

Put half the sugar and the cheese in a bowl and beat until smooth. Then beat the mixture into the semi-frozen purée. Return to the freezer until just firm.

Just before serving, whisk the egg whites until stiff but not dry then whisk in the remaining sugar. Fold the egg white lightly into the blackberry cream to give a swirled effect. Serve immediately in frosted glasses.

Serves 4

**Serving suggestion**
*Pile the cream into a bowl, surround with whipped cream and decorate with fresh blackberries.*

## Blackberry Custard Ice

*1¼ pounds (550 g) blackberries*
*3 ounces (75 g) sugar*
*½ pint (300 ml) canned dairy custard*
*¼ pint (150 ml) cream, whipped*
*Whole fresh blackberries, for decoration*

Poach the blackberries with 2 tablespoons (30 ml) water until they 'fall'. Purée then sieve the fruit into a bowl. Stir in the sugar and leave to cool.

Beat the custard into the purée then fold in the cream. Pour the mixture into a container. Cover and freeze until firm, beating twice at hourly intervals.

About 30 minutes before serving, transfer to the refrigerator. Decorate with fresh blackberries.

Serves 4–5

## Blackberry Rose Ice Cream

*9 ounces (250 g) sugar*
*1½ pounds (700 g) blackberries, puréed and sieved*
*2 tablespoons (2 × 15 ml spoons) crème de cassis*
*2 tablespoons (2 × 15 ml spoons) rose water*
*Squeeze of lemon juice, to taste*
*¾ pint (450 ml) cream, whipped*
*Whole blackberries, for decoration*

In a heavy-based saucepan, dissolve the sugar in ¾ pint (450 ml) water. Bring to the boil and boil rapidly for 2 minutes. Set aside to cool.

Stir the blackberry purée, crème de cassis, rose water and lemon juice into the syrup. Gradually pour the syrup into the cream and fold together lightly until evenly blended.

Pour the mixture into a container. Cover and freeze until firm, beating twice at hourly intervals.

About 30 minutes before serving, transfer the ice cream to the refrigerator. Decorate each portion with whole blackberries.

Serves 6–8

**Serving suggestion**
*Scoop balls into Meringue Baskets*, intermingled with fresh blackberries. Serve with a sauce made from sieved blackberry purée and cream flavoured with a touch of rose water.*

## Blackberry Sorbet

*1 pound (450 g) ripe blackberries*
*4 ounces (100 g) caster sugar*
*2 tablespoons (2 × 15 ml spoons) rose water, optional*

*For decoration*
*Blackberry leaves*
*Whole blackberries*

Cook the blackberries with 1 tablespoon (15 ml) water in a covered pan over a very low heat until the juices just begin to run and the fruit softens. Purée the fruit then pass through a fine sieve. Stir in the sugar and rose water.

Pour the mixture into a container. Cover and freeze until firm, beating 3 times at 45-minute intervals.

About 35 minutes before serving, transfer the sorbet to the refrigerator. Serve decorated with blackberry leaves and whole berries.

Serves 4

**Serving suggestion**
*Surround with fresh blackberries and serve with Cigars Russe*.*

**Dessert suggestion**
*Make into a bombe (or freeze in a cake or loaf tin) with a jacket of Apple Cream Ice (page 21).*

# Loganberry Cream Ice

*8 ounces (225 g) cream cheese*
*4 ounces (100 g) icing sugar*
*6 fluid ounces (175 ml) cream, lightly whipped*
*Juice of 1 small lemon*
*1¼ pounds (550 g) loganberries, puréed and sieved*
*Frosted\* whole loganberries, for decoration*

Beat the cheese in a bowl until it is smooth and soft then beat in the sugar. Fold in the cream, lemon juice and loganberry purée until evenly blended. Pour the mixture into a container.

Cover and freeze until firm, beating the mixture once after 1½ hours.

About 20 minutes before serving, transfer the cream ice to the refrigerator. Decorate each portion with frosted berries.

Serves 4

**Dessert suggestion**
*Just before serving, layer with circles or rectangles of Meringue\* starting and finishing with meringue. Decorate with whipped cream, flaked almonds and frosted berries.*

**Additional recipe using blackberries:** Blackberry and Orange Layer Cake (page 139).

# Blackcurrant

Blackcurrants, with their wonderfully concentrated flavour, make some of the most delicious of all ices. Puréed fruit must be sieved; one pound (450 g) blackcurrants will make about ½ pint (300 ml) purée.

**Simple Blackcurrant Ice Cream**
Add ½ pint (300 ml) blackcurrant purée, sweetened if necessary, to any of the Basic Recipes*.

## Blackcurrant Yogurt Ice

12 ounces (350 g) blackcurrants, cooked
½ pint (300 ml) plain yogurt
Juice of ½ lemon
Approximately 2 ounces (50 g) icing sugar
½ ounce (15 g) gelatine
2 egg whites

*For decoration*
Frosted* blackcurrant leaves
Whole blackcurrants

Purée the blackcurrants then pass through a sieve into a bowl. Beat in the yogurt, lemon juice and sugar.

Dissolve the gelatine in 4 tablespoons (60 ml) water in a small bowl placed over a pan of hot water. Blend this with the blackcurrant mixture and leave in a cool place until just beginning to set. Pour into a container, cover and freeze, beating twice at 45-minute intervals.

Whisk the egg whites until stiff but not dry and carefully fold into the blackcurrant mixture after the second beating. Spoon the mixture into a container. Cover and freeze until firm.

About 15 minutes before serving, transfer the ice to the refrigerator. Serve decorated with frosted blackcurrant leaves and whole blackcurrants.

Serves 4

### Low calorie version
*Substitute fructose, or a low calorie or artificial sweetener for the sugar. Use yogurt or Low Calorie Topping* instead of cream for serving.*

## Blackcurrant Sorbet

1 pound (450 g) blackcurrants
6 ounces (175 g) sugar
2 teaspoons (2 × 5 ml spoons) lemon juice
Crème de cassis, for serving

In a covered saucepan, gently cook the blackcurrants with 6 tablespoons (90 ml) water until the juices run and the fruit is soft. Reduce to a purée, with the liquid, then pass through a sieve. In a heavy-based saucepan dissolve the sugar in ½ pint (300 ml) water and bring to the boil for 10 minutes. Cool slightly, stir in the lemon juice and strain.

Mix the syrup with the blackcurrant purée and make up to 1¼ pints (700 ml) with water, if necessary. Pour the mixture into a container. Cover and freeze until firm, beating 3 times at 45-minute intervals.

About 45 minutes before serving, transfer the sorbet to the refrigerator. Pour a spoonful of crème de cassis over each portion as it is served.

Serves 6

### Serving suggestion
*For a refreshing summer starter serve intermingled with balls of Ogen, Charentais or Galia melon. Decorate with mint leaves.*

## Blackcurrant Ice Cream (with soft cheese)

6 ounces (175 g) soft cheese
3 ounces (75 g) caster sugar
½ pint (300 ml) milk
8 fluid ounces (225 ml) thick blackcurrant purée, sieved
Squeeze of lemon juice

Put the cheese with the sugar in a bowl and blend until smooth. Gradually beat in the milk making sure the mixture remains smooth. Lastly, beat in the blackcurrant purée and lemon juice.

Pour the mixture into a container. Cover and freeze until firm, beating twice at hourly intervals.

About 20 minutes before serving, transfer the ice cream to the refrigerator. Serve in frosted glasses.

Serves 4

### Serving suggestion
*Serve in a Meringue Basket* with lid. Decorate with crème de cassis-flavoured whipped cream and blackcurrants. Serve with a sauce of sieved blackcurrant purée.*

## Blackcurrant Ice Cream

1 pound (450 g) blackcurrants
5 ounces (150 g) sugar, to taste
12 fluid ounces (350 ml) cream, whipped

*For decoration*
'Pairs' of Frosted* blackcurrants
Frosted* blackcurrant leaves

In a saucepan, gently cook the blackcurrants with the sugar and ¼ pint (150 ml) water until they are soft. Reduce to a purée then pass through a fine sieve and set aside to cool. When cold fold in the cream.

Pour the mixture into a container. Cover and freeze until firm, beating twice at hourly intervals.

About 30 minutes before serving, transfer the ice cream to the refrigerator. Decorate each portion with frosted blackcurrants and blackcurrant leaves.

Serves 4

### Serving suggestion
*Pile into thin-stemmed wine glasses, interspersed with swirls of whipped cream. Decorate with fresh blackcurrants and angelica.*

### Dessert suggestion
*Layer with Peppermint Ice Cream (page 95), with crushed Meringues\* between each layer. Decorate the turned-out dessert with whipped cream flavoured with crème de menthe or crème de cassis, blackcurrants and mint leaves. Serve with Sponge Fingers\*.*

# Iced Blackcurrant Mousse

1¼ pounds (550 g) blackcurrants
5 eggs, separated
3 ounces (75 g) caster sugar
¼ pint (150 ml) cream, whipped

*For decoration*
*Whipped cream*
*Crème de cassis*
*Long thin strips of orange peel*

In a saucepan, cook the blackcurrants in 4 fluid ounces (100 ml) water until soft. Purée the blackcurrants and cooking liquid and sieve into a bowl. Set aside to cool. Whisk the egg yolks with the sugar until thick and light, fold into the blackcurrant purée with the cream. Whisk the egg whites until stiff but not dry and fold into the blackcurrant mixture.

Pour the mixture into a container. Cover and freeze until firm.

About 30 minutes before serving, transfer the mousse to the refrigerator. Serve each portion topped by a swirl of whipped cream, a little crème de cassis poured over and topped by thin shreds of orange peel.

Serves 6

### Serving suggestion
*Create a sundae with scoops of Pistachio and Green Chartreuse Ice Cream (page 101), Blackcurrant Sorbet (page 32) and tiny Meringues\*. Top with cream and flaked almonds.*

### Dessert suggestion
*Enclose the mousse in a lining of Lychee Ice Cream (page 127). Serve with fresh (or canned) lychees and sieved blackcurrant purée.*

**Additional recipes using blackcurrants:**
Blackcurrant Leaf Water Ice (page 71), Blackcurrant Rose Petal and Champagne Roll (page 136).

# Blueberry

Plump, juicy and richly flavoured, the blueberry has been described as an aristocrat among fruits. Originally gathered in the wild, blueberries are now cultivated in many parts of the world. Canned, bottled or frozen berries can be used when the fresh fruit is not available.

**Simple Blueberry Ice Cream**
Add 4 ounces (100 g) stemmed whole blueberries to any of the Basic Recipes*.

## Blueberry Yogurt Ice

12 ounces (350 g) blueberries, puréed and sieved
1/2 pint (300 ml) plain yogurt
Juice of 1/2 lemon
Approximately 2 ounces (50 g) icing sugar
1/2 ounce (15 g) gelatine, dissolved in 4 tablespoons
    (4 × 15 ml spoons) water
2 egg whites

Put the blueberry purée, yogurt, lemon juice and sugar in a bowl and beat together until smooth. Blend in the dissolved gelatine.

In another bowl, whisk the egg whites until stiff but not dry then fold into the yogurt mixture. Freeze in individual dishes until firm.

About 20 minutes before serving, transfer the ices to the refrigerator.

Serves 4

**Low calorie version**
*Use fructose or a low calorie or artificial sweetener instead of sugar. Serve with Low Calorie Topping*.*

## Blueberry Ice Cream (with whole berries)

2 eggs, separated
3 tablespoons (3 × 15 ml spoons) blackcurrant syrup
3 ounces (75 g) caster sugar
1/2 pint (300 ml) cream, whipped
8 ounces (225 g) fresh blueberries, stemmed

Whisk the egg yolks until thick in a bowl. Whisk in the blackcurrant syrup and the sugar and continue whisking until thick and light.

In another bowl, whisk the egg whites until stiff. Fold the cream into the egg yolks followed by the egg whites and lastly the blueberries.

Pour into a container. Cover and freeze until firm.

About 30 minutes before serving, transfer the ice cream to the refrigerator.

Serves 4

**Dessert suggestion**
*Freeze in a lining of Coconut and Lime Ice Cream (page 49). Warm some blueberries in brandy or Bourbon, place them on the dessert and flambé. Serve with extra blueberries and Sponge Fingers*.*

## Iced Blueberry Snow

5 ounces (150 g) full fat soft cheese, beaten
3 ounces (75 g) caster sugar
1/4 pint (150 ml) soured cream
1 pound (450 g) blueberries, puréed and sieved
2 egg whites

*For decoration*
*Sweet geranium leaves*
*Geranium flowers or crystallized roses*

Put the cheese in a bowl and gradually beat in the sugar and then the soured cream. Fold in the blueberry purée. Taste and add more sugar, if necessary.

Pour the mixture into a container. Cover and freeze to the slushy stage. Beat well in a bowl.

Whisk the egg whites until stiff but not dry and fold into the blueberry cream. Spoon into a container, cover and freeze until firm.

About 30 minutes before serving, transfer the snow to the refrigerator. Decorate each portion with sweet geranium leaves and small geranium flowers or crystallized roses.

Serves 4

**Dessert suggestion**
*Freeze in individual ring moulds, then pipe slightly softened Strawberry Soufflé (page 120) into the centre and return to the freezer. To serve, arrange blueberries around the base of the turned-out dessert and pipe small rosettes of whipped cream around the top. Place one or two strawberry slices in the centre of each soufflé.*

## Blueberry Sorbet

1 pound (450 g) jar or can blueberries
Finely grated zest and juice of 1 lemon

Purée the contents of the jar or can of blueberries with the lemon zest and juice. Pour the mixture into a container. Cover and freeze until firm, beating 3 times at 45-minute intervals.

About 15 minutes before serving, transfer the sorbet to the refrigerator.

Serves 4

**Serving suggestion**
*Serve in Coupelles* or in long-stemmed frosted wine glasses with strips of lemon and lime peel hanging from the edges. Decorate each serving with triangular segments of the lemon and lime.*

# Blueberry Ice Cream

*8 ounces (225 g) fresh blueberries, stemmed*
*4 ounces (100 g) caster sugar*
*1 pint (600 ml) single cream*
*Fresh blueberries, for decoration*

Mix the blueberries and sugar in a saucepan and cook, stirring occasionally, until the sugar dissolves and the mixture simmers. Remove from the heat and leave to cool.

Stir in the cream, mixing well. Pour the mixture into a container and cool completely. Cover and chill for at least an hour before freezing until firm, beating twice at hourly intervals.

About 20 minutes before serving, transfer the ice cream to the refrigerator. Serve decorated with the blueberries.

Serves 6

**Serving suggestion**
*Serve as a sundae with Muesli Ice Cream (page 37).*
*Top with white Wine Sauce\*.*

# Blueberry Tofu Ice Cream

*12 ounces (350 g) fresh or unsweetened frozen*
*    blueberries*
*10 ounces (300 g) tofu*
*½ ounce (15 g) fructose, or to taste*
*Few drops vanilla essence*

In a covered heavy-based saucepan, cook the blueberries over a low heat until the juice starts to run and bubble around the edges. Purée the blueberries and pass through a fine sieve. Blend the blueberry purée with the tofu, fructose and vanilla essence until smooth.

Pour the mixture into a shallow, metal container, cover and freeze until just becoming firm.

Tip the semi-frozen mixture into a bowl and beat well then return to the container, cover and freeze until firm.

About 30 minutes before serving, transfer the ice cream to the refrigerator.

Serves 3–4

# Blueberry Ripple Ice Cream

*½ pint (300 ml) milk*
*1 vanilla pod*
*3 egg yolks*
*4 ounces (100 g) sugar*
*10 ounces (300 g) fresh or unsweetened frozen*
*    blueberries*
*½ pint (300 ml) cream, whipped*

In a heavy-based saucepan, bring the milk and vanilla pod to simmering point. Remove from the heat, cover and leave for 15 minutes. Remove the vanilla pod. Put the egg yolks and half the sugar in a bowl and beat until light, then whisk in the milk. Pour the mixture into the rinsed pan and cook over a low heat, stirring constantly, until the mixture thickens. Do not allow it to boil.

Strain the custard into a bowl and leave to cool, stirring occasionally. Pour into a shallow container and chill for 30 minutes. Cover and freeze until just becoming firm.

In a covered heavy-based saucepan cook the blueberries with the remaining sugar over a low heat until the juices run and just begin to simmer. Purée the fruit then pass through a fine sieve and leave to cool.

Tip the semi-frozen custard into a bowl and beat well. Fold in the cream. Lightly fold the blueberry purée into the mixture to give a ripple effect then spoon into a washed can. Cover the ends with cling film and freeze until firm. About 30 minutes before serving, remove the ice cream from the can and leave in the refrigerator. Serve in slices.

Serves 6–8

**Serving suggestion**
*Serve with Cigars Russe\*.*

---

***To reduce your sugar intake***
Replace the sugar with half the quantity of **fructose** or with an **artificial sweetener**, provided the recipe does not call for a sugar syrup. Normally, 3–4 artificial sweeteners are the equivalent of 1 ounce (25 g) sugar but always check that you have the right degree of sweetness. Artificial sweeteners must be added to custard-based ice creams after the custard has cooled.

# Brown Bread, Cereals

Brown bread and cereals like oats and muesli add an interesting texture to ices. Toasting both breadcrumbs and oats, with sugar, gives an intriguing flavour – but watch closely and stir them with a fork while they are heating, so that they brown evenly and don't burn.

## Quick Brown Bread Ice Cream

*3 ounces (75 g) dried brown breadcrumbs*
*1¼ pints (700 ml) double cream*
*5 ounces (150 g) sugar*
*Pinch of salt*
*Few drops of vanilla essence*

Put the breadcrumbs in a bowl with ¾ pint (450 ml) of the cream and leave to soak for 15 minutes. Stir in the sugar, salt, vanilla essence and the remaining cream.

Pour the mixture into a container. Cover and freeze until firm, beating twice at hourly intervals.

About 30 minutes before serving, transfer the ice cream to the refrigerator.

Serves 6–7

### Serving suggestions
*For each serving, place a tablespoonful of Butterscotch Sauce\* in the bottom of a glass, top with a scoop or two of ice cream and trickle over some Benedictine.*

*Serve with fresh orange segments, pith and membrane removed.*

## Rich Brown Bread Ice Cream

*4 ounces (100 g) brown breadcrumbs (granary are good)*
*4 ounces (100 g) demerara sugar*
*1 pint (600 ml) double cream*
*7–8 tablespoons (7–8 × 15 ml spoons) brandy*
*1 orange, for decoration*

Mix the breadcrumbs and sugar together, spread out on a baking tray. Place in a 375°F (190°C, gas mark 5) oven for 30 minutes or until an even golden brown, stirring frequently with a fork. Leave to cool.

Pour the cream into a bowl and whisk until soft peaks form then gently fold in the brandy and cold crumbs. Spoon the mixture into a container, cover and freeze to the slushy stage. Then, if necessary, whisk vigorously to break down any ice crystals. Turn into a loaf tin lined with cling film and press down firmly. Cover and freeze until firm.

To prepare the decoration, carefully remove the peel from the orange and cut into 1 inch (25 cm) lengths and then into fine strips. Place the strips in a small saucepan of boiling water and simmer for 5 minutes. Drain, rinse in cold water and drain again. Leave to cool.

About 30 minutes before serving, transfer the ice cream to the refrigerator. Just before serving, turn the loaf out on to a cold plate, peel away the cling film and decorate with the orange strips.

Serves 4–5

### Serving suggestion
*Spoon a little hot chopped ginger in syrup beside each portion of ice cream as it is served.*

### Variation
*For a lighter ice cream, fold 2 whisked egg whites into the mixture after whisking. This quantity would then serve 6.*

### Flavour variation
*Use sherry, a coffee liqueur or crème de noyau (almond-flavoured liqueur) instead of brandy.*

## Toasted Oat and Nut Ice Cream

*3 ounces (75 g) oats*
*2 ounces (50 g) golden granulated sugar*
*2 ounces (50 g) hazelnuts, chopped*
*¼ pint (150 ml) milk*
*2 eggs, separated*
*3 ounces (75 g) light muscovado sugar*
*Approximately 6 ounce (175 g) can evaporated milk, well chilled*
*Brandy or orange liqueur, for serving*

Mix the oats, granulated sugar and hazelnuts together and place under a grill until crisp and lightly toasted. Set aside to cool.

Pour the milk into a heavy-based saucepan and bring gently to simmering point. In a bowl, whisk the egg yolks and muscovado sugar together until thick and light then whisk in the milk. Return the mixture to the rinsed pan and cook over a low heat, stirring constantly, until thickened. Remove from the heat and set aside to cool, stirring occasionally.

In a bowl, whisk the evaporated milk until thick and light. In another bowl, whisk the egg whites until stiff but not dry. Fold the evaporated milk and oat mixture into the custard followed by the egg whites.

Spoon the mixture into a container. Cover and freeze until firm.

About 30 minutes before serving, transfer the ice cream to the refrigerator. Serve with a spoonful of brandy or orange liqueur poured over.

Serves 4–6

### Serving suggestions
*Serve with Coffee Sauce\*, Sweet and Sour Treacle Sauce\* or a sauce made from sieved, puréed blackberries.*

### Dessert suggestions
*Ripple with Pineapple Sorbet (page 98) or Caribbean Sorbet (page 99).*

## Muesli Ice Cream

*4 ounces (100 g) soft brown sugar*
*4 ounces (100 g) muesli*
*Grated zest of 1 orange*
*½ pint (300 ml) thick plain yogurt*
*¼ pint (150 ml) cream, whipped*

In a heavy-based saucepan, dissolve the sugar in ½ pint (300 ml) water. Bring to the boil and boil until the temperature reaches 230–234°F (110–112°C) then leave to cool.

Mix the muesli and orange zest together then whip the yogurt into the cream followed by the syrup. Fold in the muesli and orange zest and pour into a container. Cover and freeze until firm, beating 3 times at 45-minute intervals.

About 45 minutes before serving, transfer the ice cream to the refrigerator.

Serves 4–6

**Serving suggestion**
*For each serving, place two or three scoops on a banana sliced lengthways. Pour over Chunky Marmalade Sauce\*.*

**Dessert suggestion**
*Freeze as the outer layer of a bombe with Orange*

*Sorbet De Luxe (page 84) or Seville Orange Sorbet (page 86) in the centre. Arrange thin slices (not segments) of orange, pith and membrane removed, over the surface of the turned-out dessert and pipe whipped cream around the base. Serve with Gingersnaps\* shaped like Cigars Russe\*.*

## Atholl Brose

*4 ounces (100 g) porridge oats, toasted*
*4 ounces (100 g) demerara sugar*
*½ pint (300 ml) cream, whipped*
*6–8 tablespoons (6–8 × 15 ml spoons) whisky*

Mix the oats and sugar together and fold into the cream with the whisky. Pour the mixture into a container. Cover and freeze until firm, beating after 1½ hours.

About 20 minutes before serving, transfer the Atholl Brose to the refrigerator.

Serves 4

**Serving suggestion**
*Create a coupe with Egg Nog Ice Cream (page 117) and Bitter Chocolate Sauce\*.*

**Additional recipe using cereals:** Maple Granola Ice Cream (page 81).

# Butterscotch, Caramel, Fudge

All-time favourites, these flavours appeal to children and adults alike. Butterscotch and caramel blend perfectly with a variety of bases to make tea-time treats or sophisticated desserts, while the crunchy texture of fudge complements the peanuts in one of my favourite ice creams.

## Simple Caramel Ice Cream

Add 4 ounces (100 g) caramel sweets (finely chopped in a liquidizer or food processor) to any of the Basic Recipes* or to a good-quality bought vanilla ice cream.

## Simple Chocolate Caramel Ice Cream

Add 3 ounces (75 g) finely chopped caramel sweets to Chocolate Ice Cream (page 44).

## Peanut Chocolate Fudge Ice Cream

*4 fluid ounces (100 ml) milk*
*3 eggs, separated*
*4 ounces (100 g) sugar*
*3 ounces (75 g) plain chocolate, chopped*
*1 ounce (25 g) unsalted butter*
*2 ounces (50 g) smooth peanut butter*
*Few drops vanilla essence*
*8 ounces (225 g) dark corn syrup*
*3 ounces (75 g) roasted unsalted peanuts, coarsely*
  *chopped*

In a heavy-based saucepan, gently bring the milk to boiling point. Whisk the egg yolks with the sugar in a bowl until thick. Whisk in the milk. Return the mixture to the rinsed pan and cook gently over a low heat, stirring constantly, until the custard thickens. Remove from the heat.

Melt the chocolate with the unsalted butter in a bowl set over a pan of hot water. Remove from the heat and beat in the peanut butter, vanilla essence and corn syrup. Slowly beat in the custard and leave the mixture to cool. Pour into a container, cover and freeze until just becoming firm. Beat well in a bowl.

Whisk the egg whites until stiff but not dry. Fold the egg whites into the custard with the peanuts.

Spoon the mixture back into the container. Cover and freeze until firm.

About 20 minutes before serving, transfer the ice cream to the refrigerator.

Serves 5–6

### Dessert suggestion
*Freeze in a cake or loaf tin surrounded by Genoise Cake*. Decorate the outside of the cake with peanut-butter-flavoured whipped cream and peanut brittle. Serve with Sweet and Sour Treacle Sauce*.*

## Caramel Ice Cream (with evaporated milk)

*4 ounces (100 g) sugar*
*Approximately 6 ounce (175 g) can evaporated milk*

In a heavy-based saucepan, dissolve the sugar in ¼ pint (150 ml) water and cook over a low heat until it turns a rich golden brown. Remove from the heat and gradually stir in another ¼ pint (150 ml) water. Cover your hand while doing this as the caramel splutters. Return the pan to the heat and stir until the caramel has dissolved.

Put the milk in a bowl and whisk until thick and light. Pour the caramel in, still whisking. Pour the mixture into a container. Cover and freeze until firm, beating well after 1½ hours.

About 30 minutes before serving, transfer the ice cream to the refrigerator.

Serves 4

### Dessert suggestion
*Layer with Walnut Ice Cream (page 124) and Coffee Ice Cream (page 50). Decorate the base and top of the turned-out dessert with coffee-liqueur-flavoured whipped cream and crushed caramel.*

## Butterscotch Parfait

*4 egg yolks*
*1 ounce (25 g) butter*
*3 ounces (75 g) soft brown sugar*
*½ pint (300 ml) cream, whipped*

Put the egg yolks in a bowl and whisk until light and thick. Melt the butter and sugar in a small heavy-based saucepan. Bring to the boil and boil for 1 minute. Stir in ¼ pint (150 ml) hot water – take care as the mixture will splutter – and heat until the butterscotch has dissolved. Pour on to the egg yolks, whisking, and return the mixture to the pan. Stir well to ensure all the butterscotch is incorporated and continue to stir over a low heat until the mixture thickens but do not allow it to boil. Set aside to cool.

Fold in the cream and pour the mixture into a container. Cover and freeze until firm.

About 30 minutes before serving, transfer the parfait to the refrigerator.

Serves 4

### Serving suggestion
*Sprinkle the top of the parfait with crushed almonds or Praline*.*

### Dessert suggestion
*Make a bombe or freeze in a loaf or cake tin, with the parfait encased in a layer of Rich Hazelnut Ice Cream (page 69) followed by a layer of Orange Ice Cream (page 85).*

# Iced Caramel Mousse

*2 eggs, separated*
*2 egg yolks*
*4 tablespoons (4 × 15 ml spoons) caster sugar*
*1 pint (600 ml) milk, warmed*
*9 ounces (250 g) granulated sugar*
*4 teaspoons (4 × 5 ml spoons) gelatine*
*3 tablespoons (3 × 15 ml spoons) lemon juice*
*1/2 pint (300 ml) whipping cream*
*Roughly broken walnuts, for decoration*

Put all the egg yolks and the caster sugar in a bowl and whisk together until thick. Gradually stir in the warmed milk. Pour into a heavy-based saucepan and heat gently, stirring and taking care not to let the mixture boil, until the custard thickens slightly. Leave to cool.

Dissolve the granulated sugar in 3½ fluid ounces (90 ml) water in a heavy-based saucepan. Bring to the boil and boil to a rich, dark caramel then immediately pour in another 3½ fluid ounces (90 ml) water to prevent the caramel darkening further – cover your hand while doing this as the caramel splutters. Stir over a low heat to blend in the water. Stir the caramel into the custard.

Dissolve the gelatine in the lemon juice in a small bowl placed over a pan of hot water. Remove from the heat and stir in a little of the custard then pour this mixture into the custard, stirring constantly. Leave in a cool place until just beginning to set.

Whisk the egg whites and lightly whip half the cream then fold into the custard. Pour into a 3 pint (1.7 litre) ring mould, cover and freeze until firm.

About 15 minutes before serving turn the mousse out on to a cold plate and decorate with the remaining cream and the broken walnuts. Leave in the refrigerator.

Serves 6

### Serving suggestion
*Arrange scoops in a coffee-flavoured Meringue Basket\*. Top with sliced peaches and, perhaps, some crushed Praline\*.*

# Butterscotch Ice Cream

*4 ounces (100 g) light brown sugar*
*2 ounces (50 g) golden syrup*
*2 ounces (50 g) butter*
*1/2 pint (300 ml) double cream or 50/50 single and double*
*2 ounces (50 g) butterscotch sweets, crushed*

To make the butterscotch sauce, heat the sugar, syrup and butter in a small heavy-based saucepan until the butter has melted and the sugar dissolved. Raise the heat, bring to the boil and boil for 2 minutes. Remove

from the heat and stir in 2 tablespoons (30 ml) hot water – take care as the mixture will splutter. Leave for about an hour to cool.

Pour the cream into a bowl and whisk until it stands in soft peaks. Stir in the butterscotch sauce.

Pour the mixture into a container. Cover and freeze until firm, beating well and folding in half the butterscotch sweets after 1½ hours.

Serve straight from the freezer decorated with the remaining crushed butterscotch sweets.

Serves 4–6

### Serving suggestion
*Serve in Gingersnap Baskets\*, intermingled with scoops of Apple and Raisin Ice Cream (page 21).*

### Dessert suggestion
*Ripple with Apricot Yogurt Ice (page 24).*

# Caramel Ice Cream

*5 ounces (150 g) sugar*
*8 fluid ounces (225 ml) double cream*
*12 fluid ounces (350 ml) milk*
*4 egg yolks*

Heat the sugar in a heavy-based saucepan, stirring constantly, until it melts and turns a rich golden brown. Remove from the heat immediately and plunge the base of the pan into cold water, take care as this may splutter. In another saucepan, bring cream and milk to the boil. Slowly pour the mixture into the caramel, stirring constantly, making sure the caramel is dissolved and the mixture is smooth.

Put the egg yolks in a bowl and whisk until thick then slowly whisk in some of the hot cream and caramel mixture. When the yolks have become warm whisk them into the cream mixture. Cook over a very low heat until the mixture thickens slightly. Leave to become cold. Pour the mixture into a container. Cover and freeze until firm, beating twice at hourly intervals.

About 30 minutes before serving, transfer the ice cream to the refrigerator.

Serves 4

### Dessert suggestion
*Freeze in a crust of ground amaretti and very finely chopped hazelnuts bound with melted butter. Decorate the turned-out bombe with Chocolate Curls\*.*

**Additional recipe using fudge:** Banana and Chocolate Fudge Ripple Ice Cream (page 29).

# Cherry

The dark varieties of cherries make the prettiest-coloured ices, but do make sure the flavour matches up to the colour.

### Simple Cherry Ice Cream
Add 1 pound (450 g) stoned black cherries, puréed and sieved, to any of the Basic Recipes* or to a good-quality bought vanilla ice cream.

## Victorian Cherry Ice

1 pound (450 g) Morello cherries
10 ounces (275 g) sugar
6 blanched almonds
Juice of 1 lemon
4 tablespoons (4 × 15ml spoons) kirsch, optional
2 egg whites

Remove the stones from the cherries, crack them and remove and bruise the kernels. In a saucepan, dissolve the sugar in 1 pint (600 ml) water. Add the kernels and the almonds and bring to the boil. Remove from the heat, cover and leave to infuse for 30 minutes.

Remove and discard the kernels and almonds. Purée the cherries with the syrup. Stir in the lemon juice and kirsch, if you are using it. When cold pour the mixture into a container. Cover and freeze until just becoming firm. Lightly whisk the egg whites and fold into the purée. Cover and freeze until firm. About 35 minutes before serving, transfer the ice to the refrigerator.

Serves 4–5

### Dessert suggestion
*Encase in Iced Kirsch Soufflé (page 131). Decorate the turned-out dessert with piped, very slightly softened Cherry Ice Cream (page 41).*

## Black Cherry Ice Cream (with pie filling)

Approximately 14 ounce (400 g) can black cherry pie filling
2 tablespoons (2 × 15 ml spoons) kirsch
2 tablespoons (2 × 15 ml spoons) plain yogurt
1/2 pint (300 ml) cream, whipped
Large Macaroons*, for serving

Put the pie filling and kirsch in a bowl and beat together. Fold the yogurt into the cream then fold into the pie filling. Pour the mixture into a container. Cover and freeze until firm, beating after 1½ hours.

About 20 minutes before serving, transfer the ice cream to the refrigerator. Serve with macaroons.

Serves 4

**Dessert suggestion**
*Freeze in a jacket of Genoise Cake*, sprinkled with kirsch. Decorate the turned-out dessert with mint-flavoured whipped cream and sieved cocoa powder.*

## Cherry Frost

12 ounces (350 g) ripe cherries, preferably a dark variety, stoned
3 ounces (75 g) sugar
1/2 pint (300 ml) plain yogurt
5 ounces (150 g) soft cheese or 1/4 pint (150 ml) crème fraîche, whipped
2 egg whites
2 tablespoons (2 × 15 ml spoons) icing sugar
6 pairs of cherries joined together by their stalks, for decoration

Put the cherries with the sugar in a saucepan. Add about 2 fluid ounces (50 ml) water and simmer for about 4 minutes. Reduce to a purée and leave to cool completely.

Put the yogurt and cheese in a bowl and beat until smooth or whip it lightly with the crème fraîche. Fold into the fruit purée. Pour the mixture into a container. Cover and freeze to the slushy stage. Beat well in a bowl. Whisk the egg whites until stiff. Gradually whisk in the icing sugar and continue whisking until stiff peaks are formed. Carefully fold into the fruit mixture. Spoon back into the container, cover and freeze until firm.

About an hour before serving, transfer the cherry frost to the refrigerator. Serve decorated with pairs of cherries.

Serves 6

**Serving suggestion**
*Freeze in individual containers. Serve on white plates, accompanied by Sponge Fingers*.*

**Low calorie version**
*Use fructose or a low calorie or artificial sweetener instead of sugar.*

## Black Cherry Ice Cream

1 pound (450 g) ripe black cherries, stoned
Approximately 5 ounces (150 g) caster sugar
1/2 pint (300 ml) double cream, whipped
Lemon juice, optional

For decoration
Frosted* black cherries
Frosted* mint leaves

Purée the cherries with the sugar into a bowl. Fold in the cream then taste the mixture and add more sugar or some lemon juice, if necessary. Pour the mixture into a container. Cover and freeze until firm, beating well after 1½ hours.

About 30 minutes before serving, transfer the ice cream to the refrigerator. Serve decorated with frosted cherries and mint leaves.

Serves 4

**Serving suggestions**
*Serve in chocolate-coated Meringue Baskets* or chocolate-covered Ice Cream Cones*.*

**Dessert suggestion**
*Freeze in a Chocolate Case* then decorate the top with whipped cream flavoured with Cherry Heering and Chocolate Shapes* or Curls*. Arrange black cherries around the base.*

## Cherry Ice Cream

1/2 pint (300 ml) milk
3 egg yolks
5 ounces (150 g) sugar
1/4 pint (150 ml) single cream
1/4 pint (150 ml) crème fraîche
1 pound (450 g) ripe cherries, stoned
Pairs of cherries joined together by their stalks, for decoration

In a heavy-based saucepan, heat the milk to just below boiling point. Put the egg yolks and sugar in a bowl and whisk together until thick and light then whisk in the hot milk. Return to the rinsed pan and cook over a low heat, stirring constantly, until the mixture thickens. Cool, stirring occasionally.

Stir in the single cream and crème fraîche. Pour the mixture into a container. Cover and freeze until firm, beating twice at hourly intervals, and adding the cherries after the second beating.

About 30 minutes before serving, transfer the ice cream to the refrigerator. Serve decorated with pairs of cherries.

Serves 4–6

**Serving suggestion**
*Ripple with Vanilla Ice Cream (page 123) and serve with Sponge Fingers*.*

# Chestnut

Chestnuts can be used fresh, dried, puréed or – for a touch of luxury – in the form of marrons glacés. The purée is available in cans and can be either sweetened or unsweetened. Check which type a recipe calls for and make sure you buy the right one.

**Simple Chestnut Ice Cream**
Add either 4 ounces (100 g) chopped marrons glacés or about 6 ounces (175 g) unsweetened chestnut purée to any of the Basic Recipes*.

## Chestnut and Chocolate Ice Cream

8 ounces (225 g) dried chestnuts
Vanilla pod
2 tablespoons (2 × 15 ml spoons) honey
2 eggs
2 egg yolks
3 ounces (75 g) muscovado sugar
1 pint (600 ml) milk
1/4 pint (150 ml) cream, whipped
6 ounces (175 g) plain chocolate

For decoration
Grated chocolate
Crystallized violets

Put the chestnuts in a saucepan with the vanilla pod and honey. Cover with water and simmer for about 2 hours until tender, adding a little more water if necessary. Remove the vanilla pod and purée the chestnuts, adding a little more water if the mixture is too dry.

Put the eggs, egg yolks and sugar in a bowl and beat together. Put the milk in a heavy-based saucepan and heat to just below boiling point then stir into the eggs. Return the mixture to the rinsed pan and cook over a low heat, stirring constantly, until the mixture thickens. Leave to cool.

Fold in the cream. Melt the chocolate in a bowl over a pan of hot water then blend into the chestnut purée. Fold into the custard. Pour the mixture into a container. Cover and freeze until firm, beating twice at hourly intervals.

About 30 minutes before serving, transfer the ice cream to the refrigerator. Decorate each portion with grated chocolate and crystallized violets.

Serves 6–8

**Dessert suggestion**
*Freeze in a loaf or cake tin around a centre of Ginger Wine Sorbet (page 60). Decorate the turned-out dessert with lavish swirls of whipped cream, chopped crystallized ginger and Chocolate Shapes*.*

## Chestnut and Apple Meringue Mousse

8 ounces (225 g) unsweetened chestnut purée
2 ounces (50 g) icing sugar
1/4 pint (150 ml) apple juice
1/4 pint (150 ml) double or whipping cream, whipped
2 egg whites
2 ounces (50 g) made Meringues*, roughly broken

For decoration
Whipped cream
Marrons glacés

Put the chestnut purée in a bowl with the sugar and beat until smooth. Gradually whisk in the apple juice to give a soft, smooth consistency. Pour the mixture into a container, cover and freeze until just becoming firm. Fold in the whipped cream.

Whisk the egg whites until stiff but not dry and carefully fold into the chestnut cream. Lastly fold in the meringues. Spoon the mixture back into the container. Cover and freeze until firm.

About 30 minutes before serving, transfer the ice cream to the refrigerator. Decorate each portion with whipped cream and marrons glacés.

Serves 4

**Serving suggestion**
*Serve with poached apple chunks sprinkled with chopped Praline*.*

**Dessert suggestion**
*Pile into apple shells and freeze. Decorate with slices of marrons glacés.*

**Flavour variations**
*Use Macaroons* or hazelnut macaroons instead of meringues.*

---

***To reduce your sugar intake***
Replace the sugar with half the quantity of **fructose** or with an **artificial sweetener**, provided the recipe does not call for a sugar syrup. Normally, 3–4 artificial sweeteners are the equivalent of 1 ounce (25 g) sugar but always check that you have the right degree of sweetness. Artificial sweeteners must be added to custard-based ice creams after the custard has cooled.

---

Recipes for cakes, sauces, etc., asterisked in the dessert and serving suggestions, are given on pages 145 to 152. For instructions on layering, lining and other techniques involved in creating desserts, see pages 152 to 155. Basic recipes are on pages 16 and 17.

# Chestnut and Cinnamon Circle

7 ounces (200 g) unsweetened chestnut purée
2 eggs
1/2 pint (300 ml) single cream
2 ounces (50 g) caster sugar
1/2 teaspoon (2.5 ml spoon) ground cinnamon
1 pound (450 g) whole chestnuts
1 ounce (25 g) granulated sugar
2 tablespoons (2 × 15 ml spoons) Grand Marnier or
    other orange liqueur

Put the chestnut purée, eggs, cream, caster sugar and cinnamon in a bowl and beat together until thoroughly blended. Pour into a container, cover and freeze until just becoming firm. Beat well. Pour into a cold 1½ pint (850 ml) ring mould, cover and freeze until firm.

With a small, sharp knife cut a cross through the skins of the chestnuts. Put the chestnuts in a saucepan, cover with water and boil for 10 minutes. Drain and remove the skins. Return the chestnuts to the pan, cover with water and simmer for 20–25 minutes until tender. Drain well.

In a heavy-based saucepan, heat the granulated sugar until it caramelizes and turns golden brown. Remove from the heat and stir in the Grand Marnier and 2 tablespoons (30 ml) water – take care as it will splutter. Reheat, stirring, until the caramel dissolves. Stir in the chestnuts and leave to cool.

Thirty to forty minutes before serving, turn the chestnut ring out on to a cold serving plate and leave in the refrigerator. Immediately before serving spoon the chestnuts into the centre of the ring and trickle the syrup over the ice cream.

Serves 6–8

# Chestnut and Molasses Ice Cream

2 ounces (50 g) caster sugar
4 ounces (100 g) cooked, peeled chestnuts, chopped
    and toasted
3 large eggs, separated
3 ounces (75 g) molasses
2 ounces (500 g) icing sugar
Few drops vanilla essence
8 fluid ounces (225 ml) double cream, whipped

Dissolve the caster sugar in 2½ fluid ounces (65 ml) water in a small heavy-based pan. Then boil until it becomes a light caramel. Stir in the chestnuts until evenly coated. Pour the mixture on to a cold oiled surface. Leave to become cold. Break into small pieces that resemble coarse breadcrumbs.

Put the egg yolks into a bowl and whisk until very thick and pale. Whisk in the molasses. In another bowl, whisk the egg whites until they stand in soft peaks. Whisk in the icing sugar and vanilla essence a little at a time and continue whisking until the mixture is very thick. Carefully fold the cream into the egg yolks with the crumbled chestnuts followed by the egg whites. Pour the mixture into a container. Cover and freeze until firm.

About 30 minutes before serving, transfer the ice cream to the refrigerator.

Serves 4

**Dessert suggestion**
*Encase in a jacket of Whisked Sponge Cake\*. Decorate the turned-out dessert with whipped cream and sultanas, soaked in rum if liked.*

# Nesselrode Pudding

2 ounces (50 g) sugar
2 egg yolks
1/2 pint (300 ml) single cream
1/4 pint (150 ml) whipping cream
6 ounces (175 g) unsweetened chestnut purée
1 ounce (25 g) seedless raisins
1 ounce (25 g) sultanas
1 ounce (25 g) candied orange and lemon peel
1 ounce (25 g) glacé cherries, roughly chopped
Vanilla syrup made by dissolving a little sugar in a
    small amount of water and adding a few drops of
    vanilla essence

For decoration
Whipped cream
Marrons glacés

Whisk the sugar and egg yolks together in a bowl until thick. In a heavy-based saucepan, bring the single cream to just below boiling point. Gradually pour the hot cream on to the egg yolks, stirring constantly. Return the mixture to the rinsed pan and heat gently, stirring constantly and taking care that the mixture does not boil, until it thickens slightly. Leave to cool, stirring occasionally to prevent a skin forming.

Whip the whipping cream in a bowl until thick. Gradually beat the custard into the chestnut purée then fold in the whipped cream.

Pour the mixture into a container. Cover and freeze until just becoming firm but not hard.

Lightly poach the dried fruit, peel and glacé cherries in sufficient vanilla syrup to cover them for 15 minutes. Remove with a slotted spoon and leave to drain and cool. Gently fold into the chestnut ice cream making sure they are evenly distributed. Spoon the ice cream into a charlotte or other mould, cover and freeze until firm.

About 15 minutes before serving turn out on to a cold plate and decorate with whipped cream and marrons glacés, either whole or cut in half. Leave in the refrigerator.

Serves 4

**Additional recipes using chestnuts:** Chestnut and Chocolate Bombe (page 142).

# Chocolate

Plain or lavish, chocolate ices are among the most luscious of all ice creams. They can be made from dark, bitter and white chocolate, but cake-covering and milk chocolate are not really suitable. Cooking chocolate must be heated in cream or milk to avoid imparting a raw, grainy flavour to the finished ice.

Powdered drinking chocolates and malted chocolate drink powders are also useful – and are very simple to use. They are invariably sweetened, so you may have to reduce the amount of sugar called for in a recipe. Cocoa powder, like cooking chocolate, must be cooked in milk or cream for several minutes.

To melt chocolate, heat it in milk or cream, or in a bowl placed over a pan of hot water – never over direct heat.

### Simple Chocolate Ice Cream

Add 4 ounces (100 g) very finely chopped plain chocolate to any of the Basic Recipes* or to a good-quality bought vanilla ice cream.

## Chocolate Ice Cream

4 ounces (100 g) unsalted butter, chopped
8 fluid ounces (225 ml) milk
3 ounces (75 g) sugar
Few drops of vanilla essence
2 ounces (50 g) plain chocolate, chopped

Put the butter, milk and sugar in a saucepan and stir to dissolve over low heat. Then bring to just boiling point. Pour into a blender and mix in 4 bursts of 10 seconds each. Add the vanilla essence and chocolate and blend until smooth. Pour the mixture into a container. Cover and freeze until firm, beating twice at hourly intervals.

About 30 minutes before serving, transfer the ice cream to the refrigerator.

Serves 3–4

### Serving suggestion

*For each serving, place a pear half, rounded side uppermost, on a circle of Genoise Cake* sprinkled with kirsch. Coat in the ice cream followed by Meringue*. Flash under a hot grill just long enough to brown the surface.*

## Chocolate Ice Cream (with condensed milk)

4 ounces (100 g) plain chocolate, broken into small pieces
Approximately 6 ounce (175 g) can condensed milk
½ teaspoon (2.5 ml spoon) vanilla essence
½ pint (300 ml) whipping or double cream

Dissolve the chocolate in the condensed milk in a bowl over a pan of hot water, stirring occasionally. This takes about 10 minutes. Remove from the heat

and gradually stir in the vanilla essence and 4 tablespoons (60 ml) water. Leave until completely cold.

Pour the cream into a bowl and whisk until soft peaks form then fold into the chocolate mixture. Pour the mixture into a container. Cover and freeze until firm.

About 20 minutes before serving, transfer the ice cream to the refrigerator.

Serves 6

### Dessert suggestion

*Layer with Iced Orange and Almond Mousse (page 85). Decorate the turned-out dessert with orange-liqueur-flavoured whipped cream, flaked almonds and slices of glacé orange.*

## Carob, Soya Milk and Tofu Ice Cream

3 tablespoons (3 × 15 ml spoons) unsweetened carob powder
1 pound (450 g) tofu
8 fluid ounces (225 ml) soya milk
4 fluid ounces (100 ml) oil
3 ounces (75 g) brown sugar
Few drops vanilla essence

Blend all the ingredients together in 2 or 3 batches until smooth. Pour into a container, cover and freeze until firm, beating 3 times at 45-minute intervals.

About 30 minutes before serving, transfer the ice cream to the refrigerator.

Serves 6

## Chocolate-Mint Ice Cream

1 ounce (25 g) sugar
6 ounces (75 g) slim chocolate mint creams
3 egg yolks
¼ pint (150 ml) double cream
2 fluid ounces (50 ml) cognac, optional

Put the sugar and 4 fluid ounces (100 ml) water into a small saucepan and stir to dissolve over low heat. Bring to the boil and boil for 3 minutes. Pour the syrup into a blender, add the chocolates and process until smooth.

Put the egg yolks in a bowl and whisk until very light. Fold in the chocolate mixture. Lightly whip the cream with the cognac, if used, and lightly fold into the chocolate mixture.

Pour the mixture into a container. Cover and freeze until firm.

About 20 minutes before serving, transfer the ice cream to the refrigerator.

Serves 4–6

# Rich Chocolate Ice Cream

8 ounces (225 g) good-quality plain chocolate,
    chopped
2 eggs
2 ounces (50 g) caster sugar
1/4 pint (150 ml) double cream
2 1/2 fluid ounces (65 ml) single cream
1 tablespoon (15 ml spoon) Grand Marnier, optional
Twisted fine strips of orange peel, to decorate

Melt the chocolate in a bowl over a pan of hot water.
Put the eggs and sugar into a bowl and whisk together
until very light and fluffy then quickly but lightly fold
in the chocolate.

In another bowl, lightly whip the creams and Grand
Marnier, if used, together and fold into the chocolate
mixture. Pour the mixture into a loaf tin, cover and
freeze until firm, beating well after 1 1/2 hours.

About 15 minutes before serving, turn the ice cream
out on to a cold plate and leave in the refrigerator.
Serve decorated with twists of orange peel.

Serves 4

### Dessert suggestion
*Freeze in a crust of ground almonds worked to a stiff
paste with caster sugar and egg white, around a centre
of Iced Nectarine Mousse (page 89). Decorate the
turned-out dessert with Chocolate Shapes\* and
nectarine slices.*

# Cocoa Ice Cream

3 tablespoons (3 × 15 ml spoons) unsweetened cocoa
    powder
1 1/4 pints (700 ml) milk
7 ounces (200 g) caster sugar
6 egg yolks
3 ounces (75 g) toasted hazelnuts, finely chopped

Put the cocoa powder in a heavy-based saucepan.
Blend in a little milk until smooth. Then stir in the
remaining milk. Bring to the boil over a medium heat.

Put the sugar and egg yolks in a bowl and whisk
until thick and light. Whisk in the hot milk. Return the
custard to the pan and gently heat, stirring constantly,
until thickened, but do not allow it to boil. Remove
from the heat and leave to cool, stirring occasionally,
to prevent a skin forming. Stir in the nuts and chill for
about an hour. Pour the mixture into a container.
Cover and freeze until firm, beating twice at hourly
intervals.

About 20 minutes before serving, transfer the ice
cream to the refrigerator.

Serves 6

### Serving suggestion
*Serve as a sundae with Pina Colada Ice Cream (page
98), chopped marshmallows, lightly toasted chopped
hazelnuts and Sweet and Sour Treacle Sauce\*.*

# Iced Chocolate Soufflé

6 ounces (175 g) bitter chocolate, chopped
4 egg whites
6 ounces (175 g) icing sugar
2 tablespoons (2 × 15 ml spoons) orange liqueur
3/4 pint (450 ml) cream, whipped

Melt the chocolate in a bowl over a pan of hot water.
Leave to cool.

Put the egg whites in a bowl and whisk until stiff.
Gradually add the sugar, whisking well after each
addition. Continue to whisk until a thick, light
meringue is formed. Carefully fold in the liqueur,
chocolate and then the cream. Pour into a container.
Cover and freeze until firm. About 15 minutes before
serving, transfer to the refrigerator.

Serves 8

### Dessert suggestion
*Freeze in individual containers, then turn out and
coat in Rich Hazelnut Ice Cream (page 69). Decorate
with Chocolate Shapes\* and small scrolls of whipped
cream flavoured with hazelnut liqueur.*

# Chocolate-Peppermint Ripple

5 ounces (150 g) plain chocolate, chopped
2 tablespoons (2 × 15 ml spoons) milk
4 eggs
4 ounces (100 g) caster sugar
3/4 pint (450 ml) whipping cream
1/2 pint (300 ml) plain yogurt
1 teaspoon (5 ml spoon) peppermint oil
Green food colouring, optional

Melt the chocolate in the milk in a bowl placed over a
pan of hot water. Stir until smooth and remove from
the heat. Put the eggs and sugar in a bowl and whisk
together until thick and light.

In another bowl, whip the cream and yogurt
together until soft peaks are formed then fold into the
egg mixture. Fold two-thirds of the egg and cream
mixture into the melted chocolate. Stir the peppermint
oil and a few drops of green colouring, if you are using
it, into the remaining mixture.

Place the chocolate mixture into a container, cover
and place in the freezer for about an hour. Put the
peppermint mixture in the refrigerator. Swirl the
peppermint mixture through the chocolate to give a
rippled effect then freeze until firm.

About 30 minutes before serving, transfer the ice
cream to the refrigerator.

Serves 8

### Serving suggestion
*Freeze in a can. Serve with Marshmallow Sauce\* and
Cigars Russe\*.*

# Chocolate Ice Cream (with evaporated milk)

*Approximately 14 ounce (398 g) can evaporated milk, well chilled*
*7 fluid ounces (200 ml) milk or single cream*
*4 ounces (100 g) caster sugar*
*4 tablespoons (4 × 15 ml spoons) drinking chocolate*

Pour the evaporated milk and milk or cream into a bowl. Add the sugar and whisk until very light and thick. Whisk in the drinking chocolate until just evenly combined. Pour the mixture into a container. Cover and freeze until firm, beating well after 1½ hours.

About 30 minutes before serving, transfer the ice cream to the refrigerator.

Serves 4

### Dessert suggestion
*Serve in a chequerboard with Vanilla Ice Cream (page 123).*

### Flavour variation
*Use a malted chocolate drink powder instead of drinking chocolate.*

# Chocolate Cream Ice

*1 pint (600 ml) single cream*
*1 vanilla pod*
*4 ounces (100 g) sugar*
*4 ounces (100 g) plain chocolate, melted*

Put the cream with the vanilla pod in a heavy-based saucepan and heat gently to just below simmering point. Remove from the heat, stir in the sugar, cover and leave for 30 minutes.

Remove the vanilla pod then gradually stir the cream into the melted chocolate. Pour the mixture into a container. Cover and freeze until firm, beating twice at hourly intervals.

About 30 minutes before serving, transfer the cream ice to the refrigerator.

Serves 4

### Serving suggestion
*Serve in Ice Cream Cones\* coated in desiccated coconut. Accompany with Chunky Marmalade Sauce\*.*

---

**To reduce your sugar intake**
Replace the sugar with half the quantity of **fructose** or with an **artificial sweetener**, provided the recipe does not call for a sugar syrup. Normally, 3–4 artificial sweeteners are the equivalent of 1 ounce (25 g) sugar but always check that you have the right degree of sweetness. Artificial sweeteners must be added to custard-based ice creams after the custard has cooled.

---

# White Chocolate Ice Cream

*4 egg yolks*
*2 ounces (50 g) caster sugar*
*9 fluid ounces (250 ml) milk*
*8 ounces (225 g) white couveture chocolate, chopped*
*9 fluid ounces (250 ml) cream, whipped*
*2 tablespoons (2 × 15 ml spoons) Cointreau, optional*
*Grated bitter chocolate, for decoration*

Put the egg yolks and sugar in a bowl and whisk until thick and light. Pour the milk into a heavy-based saucepan and heat to just below simmering point. Whisk the milk into the egg yolks and return the mixture to the rinsed pan. Cook over a low heat, stirring constantly, until the mixture thickens. Remove from the heat.

Put the chocolate into a bowl over a pan of hot water and stir in the custard. When the chocolate has melted remove the bowl from the heat and leave to cool, stirring occasionally. Fold in the cream and Cointreau, if you are using it. Pour the mixture into a container. Cover and freeze until firm, beating twice at hourly intervals.

About 30 minutes before serving, transfer the ice cream to the refrigerator. Serve each portion decorated with grated bitter chocolate.

Serves 6

### Dessert suggestion
*Form into 6 balls around a small amount of Raspberry Sorbet (page 104) and coat in cocoa powder. Serve with Langues de Chat\*.*

### Flavour variation
*At Inigo Jones restaurant, Garrick Street, in London's Covent Garden, where this recipe was created, they flavour the ice cream with 2 tablespoons (2 × 15 ml spoons) truffle juice and 1 finely chopped fresh, small truffle instead of Cointreau. Needless to say, it's quite heavenly.*

**Additional recipes using chocolate:** Simple Chocolate Caramel Ice Cream (page 38), Chestnut and Chocolate Ice Cream (page 42), Ginger and Chocolate Chip Ice Cream (page 61), Mint and Chocolate Ice Cream (page 95), Chestnut and Chocolate Bombe (page 142), Chocolate Truffle and Hazelnut Ring (page 142).

---

*CIDER: see WINES, LIQUEURS*
*CINNAMON: see SPICES*
*CLOVE: see SPICES*

# Coconut

Coconut ices can be made from fresh coconut water and flesh, creamed coconut (which comes in a solid, compressed block) and coconut cream (a liquid, available in cans). To toast coconut, spread fresh strands, or shreds of desiccated coconut, on a tray in a 350°F (180°C, gas mark 4) oven for about 20 minutes. Watch carefully, and stir, to make sure it doesn't get too brown.

### Simple Coconut Ice Cream
Add 8 ounces (225 g) desiccated coconut to any of the Basic Recipes*.

## Coconut Ice Cream

*¾ pint (450 ml) milk*
*3 egg yolks*
*2 ounces (50 g) golden syrup, warmed*
*1½ ounces (40 g) butter, melted*
*Few drops vanilla essence*
*4 ounces (100 g) desiccated coconut*
*Toasted coconut, for decoration*

Pour the milk into a heavy-based saucepan and bring to just below boiling point. Put the egg yolks with the syrup into a bowl and whisk until thick. Whisk in the hot milk and the butter.

Return the mixture to the rinsed pan and cook over a low heat until the custard thickens, stirring constantly – do not allow it to boil. Remove from the heat and add the vanilla essence and coconut and leave to cool, stirring occasionally.

Pour the mixture into a container. Cover and freeze until firm, beating twice at hourly intervals.

About 40 minutes before serving, transfer the ice cream to the refrigerator. Serve each portion decorated with a sprinkling of toasted coconut.

Serves 4

### Serving suggestions
*Serve with Black Cherry Sauce\*, Hot Chocolate Sauce\*, Coffee Sauce\*, Mars Bar Sauce\* or Orange Flower Sauce\*.*

## Coconut and Lime Ice Cream

*5 eggs, separated*
*3 ounces (75 g) caster sugar*
*Juice and finely grated zest of 2 limes*
*12 fluid ounces (350 ml) canned coconut cream or*
*    4½ ounce (115 g) block creamed coconut*
*    dissolved in 8 fluid ounces (225 ml) hot water*

*For decoration*
*Toasted coconut*
*Twisted lime or lemon slices*

Put the egg yolks, sugar and lime juice in a bowl and whisk until very thick and light. Whisk in the coconut cream and fold in the lime zest. Pour into a container, cover and freeze until just becoming firm. Beat well in a bowl. Whisk the egg whites until stiff but not dry and fold into the coconut mixture.

Spoon the mixture back into its container. Cover and freeze until firm.

About 30 minutes before serving, transfer the ice cream to the refrigerator. Serve each portion decorated with toasted coconut and a twisted slice of lime.

Serves 6–8

### Dessert suggestion
*Make with lemon juice instead of lime and use as the jacket of a bombe. Follow with a layer of Coconut Cake\* soaked in orange liqueur and a centre of Iced Apricot Mousse (page 24). Decorate the turned-out dessert with coffee-flavoured whipped cream, shreds of toasted coconut and quarters of poached apricots.*

## Smooth Coconut Ice Cream

*6 ounces (175 g) desiccated coconut*
*8 fluid ounces (225 ml) single cream*
*3–4 ounces (75–100 g) caster sugar*
*½ pint (300 ml) plain yogurt*

*To serve*
*Fresh\* raspberry sauce*
*Fresh raspberries*
*Strands of toasted coconut*

Put the coconut and cream in a saucepan and bring slowly to the boil. Turn off the heat, cover the pan and leave to infuse for 30 minutes. Reduce the mixture to as fine a purée as possible in a food processor or blender then pass through a sieve. Pour about ¼ pint (150 ml) very hot water through the sieve at the end to wash as much of the liquor through as possible. Stir in the sugar. Pour the mixture into a container. Cover and freeze until just becoming firm. Whip in the yogurt and freeze until firm.

About 35 minutes before serving, transfer the ice cream to the refrigerator. Serve with fresh raspberry sauce poured over and surrounded by fresh raspberries. Strew a few toasted coconut strands over the surface.

Serves 4–5

### Serving suggestion
*Spoon into Almond Tuiles\* and surround with poached cranberries.*

*Form the ice cream into 4 balls and surround each with swirls of whipped cream. Decorate with butterfly-like Chocolate Shapes\* and mint leaves.*

## Smooth Coconut Ice Cream (with fresh coconut)

*1 coconut*
*¼ pint (150 ml) milk*
*2 ounces (50 g) coconut cream*
*3 ounces (75 g) sugar*
*½ pint (300 ml) cream, whipped*
*Marshmallows dipped in toasted coconut shreds, for*
*    decoration*

Crack open the coconut, scrape out the flesh and reserve the water. Cut the flesh into small pieces and put in a saucepan with the coconut water, milk, coconut cream and sugar and cook until soft. Reduce to a purée in a blender or food processor then pass through a fine sieve. Fold in the cream. Pour the mixture into a container. Cover and freeze until firm, beating twice at hourly intervals.

About 30 minutes before serving transfer the ice cream to the refrigerator. Serve decorated with the marshmallows dipped in coconut.

Serves 4

### Serving suggestion
*Form the ice cream into 4 balls, roll in cocoa powder, and make a small indentation in the top of each. Pour some coffee or chocolate liqueur into the indentation and cap with a coconut-coated marshmallow.*

**Additional recipes using coconut:** Coffee and Coconut Ice Cream (page 53), Mango and Coconut Ice Cream (page 79), Pina Colada Ice Cream (page 98), Pineapple and Coconut Macaroon Cake (page 137).

Recipes for cakes, sauces, etc., asterisked in the dessert and serving suggestions, are given on pages 145 to 152. For instructions on layering, lining and other techniques involved in creating desserts, see pages 152 to 155. Basic recipes are on pages 16 and 17.

# Coffee

Freshly roasted, freshly ground coffee steeped in milk or cream which is then strained through a fine sieve gives the ultimate in coffee flavours. An infusion of coffee beans is also delicious, but good instant coffees – and even coffee essence – are by no means to be despised or dismissed. For a softer, more rounded flavour, sweeten the ice with vanilla sugar or add a few drops of vanilla essence.

**Simple Coffee Ice Cream**
Add 2 tablespoons (2 × 15 ml spoons) instant coffee to any of the Basic Recipes*.

## Coffee Granita

*About 3 ounces (75 g) sugar*
*1/2 pint (300 ml) fresh, hot, very strong black coffee*
*4–6 ice cubes*
*1/4 pint (150 ml) double cream, whipped*

Dissolve sufficient sugar to taste in the coffee – the granita should not be very sweet. Add 1/2 pint (300 ml) cold water and the ice cubes and stir until the cubes have melted.

Pour the mixture into a container. Cover and freeze until the mixture has the appearance of a mass of small, light crystals. Stir the granita and spoon into 6 tall glasses. Top each with whipped cream and serve at once with long spoons.

Serves 6

***Coffee granita de luxe***
*Add 1 1/2 tablespoons (1 1/2 × 15 ml spoons) Benedictine and adjust the sugar level.*

## Coffee Ice Cream

*6 ounces (175 g) unsalted butter, chopped*
*12 fluid ounces (350 ml) milk*
*4 1/2 ounces (115 g) caster sugar*
*Few drops of vanilla essence*
*2 tablespoons (2 × 15 ml spoons) instant coffee granules*

Put the butter, milk and sugar in a saucepan and heat gently until the butter has melted and the sugar dissolved. Then bring to just boiling point. Pour into a blender, add the vanilla essence and coffee and blend in 4 bursts of 10 seconds each. Leave to cool. Pour the mixture into a container. Cover and freeze until firm, beating twice at hourly intervals.

About 30 minutes before serving, transfer the ice cream to the refrigerator.

Serves 4–5

***Serving suggestion***
*Scoop into individual dishes and decorate with grated chocolate and chocolate-covered coffee beans.*

## Coffee Ice Cream (with condensed milk)

*Approximately 6 ounce (175 g) can full cream condensed milk*
*1 1/2 tablespoons (1 1/2 × 15 ml spoons) instant coffee granules, dissolved in 1 tablespoon (15 ml spoon) boiling water*
*1/2 teaspoon (2.5 ml spoon) vanilla essence*
*1/2 pint (300 ml) whipping or double cream*

Put the condensed milk and dissolved coffee in a bowl over a pan of gently simmering water. Cook for 15 minutes, stirring occasionally, until slightly thickened. Remove from the heat, stir in the vanilla essence and leave to cool before chilling in the refrigerator.

Whip the cream until soft peaks are formed then fold into the coffee mixture. Pour the mixture into a container. Cover and freeze until firm, beating well after 1 1/2 hours.

About 15 minutes before serving, transfer the ice cream to the refrigerator.

Serves 4

***Serving suggestions***
*Serve with Black Cherry Sauce*, Hot Fudge Sauce* or Burnt Honey Sauce*.*

## Traditional Coffee Parfait

*3 ounces (75 g) sugar*
*4 egg yolks*
*3/4 pint (450 ml) double cream*
*Few drops of vanilla essence*
*2 tablespoons (2 × 15 ml spoons) instant coffee*
*Grated plain chocolate, for decoration*

Put the sugar and 2 1/2 fluid ounces (65 ml) water in a small heavy-based saucepan. Stir to dissolve over low heat then bring to the boil and boil until the temperature reaches 230°F (110°C).

Whisk the egg yolks in a bowl until thick and light. Gradually whisk in the syrup. Leave to cool then chill for 30 minutes.

Put the cream in a bowl with the vanilla essence and coffee and whip until soft peaks are formed. Carefully fold into the egg yolk mixture. Spoon or pipe into tall, freezer-proof glasses, if available, or into individual dishes, and freeze until firm.

About 15 minutes before serving, transfer the parfaits to the refrigerator. Decorate the tops of the parfaits with grated chocolate.

Serves 4–6

***Dessert suggestion***
*Form into 4–6 balls, each with a tablespoonful (15 ml spoon) Nougat Glace à l'Orange (page 57) in the centre. Roll in desiccated coconut, crushed hazelnut Macaroons* or cocoa powder.*

# Iced Mocha Soufflé

3 ounces (75 g) freshly ground coffee
1/2 pint (300 ml) milk
8 ounces (225 g) plain bitter chocolate, chopped
4 egg whites
8 ounces (225 g) icing sugar
3/4 pint (425 ml) cream, whipped
8 Meringue Baskets*

Put the coffee and milk in a saucepan and heat to boiling point. Remove from the heat, cover and leave to infuse for 15 minutes. Strain over the chocolate and stir until the chocolate has melted and the liquid is smooth. Leave to cool.

Whisk the egg whites in a bowl over a pan of hot water until thick then gradually whisk in the sugar. Continue whisking off the heat until the meringue is thick, very light and cold.

Lightly fold the cream and chocolate together then fold into the meringue. Freeze until firm in individual meringue baskets. Serve straight from the freezer.

Serves 8

### Dessert suggestion
Fold 2 ounces (50 g) chopped walnuts into the soufflé mixture just before freezing. Make a bombe with a jacket of Genoise Cake* sprinkled with rum, followed by a layer of Vanilla Ice Cream (page 123). Fill the centre with the soufflé. Decorate the turned-out dessert with coffee- or chocolate-flavoured whipped cream, coffee dragées and Chocolate Shapes*.

# Iced Capuccino

1 tablespoon (15 ml spoon) gelatine
1 pint (600 ml) strong black coffee
1 ounce (25 g) plain chocolate, chopped
4 1/2 ounces (115 g) sugar
8 fluid ounces (225 ml) double cream
2–3 tablespoons (2–3 × 15 ml spoons) coffee liqueur
Finely grated chocolate, for decoration

Dissolve the gelatine in a little of the coffee in a bowl. Put the chocolate and half the coffee in a saucepan and stir to melt over very low heat. Stir in the sugar and gradually stir the mixture into the gelatine. Stir in the remaining coffee and chill. Stir in the cream and liqueur and pour into a container. Cover and freeze until firm.

About 45 minutes before serving, transfer the ice cream to the refrigerator. Serve decorated with grated chocolate.

Serves 6–8

### Serving suggestion
Serve in tall glasses with long-handled spoons, accompanied by Sponge Fingers*.

# Coffee and Hazelnut Ice Cream

3 egg yolks
3 ounces (75 g) icing sugar
3/4 pint (450 ml) cream, whipped
1 tablespoon (15 ml spoon) hazelnut liqueur or
    1 ounce (25 g) hazelnuts, toasted and chopped
1 teaspoon (5 ml spoon) instant coffee granules
1 1/2 ounces (40 g) raisins
3 tablespoons (3 × 15 ml spoons) flaked almonds, toasted
Cocoa powder, for decoration

Whisk the egg yolks and icing sugar together in a bowl until very light. Fold in 9 fluid ounces (250 ml) of the cream and the liqueur or hazelnuts. Spoon half the mixture into a ring mould or loaf tin, cover and freeze for 2 hours.

Fold the coffee into the remaining cream until evenly blended. Sprinkle the raisins then the almonds evenly over the frozen cream mixture and cover with the coffee cream. Finally, spoon in the remaining hazelnut cream. Return to the freezer until firm.

About 20 minutes before serving, turn the ice cream out on to a cold plate and leave in the refrigerator. Sprinkle a little cocoa powder over the top just before serving.

Serves 4–5

### Dessert suggestion
Freeze in a ring mould. Fill the centre of the turned-out mould with small orange segments and chopped marshmallows. Pipe brandy-flavoured whipped cream around the base of the dessert and finish with chopped hazelnuts.

# Coffee Almond Ice Cream

2 tablespoons (2 × 15 ml spoons) coffee essence
2 tablespoons (2 × 15 ml spoons) soft brown sugar
1/2 pint (300 ml) plain yogurt
2 ounces (50 g) ground almonds
2 egg whites

Put the coffee essence, brown sugar and yogurt in a bowl and beat until well mixed. Fold in the ground almonds.

In another bowl, whisk the egg whites until stiff but not dry and fold into the coffee mixture. Pour into individual dishes, cover and freeze.

About 20 minutes before serving, transfer the ice cream to the refrigerator.

Serves 4

### Low calorie version
Use fructose, or a low calorie or artificial sweetener instead of sugar.

# Italian Coffee Ice Cream

*4 egg yolks*
*4½ ounces (115 g) caster sugar*
*11 fluid ounces (325 ml) strong espresso coffee made*
*   with milk instead of water*
*8 fluid ounces (225 ml) double cream, lightly whipped*

*For serving*
*Sambuca*
*Coffee dragées*

Put the egg yolks and sugar in a bowl and whisk until thick and light. Whisk in the coffee then fold in the cream.

Pour the mixture into a saucepan and warm over low heat, stirring constantly, until it swells to nearly twice its original volume. Leave to cool completely.

Pour the mixture into a container. Cover and freeze until firm, beating twice at hourly intervals.

About 40 minutes before serving, transfer the ice cream to the refrigerator. Pour a little Sambuca over each portion and finish with coffee dragées.

Serves 6

# Coffee and Coconut Ice Cream

*2 ounces (50 g) coffee beans*
*¾ pint (450 ml) double or whipping cream*
*1 teaspoon (5 ml spoon) vanilla essence*
*3 large eggs, separated*
*2 ounces (50 g) sugar*
*3 ounces (75 g) lightly toasted desiccated coconut*
*Bitter Chocolate Sauce\*, for serving*

Put the coffee beans and half the cream in a saucepan and bring to just below boiling. Remove from the heat, cover and leave for 30 minutes. Strain the cream, discard the coffee beans and whisk in the remaining cream with the vanilla essence.

Put the egg yolks in a bowl and whisk until thick and light. In a small heavy-based saucepan, dissolve the sugar in 3 fluid ounces (75 ml) water. Then boil until the temperature reaches 220°F (104°C). Pour the syrup on to the egg yolks in a steady stream, whisking constantly, and continue to whisk until thick and cold.

Fold in the cream and coconut. Whisk the egg whites until stiff but not dry and fold into the mixture. Pour the mixture into a container. Cover and freeze until firm.

About 20 minutes before serving, transfer to the refrigerator. Serve with chocolate sauce.

Serves 4–5

**Serving suggestion**
*Serve as a sundae with pineapple cubes soaked in kirsch, Melon-Lime Ice (page 83) and coarsely chopped plain chocolate. Top with Coffee Sauce\*.*

# Fresh Coffee Ice Cream

*4 fluid ounces (100 ml) milk*
*¾ ounce (20 g) finely ground coffee*
*3 ounces (75 g) sugar*
*2 small or 1½ large eggs, lightly beaten*
*Pinch of salt*
*Few drops vanilla essence*
*12 fluid ounces (350 ml) single or whipping cream*

Put the milk in a heavy-based saucepan and bring to just on boiling point. Stir in the coffee and the sugar. Slowly pour the coffee-milk mixture on to the eggs, beating constantly. Pour back into the pan, add the salt and vanilla essence and cook over a very gentle heat, stirring constantly, until it thickens, taking care not to let the mixture boil. Remove from the heat, stir in half the cream and leave until cool, stirring occasionally.

Strain the custard through cheesecloth or muslin. Blend in the remaining cream and pour into a container. Cover and freeze until firm, beating twice at hourly intervals.

About 30 minutes before serving, transfer the ice cream to the refrigerator.

Serves 5

**Serving suggestion**
*Make ice cream sodas by putting 2 tablespoons (2 × 15 ml spoons) chocolate topping in the base of a tall glass for each serving. Mix with soda water, add a scoop of ice cream and finish with more chocolate topping.*

**Dessert suggestion**
*Carefully fold small Meringues\* into the ice cream when it has been beaten for the second time and freeze in a loose-bottomed cake tin. Decorate the turned-out dessert with large swirls of slightly softened Chocolate Ice Cream (page 44). Finish with small meringues and hazelnuts.*

**Additional recipes using coffee:** Walnut Mocha Ice Cream (page 125), Coffee Ice Cream Slice (page 137), Chocolate-coated Coffee Ice Cream Balls (page 138).

Recipes for cakes, sauces, etc., asterisked in the dessert and serving suggestions, are given on pages 145 to 152. For instructions on layering, lining and other techniques involved in creating desserts, see pages 152 to 155. Basic recipes are on pages 16 and 17.

CRAB-APPLE:     see OLD-FASHIONED
                    FAVOURITES

# Cranberry

Either fresh or frozen cranberries can be used for the purées in these recipes (which make some of the most beautifully coloured of all ices). One pound (450 g) fresh or frozen cranberries and 4–5 ounces (100–150 g) sugar will yield about 12 fluid ounces (350 ml) purée. If the fruit itself is not available cranberry sauce, preferably home-made, is a good store-cupboard stand-by for quick ice creams.

**Simple Cranberry Ice Cream**
Add 12 fluid ounces (350 ml) cranberry sauce, sweetened if necessary, to any of the Basic Recipes*.

## Cranberry Ice Cream (with cranberry purée)

3 eggs, separated
1 ounce (25 g) caster sugar
12 fluid ounces (350 ml) sweetened cranberry purée
1/2 pint (300 ml) cream, whipped
Whole cooked fresh cranberries, for decoration

Put the egg yolks and sugar in a bowl and whisk until very thick and light. Fold in the cranberry purée, then the cream.

In another bowl, whisk the egg whites until stiff but not dry and fold into the cranberry cream. Pour the mixture into a container. Cover and freeze until firm.

About 30 minutes before serving, transfer to the refrigerator. Decorate with fresh cranberries.

Serves 4–6

### Serving suggestion
*Freeze in an ice-cube tray with the ice-cube divider in place. Pile in frosted glasses with cream or plain yogurt trickled over, with a scattering of cranberries.*

## Quick Cranberry Ice Cream

1/2 pint (300 ml) cream, whipped
10 ounces (275 g) bought cranberry sauce or 1/2 pint (300 ml) sweetened thick home-made cranberry sauce
1–2 tablespoons (1–2 × 15 ml spoons) chunky orange marmalade

Put the cream in a bowl and fold in the cranberry sauce. Mix until evenly blended. Add marmalade to taste. Pour the mixture into a container. Cover and freeze until firm. About 20 minutes before serving, transfer to the refrigerator.

Serves 4

### Texture variation
*Use a sauce made with whole cranberries.*

## Cranberry Ice Cream

*1 pound (450 g) fresh or frozen cranberries*
*4–5 ounces (100–150 g) sugar*
*½ pint (300 ml) crème fraîche or whipping cream*
*2 tablespoons (2 × 15 ml spoons) milk if crème fraîche is used or plain yogurt if whipping cream is used*

Put the cranberries in a saucepan and pour 7½ fluid ounces (215 ml) boiling water over. Cover and leave for 5 minutes. Bring to simmering point, cook for 5 minutes, turn off the heat and leave for 5 minutes. Bring to simmering point again and cook for 5 minutes. Remove from the heat, stir in the sugar and reduce to a purée. This method produces a purée with an exceptionally good colour. Leave to cool.

In a bowl, lightly whip the crème fraîche with the milk or the cream with the yogurt then fold into the purée. Pour the mixture into a container. Cover and freeze until firm, beating twice at hourly intervals.

About 20 minutes before serving, transfer the ice cream to the refrigerator.

Serves 4

### Dessert suggestion
*Freeze Smooth Coconut Ice Cream (page 49) in small foil dishes or ramekins. Turn out and cover in the ice cream. Just before serving, decorate with gin-flavoured whipped cream.*

## Cranberry Ice Cream (with cheese and yogurt)

*1 pound (450 g) fresh or frozen cranberries*
*4–5 ounces (100–150 g) sugar*
*8 ounces (225 g) soft cheese, beaten or sieved*
*4 fluid ounces (100 ml) plain yogurt*
*1 egg white*

Cook the cranberries as for Cranberry Ice Cream, then stir in the sugar, adjusting the level to taste and leave to cool.

Put the cheese into a bowl and gradually beat in the yogurt to make a smooth mixture then stir in the cranberries. Pour the mixture into a container, cover and freeze until firm. Tip into a bowl and beat well. Whisk the egg white until stiff but not dry and fold into the cranberry mixture. Spoon the mixture back into the container. Cover and freeze until firm.

About 40 minutes before serving, transfer the ice cream to the refrigerator.

Serves 4

### Dessert suggestion
*Ripple with Orange Frost (see Grapefruit Frost, page 66). Serve with Cigars Russe\*.*

### Low calorie version
*Use fructose, or a low calorie or artificial sweetener instead of sugar.*

## Cranberry and Pistachio Ripple

*1 pound (450 g) fresh or frozen cranberries*
*Finely grated zest and juice of 2 oranges*
*4 ounces (100 g) sugar*
*½ pint (300 ml) cream, whipped*
*2 × approximately 1½ ounce (40 g) packets dessert topping mix*
*½ pint (300 ml) milk*
*1 ounce (25 g) pistachio nuts*
*3 tablespoons (3 × 15 ml spoons) Cointreau, optional*

Cook the cranberries with the orange zest and juice as for 'Cranberry Ice Cream'. Purée, sieve, stir in the sugar and leave to cool. Fold in the cream then freeze in a covered container until just becoming firm.

Make up the topping mix with the milk in a bowl. Stir in the nuts and liqueur. Carefully fold through the cranberry cream to give a rippled effect. Return to the freezer until firm.

About 30 minutes before serving, transfer the ice cream to the refrigerator.

Serves 8–12

### Dessert suggestion
*Freeze in individual ring moulds. Fill the centres with cubes of white marshmallow lightly mixed with cranberry sauce. Pipe small rosettes of whipped cream, brandy flavoured if wished, around the base of each serving.*

**Additional recipe using cranberries:** Cranberry Snowballs (page 138).

CRYSTALLIZED FRUIT:  *see DRIED, CANDIED and GLACÉ FRUITS*
CUCUMBER:  *see SAVOURY*
CUSTARD:  *see VANILLA, CUSTARD*
DAMSON:  *see PLUM, PRUNE*
DATE:  *see DRIED, CANDIED and GLACÉ FRUITS*

# Dried, Candied & Glacé Fruits

All kinds of dried fruits – apples, pears, peaches and even bananas – are suitable for ices. They can be the main ingredient, as in the recipes on these pages, or added to other recipes for extra interest (preferably soaked for a while beforehand in a spirit or liqueur, to plump them up).

Glacé and candied fruits (steeped in a rich sugar syrup for up to 14 days) and crystallized fruits (steeped in syrup and then given an outer coating of crunchy sugar) make equally delicious ices, either on their own as in a number of the recipes that follow, or combined with dried fruits.

**Simple Dried Fruit Ice Cream**
Soak 4 ounces (100 g) chopped dried fruit overnight in brandy or liqueur. Add to any of the Basic Recipes* or to a good-quality bought vanilla ice cream.

## Tutti-Frutti Ice Cream

4 ounces (100 g) mixed sultanas, raisins and currants
1 ounce (25 g) glacé cherries, chopped
1 ounce (25 g) crystallized pineapple, chopped
1 ounce (25 g) crystallized orange or citron peel,
    chopped
1/2 ounce (15 g) angelica, chopped
Long strip of lemon peel
4 tablespoons (4 × 15 ml spoons) brandy or orange
    liqueur
4 eggs, separated
4 ounces (100 g) icing sugar, sieved
1/2 pint (300 ml) double cream, whipped
1 1/2 ounces (40 g) flaked almonds

For decoration
'Leaves' cut from angelica
Glacé cherries, quartered

Soak the fruits and lemon peel in the brandy or liqueur for at least 4 hours.

Put the egg yolks and sugar in a bowl and whisk until thick and light. In another bowl, whisk the egg whites until stiff but not dry. Fold the egg whites into the egg yolks with the cream.

Pour the mixture into a container. Cover and freeze until beginning to become firm around the edges.

Remove and discard the lemon peel from the fruits. Mix the fruits, the soaking liquor, and the almonds into the ice cream.

Spoon into a 2 pint (1.1 litre) pudding bowl. Cover and freeze until firm.

About 20 minutes before serving, turn out on to a cold plate and leave in the refrigerator. Decorate with the angelica 'leaves' and quartered cherries arranged in the shapes of flowers.

Serves 6–8

**Dessert suggestion**
*Fill a Swiss Roll\* with the ice cream, then coat the outside in Smooth Pistachio Ice Cream (page 101). Decorate with whole pistachio nuts.*

## Frozen Fruit Cake

3 eggs, beaten
3 1/2 ounces (90 g) sugar
3/4 pint (450 ml) milk
6 ounces (175 g) sultanas
4 ounces (100 g) pecans or walnuts, chopped
6 ounces (175 g) Macaroons*, crushed
3 ounces (75 g) glacé cherries, chopped
1 teaspoon (5 ml spoon) vanilla essence
8 fluid ounces (225 ml) cream, whipped

Put the eggs and sugar in a bowl and beat until thick and light. Pour the milk into a heavy-based saucepan and bring to just simmering point. Gradually pour on to the eggs, stirring. Return to the rinsed pan and cook over low heat, stirring constantly, until thickened. Remove from the heat and set aside to cool. Pour into a container, cover and freeze to the slushy stage. Turn into a bowl, beat well, then stir in the sultanas, nuts, macaroons, cherries and vanilla and fold in the cream. Spoon the mixture back into the container. Cover and freeze until firm.

About 30 minutes before serving, transfer the ice cream to the refrigerator.

Serves 6

**Dessert suggestion**
*Fill a Swiss Roll\* with the frozen cake, then coat the outside with Maple Ice Cream (page 81), Rich Hazelnut Ice Cream (page 69) or Chocolate Ice Cream (page 44).*

## Fruit Cake Ice Cream

2 eggs
2 ounces (50 g) soft brown sugar or other brown
    sugar
8 fluid ounces (225 ml) milk
7 fluid ounces (200 ml) cream
1 1/2 ounces (40 g) marzipan, finely chopped or
    1 ounce (25 g) ground almonds
3 ounces (75 g) fruit cake, finely chopped
1 fluid ounce (25 ml) brandy, sherry or rum

Whisk the eggs and sugar together in a large bowl.

Bring the milk and cream to simmering point in a saucepan. Pour on to the eggs in a slow steady stream, whisking constantly, and continue to whisk until the mixture is very thick and light.

Whisk in the marzipan or ground almonds then fold in the fruit cake and brandy, sherry or rum.

Spoon the mixture into a container. Cover and freeze until firm.

About 20 minutes before serving, transfer the ice cream to the refrigerator.

Serves 6

## Simple Crystallized Fruit Ice Cream

*4 ounces (100 g) mixed crystallized or glacé fruits, chopped if necessary*
*Grated zest of 1 large lemon*
*1 × approximately 1½ ounce (40 g) packet instant dessert topping*
*¼ pint (150 ml) milk*
*½ pint (300 ml) cream, whipped*

Mix the crystallized or glacé fruit together with the lemon zest. Make up the dessert topping with the milk in a bowl. Fold in the cream and the fruits.

Spoon the mixture into a container. Cover and freeze until firm, beating twice at hourly intervals.

About 30 minutes before serving, transfer the ice cream to the refrigerator.

Serves 4

**Serving suggestion**
*Sandwich each portion between two Meringues\* and freeze. Just before serving, pour a little Mars Bar Sauce\* over each one, and sprinkle with finely chopped hazelnuts.*

## Nougat Glace à l'Orange

*2¾ ounces (70 g) granulated sugar*
*2 egg whites*
*½ ounce (15 g) caster sugar*
*1½ pints (850 ml) double or whipping cream*
*1½ fluid ounces (40 ml) Cointreau*
*1½ ounces (40 g) crystallized orange peel, chopped*
*1 ounce (25 g) Praline\**
*Fresh\* raspberry sauce, for serving*

In a heavy-based saucepan, dissolve the granulated sugar in 1 fluid ounce (25 ml) water then boil until a temperature of 250°F (120°C) is reached.

Whisk the egg white in a bowl with the caster sugar until stiff but not dry. Slowly pour in the syrup, whisking constantly and continue to whisk until the mixture is very thick and cold.

In another bowl whip the cream together with the Cointreau until soft peaks form then fold into the meringue with the orange peel and the praline.

Pour into an oblong mould, cover and freeze until firm.

About 20 minutes before serving, turn the ice cream out on to a chilled plate and leave in the refrigerator. Serve cut into slices surrounded with raspberry sauce.

Serves 6

**Serving suggestion**
*Sprinkle with grated chocolate.*

## Crystallized Fruit Ice Cream

*8 ounces (225 g) crystallized fruits*
*6 tablespoons (6 × 15 ml spoons) kirsch, brandy or sherry*
*8 boudoir or other dry sponge biscuits, cut into ½ inch (12 mm) pieces*
*1¼ pints (700 ml) cream, lightly whipped*
*4 ounces (100 g) icing sugar*
*Few drops of vanilla essence*
*Fresh\* orange sauce for serving*

Soak the fruit in the kirsch, brandy or sherry for 30 minutes.

Put the sponge biscuits in a bowl and drain the liquor over them. Pour the liquid off again. Whip the liquid into the cream with the sugar and vanilla essence then fold in the fruit and biscuits. Spoon into a chilled 1½ pint (850 ml) domed mould or pudding bowl, cover and freeze until firm.

About 15 minutes before serving, turn the dessert out on to a chilled plate and leave in the refrigerator. Serve each portion with some fresh orange sauce.

Serves 6–8

## Winter Fruit Ice Cream

*6 ounces (175 g) dried fruits – figs, peaches, dates, pears, apples etc., chopped*
*4 tablespoons (4 × 15 ml spoons) brandy or rum*
*¾ pint (450 ml) milk*
*1 cinnamon stick*
*3 eggs*
*4 ounces (100 g) demerara sugar*
*¾ pint (450 ml) whipping cream*

Soak the fruits in the brandy or rum overnight.

Pour the milk into a heavy-based saucepan, add the cinnamon and bring to just below boiling point. Remove from the heat, cover and leave for 30 minutes. Remove the cinnamon stick.

Put the eggs and sugar in a bowl and whisk together. Bring the milk to just below boiling point again and slowly pour on to the eggs, whisking constantly. Cook the mixture gently, stirring constantly, until it thickens but do not allow it to boil. Remove from the heat and leave to cool, stirring frequently.

Whip the cream in a bowl until soft peaks form then fold into the custard with the fruits and soaking liquor. Pour into a container. Cover and freeze until firm.

About 30 minutes before serving, transfer the ice cream to the refrigerator.

Serves 6–8

**Serving suggestion**
*Layer with crushed ginger biscuits in tall glasses. Pour over Burnt Honey Sauce\* or Chunky Marmalade Sauce\*.*

# Candied Peel Ice Cream

*½ pint (300 ml) whipping or double cream*
*4–5 tablespoons (4–5 × 15 ml spoons) advocaat*
*1–2 ounces (25–50 g) icing sugar*
*1–2 tablespoons (1–2 × 15 ml spoons) orange juice*
*3 heaped tablespoons (3 × 15 ml spoons) chopped*
*candied peel*
*Orange segments or Caramelized\* orange strips, for*
*serving*

Whip the cream in a bowl with the advocaat, icing sugar and orange juice, adjusting the amounts of these to taste, until soft peaks are formed. Spoon into a container, cover and freeze until just becoming firm. Turn into a bowl and beat well. Fold in the candied peel.

Spoon the mixture back into the container. Cover and freeze until firm.

About 20 minutes before serving, transfer the ice cream to the refrigerator. Serve with fresh orange segments or caramelised orange strips.

Serves 4

# Date and Fig Ice Cream

*3 ounces (75 g) dates, chopped*
*3 ounces (75 g) figs, chopped*
*¼ pint (150 ml) sherry*
*Finely grated zest and juice of 1 orange*
*4 ounces (100 g) brown sugar*
*7 fluid ounces (200 ml) double or whipping cream*
*7 fluid ounces (200 ml) soured cream*
*2 egg whites*

Put the dates, figs and sherry in a small saucepan and heat gently to just below simmering point. Stir in the orange zest and juice and the sugar, cover and leave for at least 4 hours.

Put the creams in a bowl with the liquor drained from the fruit and whip until soft peaks form. In another bowl, whisk the egg whites until stiff. Fold the fruit into the cream and then the egg whites. Spoon the mixture into a container. Cover and freeze until firm.

About 30 minutes before serving, transfer the ice cream to the refrigerator.

Serves 4–6

### Serving suggestions
*Spoon into small Crêpes\* with orange segments soaked in a liqueur or spirit. Deep fry briefly, sprinkle with a thick coating of icing sugar, and serve with a white Wine Sauce\*.*

### Dessert suggestion
*Freeze in a fluted container. Decorate the turned-out dessert with swirls of whipped cream, chocolate drops and walnuts.*

# Date Ice Cream

*3 ounces (75 g) stoned dates, chopped*
*4 tablespoons (4 × 15 ml spoons) rum*
*2 eggs, separated*
*4 ounces (100 g) sugar*
*¼ pint (150 ml) milk*
*12 ounces (350 g) cottage or curd cheese, sieved*
*Finely grated zest and juice of 1 lemon*
*¼ pint (150 ml) cream, whipped*
*1 ounce (25 g) stem ginger, finely chopped*

Soak the dates in the rum for about 4 hours. Put the egg yolks and sugar in a bowl and whisk until light. Heat the milk to simmering point in a saucepan then whisk into the egg yolks. Return the mixture to the rinsed pan and cook over a low heat, stirring constantly, until thickened. Cool, stirring occasionally.

Process the cottage or curd cheese, lemon zest and juice and the rum strained from the dates together in a blender or food processor until smooth then mix with the custard. Pour the mixture into a container, cover and freeze until just becoming firm. Turn into a bowl, beat well, then fold in the cream, dates and ginger. Whisk the egg whites in a bowl until stiff but not dry and fold into the fruit mixture.

Spoon the mixture back into the container. Cover and freeze until firm.

About 30 minutes before serving, transfer the ice cream to the refrigerator.

Serves 6

### Dessert suggestion
*Freeze between layers of chocolate-flavoured Meringue\*. Cover the turned-out dessert with whipped cream. Decorate with pieces of candied orange peel or shapes cut from fresh orange peel.*

**Additional recipes using dried, candied and glacé fruits:** Old English Raisin Ice Cream (page 64), Raisin Ice Cream (page 64), Sultana Ice Cream (page 65), Honey and Fig Sorbet (page 73), Prune Sorbet (page 103), Prune Custard Ice (page 103), Prune Ice Cream with Brandy (page 116), Prune Ice Cream with Wine and Brandy (page 130), Mince Meat Ice Cream (page 141), Cassata (page 135), Iced Christmas Pudding (page 139).

*ELDERBERRY:   see OLD-FASHIONED*
*FAVOURITES*
*FLOWERS:   see HERBS, FLOWERS,*
*LEAVES*
*FUDGE:   see BUTTERSCOTCH,*
*CARAMEL, FUDGE*
*GERANIUM LEAF:   see HERBS,*
*FLOWERS, LEAVES*

# Ginger

Traditionally used in sweet dishes as well as savoury ones, ginger makes some of the freshest-tasting of all ices. Ginger wine gives a particularly rich, smooth flavour, while the syrup from a jar of preserved ginger is sweeter but equally refreshing. Chopped crystallized or preserved ginger provides 'bite' and texture, while freshly chopped fresh root ginger is well worth trying. Powdered or ground ginger can also be used and is probably a more practical ingredient.

**Simple Ginger Ice Cream**
Add 3 ounces (75 g) chopped crystallized ginger or 3 ounces (75 g) Chow Chow to any of the Basic Recipes* or to a good-quality bought vanilla ice cream.

## Ginger Wine Sorbet

*12 fluid ounces (350 ml) ginger wine*
*2 tablespoons (2 × 15 ml spoons) lime juice*
*7 ounces (200 g) sugar*
*¼ teaspoon (1.25 ml spoon) cream of tartar*
*2 egg whites*

*For decoration*
*Crystallized ginger*
*Long, thin, twisted strips of lemon peel*

Mix the ginger wine and lime juice with 12 fluid ounces (350 ml) water and pour either into an 8 inch (20 cm) cake tin or into an ice cream maker and freeze until slushy.

In a heavy-based saucepan, dissolve the sugar with the cream of tartar in 2½ fluid ounces (65 ml) water over low heat. Bring to the boil and boil rapidly for 4 minutes. Remove from the heat.

Whisk the egg whites in a bowl until firm then slowly pour in the hot syrup whisking all the time. Beat the ginger wine mixture then fold in the meringue.

Return the mixture to the container, cover and freeze until firm.

About 15–20 minutes before serving, transfer the sorbet to the refrigerator. Decorate each portion with crystallized ginger and prettily twisted strips of lemon peel.

Serves 6

**Serving suggestion**
*Flake the sorbet and serve on top of a fresh fruit salad.*

## Ground Ginger Ice Cream

*3 eggs, separated*
*3 ounces (75 g) caster sugar*
*1 teaspoon (5 ml spoon) ground ginger*
*4 ounces (100 g) full fat soft cheese*
*¼ pint (150 ml) milk*
*1 ounce (25 g) crystallized or preserved ginger, finely chopped*

Whisk the egg yolks, sugar and ginger together in a bowl until very light.

In another bowl, beat the cheese with the milk until fluffy. In a third bowl, whisk the egg whites until stiff but not dry.

Fold the cheese and milk into the egg yolk mixture with the chopped ginger. Then fold in the egg whites.

Spoon the mixture into a container. Cover and freeze until firm.

About 30 minutes before serving, transfer the ice cream to the refrigerator.

Serves 4

**Dessert suggestion**
*Layer with Whisked Sponge Cake* or Sponge Fingers* and Gooseberry Mallow Ice Cream (page 62). Decorate the turned-out dessert with whipped cream and walnuts.*

## Ginger Ice Cream (with whisky and marmalade)

*2 tablespoons (2 × 15 ml spoons) whisky*
*4 tablespoons (4 × 15 ml spoons) ginger marmalade*
*2 tablespoons (2 × 15 ml spoons) brown sugar*
*Finely grated zest of 1 lemon*
*½ pint (300 ml) whipping or double cream*
*2 egg whites*

Put the whisky, marmalade, sugar and lemon zest in a bowl and leave for at least 15 minutes. Whip in the cream until soft peaks are formed.

In another bowl, whisk the egg whites until stiff but not dry. Fold into the ginger cream.

Pour into a container. Cover and freeze until firm.

About 20 minutes before serving, transfer the ice cream to the refrigerator.

Serves 4

**Serving suggestion**
*Serve in Almond Tuiles*. Decorate with whipped cream, fresh lime segments, pith and membrane removed, and a sprinkling of brown sugar crystals.*

---

Recipes for cakes, sauces, etc., asterisked in the dessert and serving suggestions, are given on pages 145 to 152. For instructions on layering, lining and other techniques involved in creating desserts, see pages 152 to 155. Basic recipes are on pages 16 and 17.

# Ginger Crush

*3 egg yolks*
*2 ounces (50 g) sugar*
*½ pint (300 ml) milk*
*¼ pint (150 ml) cream, whipped*
*3 ounces (75 g) crystallized or stem ginger, drained*
  *and chopped*
*3 ounces (75 g) Meringues\*, roughly broken*
*Slices of stem ginger, for decoration*

Put the egg yolks and sugar in a bowl and beat together until thick and light.

In a heavy-based saucepan, heat the milk to just below boiling point. Slowly pour the milk on to the eggs, beating constantly. Return to the rinsed pan and heat gently, stirring constantly, until the custard thickens – but do not allow it to boil. Allow to cool completely.

Pour the custard into a container, cover and freeze to the slushy stage. Beat well in a bowl.

Whip the cream in a bowl until soft peaks form. Fold the cream into the ice cream with the ginger and meringues. Return the mixture to the container, cover and freeze until firm.

About 30 minutes before serving, transfer the ice cream to the refrigerator. Serve decorated with the slices of stem ginger.

Serves 6

### Dessert suggestion
*Make into a bombe or freeze in a loaf or cake tin with a centre of Pear Sorbet (page 93). Serve with Sponge Fingers\*.*

# Ginger and Lime Granita

*12 ounces (350 g) sugar*
*½ ounce (15 g) fresh root ginger, grated*
*Finely grated zest of 2 limes*
*Juice of 6 limes*

Put the sugar in a saucepan with 18 fluid ounces (500 ml) water. Stir to dissolve over low heat. Add the ginger and lime zest and bring to the boil. Remove from the heat, cover and leave to infuse for 15 minutes. Add the lime juice and leave to cool completely. Pour into a large, shallow container, cover and chill before freezing. Stir occasionally from the outside edges to the middle until it forms into a mass of ice crystals. Serve immediately – a good palate cleanser between the courses of a long and/or rich meal.

Serves 5–6

# Ginger Ice Cream

*2 ounces (50 g) sugar*
*3 large egg yolks*
*5 tablespoons (5 × 15 ml spoons) syrup from jar of*
  *preserved ginger*
*1 pint (600 ml) cream, whipped*
*4 ounces (100 g) preserved ginger, chopped*

In a heavy-based saucepan, dissolve the sugar in 4 fluid ounces (100 ml) water. Bring to the boil and boil until the temperature reaches 215°F (101°C).

Meanwhile whisk the egg yolks in a bowl until very thick. Whisk in the syrup in a slow, continuous stream. Whisk in the ginger syrup. Fold in the cream and ginger.

Pour the mixture into a container. Cover and freeze until firm, beating the mixture twice at hourly intervals.

About 30 minutes before serving, transfer the ice cream to the refrigerator.

Serves 6

# Ginger and Chocolate Chip Ice Cream

*½ pint (300 ml) milk*
*3 egg yolks*
*4 ounces (100 g) sugar*
*¼ pint (150 ml) ginger wine*
*Juice of 1 lemon*
*½ pint (300 ml) double cream, whipped*
*3 ounces (75 g) bitter chocolate, finely chopped*

In a heavy-based saucepan, gently heat the milk to just below simmering point.

Put the egg yolks and sugar in a bowl and beat together until thick, then whisk in the hot milk. Return the mixture to the rinsed pan and cook over a low heat, stirring constantly, until the mixture thickens. Remove from the heat and leave to cool slightly. Stir in the ginger wine and lemon juice and leave to cool completely, stirring occasionally.

Pour the custard into a shallow metal container, cover and freeze until just becoming firm. Tip the semi-frozen mixture into a bowl and beat well. Fold in the cream and chocolate then spoon back into the container, cover and freeze until firm.

About 20 minutes before serving, transfer the ice cream to the refrigerator.

Serves 6

*GLACÉ FRUITS:   see DRIED, CANDIED*
*and GLACÉ FRUITS*

# Gooseberry

Gooseberries are always sieved when they are used in ices, so there is no need to go through the tiresome process of topping and tailing them. If possible, use mid- or late season berries which will impart a sweet, full flavour to the ice. For an additional, subtle taste add a sprig of elderflowers to the poaching liquid.

**Simple Gooseberry Ice Cream**
Add ½ pint (300 ml) sieved gooseberry purée made from a 14 ounce (400 g) can of gooseberries (drained) to any of the Basic Recipes*, or to a good-quality bought vanilla ice cream.

## Gooseberry Sorbet

*1 pound (450 g) gooseberries*
*6 ounces (175 g) sugar*
*Juice of ½ lemon*
*Green colouring, optional*
*2 fluid ounces (50 ml) gin, optional*

In a saucepan gently cook the gooseberries with the sugar, lemon juice and ¼ pint (150 ml) water until soft. Reduce to a purée then pass through a sieve. Add a few drops of green colouring, if you are using it. Set aside to cool completely.

Stir in the gin, if you are using it. Pour the mixture into a container, cover and chill. Freeze until firm, beating 3 times at 45-minute intervals.

About 30 minutes before serving, transfer the sorbet to the refrigerator.

Serves 4

**Serving suggestion**
*Serve in Almond Tuiles* surrounded by fresh gooseberries marinated in dessert wine. Decorate with sweet geranium flowers or elderflowers.*

## Easy Gooseberry Ice Cream

*1¼ pounds (550 g) gooseberries*
*4 ounces (100 g) sugar*
*Long strip of orange peel*
*½ pint (300 ml) cream, whipped*

In a saucepan, poach the gooseberries with the sugar (adding more or less to taste), orange peel and about 2 tablespoons (30 ml) water until soft. Remove and discard the orange peel. Purée the gooseberries and pass through a fine sieve. Leave to cool.

Fold in the cream and pour into a container. Cover and freeze until firm, beating twice at hourly intervals.

About 30 minutes before serving, transfer the ice cream to the refrigerator.

Serves 4

**Dessert suggestion**
*Sandwich each portion between two digestive biscuits and freeze. Serve with Orange Flower Sauce*.*

## Gooseberry Mallow Ice Cream

*12 white marshmallows*
*Approximately 6 ounce (175 g) can evaporated milk*
*1 pound (450 g) fresh or frozen gooseberries*
*3 ounces (75 g) sugar*
*¼ pint (150 ml) cream, whipped*
*2 ounces (50 g) golden syrup*
*12–16 large macaroons, to serve*

Melt the marshmallows with the evaporated milk in a bowl placed over a pan of warm water, stirring until smooth.

In a saucepan, cook half the gooseberries in 2 tablespoons (30 ml) water over gentle heat for about 5 minutes or until the skins burst and the fruit softens. Stir in the sugar then sieve. Leave to cool.

Fold in the cream and pour into a container. Cover and freeze until firm.

Make a sauce by cooking the remaining gooseberries with the golden syrup and 2 tablespoons (30 ml) water in a covered pan over gentle heat until the fruit softens. Pass through a sieve and set aside.

About 45 minutes before serving, transfer the ice cream to the refrigerator. Just before serving, warm the sauce gently if necessary. Spoon the ice cream between the macaroons and pour the sauce over.

Serves 6–8

## Gooseberry and Geranium Leaf Yogurt Ice

*1 pound (450 g) dessert gooseberries*
*3½ ounces (90 g) sugar*
*6 sweet geranium leaves*
*¼ pint (150 ml) thick plain yogurt*
*Geranium flowers, for decoration*

Poach the gooseberries with the sugar, geranium leaves and 4 tablespoons (60 ml) water in a covered pan until very soft. Remove the geranium leaves. Purée the gooseberry mixture, pass through a sieve into a bowl and leave to cool.

Beat the yogurt into the gooseberry purée. Pour into a container, cover and freeze until firm, beating 3 times at 45-minute intervals.

About 40 minutes before serving, transfer the ice to the refrigerator. Serve each portion decorated with a small sprig or a single geranium flower.

Serves 4

**Serving suggestion**
*Scoop into individual dishes and surround with slices of kiwi fruit.*

**Low calorie version**
*Use fructose, or a low calorie or artificial sweetener instead of sugar.*

# Gooseberry Ice Cream

1¾ pounds (800 g) gooseberries
6 ounces (175 g) brown sugar
½ pint (300 ml) milk
3 large egg yolks
Juice of 1 lemon
¼ pint (150 ml) cream, whipped.
Green food colouring, optional

Poach the gooseberries with half the sugar and about 4 tablespoons (60 ml) water in a covered pan until soft but not mushy. Drain off the excess liquid into a small saucepan and boil until reduced and syrupy. Purée the fruit then pass through a sieve.

In a heavy-based saucepan, bring the milk to just below boiling point. Whisk the egg yolks in a bowl with the remaining sugar until thick and light then whisk in the hot milk. Return the mixture to the rinsed pan and cook over a low heat, stirring constantly, until thickened – but do not allow to boil. Leave to cool, stirring occasionally.

Beat the gooseberry purée and syrup and the lemon juice into the custard. Fold in the cream and colouring, if you are using it.

Pour the mixture into a container. Cover and freeze until firm beating twice at hourly intervals.

About 30 minutes before serving, transfer the ice cream to the refrigerator.

Serves 6–8

**Dessert suggestion**
*Layer with Moist Ginger Cake\*. Decorate with advocaat-flavoured cream and fresh orange segments.*

Recipes for cakes, sauces, etc., asterisked in the dessert and serving suggestions, are given on pages 145 to 152. For instructions on layering, lining and other techniques involved in creating desserts, see pages 152 to 155. Basic recipes are on pages 16 and 17.

# Grape

For a truly distinctive taste, choose muscat grapes with their rich, almost exotically perfumed flavour. Black grapes are also suitable – their flesh has a pink tinge which is retained in the finished ice. However, for a really good 'grape' colour, use unsweetened grape juice, available in cartons and bottles. Remember to remove the pips first if you purée the grapes in a blender or food processor; 1 pound (450 g) fruit will give about ¾ pint (450 ml) purée, depending on the type of grape. Or you can use seedless grapes, provided they have a good, strong flavour. Several recipes for dried grapes – sultanas and raisins – are included in this section.

**Simple Grape Ice Cream**
Peel, de-pip and halve 1 pound (450 g) sweet grapes and add to any of the Basic Recipes* or to a good-quality bought vanilla ice cream.

## Black Grape Granita

6 ounces (175 g) sugar
1½ pounds (700 g) black grapes, puréed and sieved
Juice of 1 lime or lemon
½ pint (300 ml) full-bodied dry white wine
Black grapes, for decoration

In a saucepan, dissolve the sugar in ¼ pint (150 ml) water. Bring to the boil and boil for 1 minute. Leave to cool.

Stir the syrup into the grape purée with the lime or lemon juice and wine. Freeze in a shallow tray, stirring from the sides to the centre with a fork to form a mass of small crystals. Serve immediately straight from the freezer.

Serves 6

**Flavour variation**
Use white instead of black grapes.

## Raisin Ice Cream

4 ounces (100 g) raisins
5 tablespoons (5 × 15 ml spoons) lemon juice
Approximately 14 ounce (400 g) can evaporated milk, well chilled
Few drops of vanilla essence
2 ounces (50 g) caster sugar

Soak the raisins in the lemon juice for at least 4 hours. Pour the evaporated milk into a bowl and whisk until very thick. Whisk in the vanilla essence and sugar. Fold in the raisins with their liquor and pour into a container. Cover and freeze until firm.

About 30 minutes before serving, transfer the ice cream to the refrigerator.

Serves 6

**Serving suggestion**
Serve with fresh orange segments, pith and membrane removed, and Orange Flower Sauce*.

## Grape Ice Cream

4½ ounces (115 g) sugar
1 pound (450 g) grapes, preferably muscat, peeled and pips removed
4 tablespoons (4 × 15 ml spoons) double cream, whipped
Frosted* grapes, for decoration

Dissolve the sugar in 8 tablespoons (120 ml) water in a small saucepan over medium heat. Then pour the syrup into a bowl and leave to cool.

Chop the grape flesh finely (do not worry if you have missed a few shreds of the skin) and mix with the syrup, adding any juice that comes out of the fruit. Pour into a container, cover and freeze until just becoming firm. Turn into a bowl, beat well then fold in the cream. Spoon back into the container, cover and freeze until firm, beating after 45 minutes. If possible, serve the ice cream immediately it is ready. If prepared in advance, transfer the ice cream to the refrigerator about 30 minutes before serving. Decorate each portion with frosted grapes.

Serves 4

**Dessert suggestion**
Line a mould or tin with Langues de Chat*. Add a layer of the ice cream and fill the centre with White Wine Sorbet (page 130). Decorate with black grapes.

## Old English Raisin Ice Cream

½ pint (300 ml) milk
4 tablespoons (4 × 15 ml spoons) clear honey
2 eggs, beaten
1½ teaspoons (1½ × 5 ml spoons) ground nutmeg
4 ounces (100 g) raisins
2 ounces (50 g) toasted flaked almonds
½ pint (300 ml) cream, whipped

In a heavy-based saucepan, heat the milk and honey to just below simmering point. Put the eggs in a bowl and whisk until light. Then whisk in the milk. Return the mixture to the rinsed pan and cook over low heat until the mixture thickens, stirring constantly. Remove from the heat, stir in the nutmeg and leave to cool, stirring occasionally. Pour into a container, cover and freeze until firm. Turn into a bowl and beat well. Stir in the raisins and almonds and fold in the cream.

Spoon the mixture back into the container. Cover and freeze until firm.

About 30 minutes before serving, transfer the ice cream to the refrigerator.

Serves 4–5

**Flavour variation**
Soak the raisins in dark rum and add the soaking liquid to the mixture, with the raisins.

## Sultana Ice Cream

*2 large juicy lemons*
*1/2 pint (300 ml) double cream*
*1/2 pint (300 ml) single cream*
*4 ounces (100 g) light muscovado sugar*
*4 tablespoons (4 × 15 ml spoons) advocaat, optional*
*3 ounces (75 g) sultanas, soaked in a spirit or liqueur if liked*
*1 ounce (25 g) chopped marrons glacés (or mixed peel)*
*Sliced marrons glacés or toasted flaked almonds, for decoration*

Remove the rind from the lemons with a potato peeler and put in a saucepan with the creams and sugar and simmer for 5 minutes. Remove from the heat, cover and leave until cold.

Strain the cream into a bowl. Add the advocaat if using, and whisk until soft peaks are formed. Pour into a container, cover and freeze until just becoming firm. Turn into a bowl, beat, then fold in the sultanas and marrons, or peel. Spoon the mixture back into the container, cover and freeze until firm.

About 30 minutes before serving, transfer the ice cream to the refrigerator. Serve each portion decorated with sliced marrons or toasted flaked almonds.

Serves 4

**Serving suggestion**
*For each serving, spoon into the centre of a spirit-soaked rum baba or a ring doughnut studded with flaked almonds. For a flamboyant flourish, flambé with a spirit or an orange liqueur.*

## Grape Yogurt Ice

*3/4 pint (450 ml) grapes (preferably muscat), puréed and sieved (see introduction)*
*Approximately 2–3 ounces (50–75 g) icing sugar*
*1/2 pint (300 ml) plain yogurt*
*Squeeze of orange juice*
*2 egg whites*

Blend the grape purée and sugar together in a bowl. Blend in the yogurt and orange juice. Taste and adjust the level of sweetness and orange juice.

Pour the mixture into a container. Cover and freeze to the slushy stage. Beat well in a bowl.

In another bowl, whisk the egg whites until stiff. Fold the egg whites into the grape yogurt ice, return the mixture to the container, cover and freeze.

About 40 minutes before serving, transfer the yogurt ice to the refrigerator.

Serves 5–6

**Low calorie version**
*Use fructose, or a low calorie or artificial sweetener instead of sugar.*

## Smooth Grape Ice Cream

*2 1/4 ounces (55 g) caster sugar*
*1/2 pint (300 ml) unsweetened grape juice, preferably red*
*1 teaspoon (5 ml spoon) lime or lemon juice*
*1 pint (600 ml) cream, whipped*

*For decoration*
*Halved black grapes*
*Leaf shapes cut from lemon peel*

Dissolve the sugar in the grape juice and lime or lemon juice. Fold into the whipped cream and pour into a container. Cover and freeze until firm, beating twice at hourly intervals.

About 20 minutes before serving, transfer to the refrigerator. Serve decorated with the grapes and lemon peel 'leaves'.

Serves 6

**Dessert suggestion**
*Layer with Provençal Honey Ice Cream (page 72) between a base and top of Hazelnut Meringue\*. Decorate the outside of the dessert with orange-liqueur-flavoured whipped cream and seedless green grapes.*

## Muscat Sorbet

*8 ounces (225 g) sugar*
*1 1/4 pounds (550 g) muscat grapes, puréed and sieved*
*Juice of 2 lemons*
*1 tablespoon (15 ml spoon) orange flower water (or use orange instead of lemon juice)*
*3 tablespoons (3 × 15 ml spoons) sweet muscat wine*
*Finely chopped pistachio nuts, for decoration*

In a heavy-based saucepan, dissolve the sugar in 1 pint (600 ml) water. Bring to the boil and boil for 10 minutes. Remove from the heat, add the lemon (or orange) juice and leave to cool.

Strain the syrup into the grape purée with the orange flower water if used and the wine.

Pour the mixture into a container. Cover and freeze until firm, beating 3 times at 45-minute intervals.

About 30 minutes before serving, transfer the sorbet to the refrigerator. Serve decorated with pistachio nuts.

Serves 6–8

**Dessert suggestion**
*Encase in Tea Ice Cream (page 71).*

**Additional recipe using grapes:** Apple and Raisin Ice Cream (page 21).

# Grapefruit

Use large, firm fruit that feels heavy for its size – a light grapefruit has more pith and less juice. The many pink varieties that are now available are comparatively sweet, with a soft, delicate flavour. However, all grapefruit make marvellously refreshing ices, giving sorbets in particular a fresh, tangy taste. Canned grapefruit segments, in syrup or unsweetened, are ideal for serving with the ices, and the unsweetened variety can, if necessary, be used instead of fresh fruit.

### Simple Grapefruit Ice Cream

Chop 4 ounces (100 g) drained, canned grapefruit segments (in syrup) and add to any of the Basic Recipes*, or to a good-quality bought vanilla ice cream.

## Grapefruit Yogurt Ice

*2 large grapefruit*
*4 ounces (100 g) sugar*
*8 fluid ounces (225 ml) plain yogurt*
*8 ounces (225 g) low fat soft cheese, beaten*
*1 tablespoon (15 ml spoon) finely chopped fresh mint*
*1 egg white*

*For decoration*
*Grapefruit segments*
*Mint leaves*

Peel the grapefruit, divide into segments and cut the flesh away from the membranes. Chop the flesh, reserving any juice.

In a heavy-based saucepan, dissolve the sugar in 6 fluid ounces (175 ml) water. Bring to the boil and boil until the temperature reaches 234°F (112°C). Set aside to cool.

Stir the grapefruit flesh and reserved juice into the syrup. Blend the yogurt and cheese together until smooth, then mix in the grapefruit mixture and mint.

Pour the mixture into a container, cover and freeze to the slushy stage. Beat well in a bowl.

Whisk the egg white in a small bowl until stiff but not dry. Fold into the grapefruit-yogurt mixture.

Spoon the mixture into individual dishes, cover and return to the freezer.

About 40 minutes before serving, transfer the ices to the refrigerator. Decorate each dish with grapefruit segments and mint leaves.

Serves 4

### Serving suggestion
*Serve in chilled grapefruit or avocado shells, intermingled with small scoops of Avocado Ice Cream (page 27), quartered grapefruit segments, pith and membrane removed, chopped hazelnuts and sprigs of mint.*

### Low calorie version
*Use fructose, or a low calorie or artificial sweetener instead of sugar.*

## Grapefruit Sorbet

*2 ounces (50 g) cube sugar*
*2 large juicy grapefruit*
*1 egg white*

Rub the sugar cubes over the skins of the grapefruit until they are soaked in the flavouring oil. Dissolve the cubes in ¼ pint (150 ml) water.

Squeeze the juice from the grapefruit – there should be about ½ pint (300 ml) – into a bowl. Stir the syrup into the juice and pour into a container. Cover and freeze until just becoming firm around the edges. Beat well in a bowl.

In another bowl, whip the egg white until stiff but not dry. Fold it into the juice. Return to the container, cover and freeze until firm.

About 30 minutes before serving, transfer the sorbet to the refrigerator.

Serves 4

### Flavour variation
*Add approximately 2 tablespoons (2 × 15 ml spoons) of chopped fresh mint.*

## Grapefruit Frost

*1 tablespoon (15 ml spoon) gelatine*
*6¼ fluid ounce (184 ml) can frozen concentrated grapefruit juice, thawed*
*½ pint (300 ml) plain yogurt*
*Finely grated zest of 1 large grapefruit*
*2 egg whites*
*Fine strips of twisted grapefruit peel, for decoration*

Dissolve the gelatine in 4 tablespoons (60 ml) water in a small bowl placed over a pan of hot water. Beat the grapefruit juice, yogurt and grapefruit zest together then gradually blend with the gelatine.

Pour the mixture into a container, cover and freeze until slushy. Beat well in a bowl.

Put the egg whites in a bowl and whisk until stiff but not dry. Fold the egg whites into the grapefruit mixture. Return the mixture to the container, cover and freeze until firm.

About 40 minutes before serving, transfer the frost to the refrigerator. Decorate each portion with twists of grapefruit peel.

Serves 4

### Flavour variation
*Substitute frozen orange juice and the finely grated zest of 2 oranges for the grapefruit juice and zest.*

# Grapefruit Ice Cream

*8 fluid ounces (225 ml) grapefruit juice*
*6 ounces (175 g) icing sugar*
*1/2 pint (300 ml) double cream, whipped*

Put the juice and sugar into a bowl and stir until the sugar has dissolved. Fold the juice into the cream and pour into a container. Cover and freeze until firm, beating twice at hourly intervals.

About 30 minutes before serving, transfer the ice cream to the refrigerator.

Serves 4

### Serving suggestion
*Put scoops in small éclairs and cover with Hot Chocolate Sauce\* or Bitter Chocolate Sauce\*.*

### Dessert suggestion
*Form into 4 balls with a tablespoon (15 ml spoon) of Mint Sorbet (page 71) in the centre of each one. Serve in Gingersnap Baskets\* or Coupelles\*. Surround with grapefruit segments, pith and membrane removed, sprinkled with crème de menthe.*

# Grapefruit and Vermouth Granita

*6 ounces (175 g) sugar*
*2 large juicy grapefruit*
*5 tablespoons (5 × 15 ml spoons) dry vermouth*
*Fine strips of grapefruit peel, blanched, for decoration*

In a heavy-based saucepan, dissolve the sugar in 1/2 pint (300 ml) water. Bring to the boil then simmer for 5 minutes. Leave to cool.

Peel the grapefruit, divide into segments and remove any pips. Purée the grapefruit with the vermouth then mix in the sugar syrup. Pour this mixture into a shallow tray and place in the freezer. Stir occasionally from the outside to the middle until the mixture forms into a mass of small ice crystals. Serve immediately, decorated with grapefruit peel.

Serves 6

### Flavour variation
*Use gin instead of vermouth.*

# Pink Grapefruit Sorbet

*3 ounces (75 g) caster sugar*
*4 pink grapefruit*

Dissolve the sugar in 3 tablespoons (45 ml) water in a small heavy-based saucepan. Bring to the boil and boil for 5 minutes. Leave to cool.

Squeeze the grapefruit and strain the juice into the syrup. Pour into a container, cover and freeze until firm, beating 3 times at 45-minute intervals.

About 30 minutes before serving, transfer the sorbet to the refrigerator.

Serves 4–5

### Serving suggestion
*Serve in chilled grapefruit shells decorated with swirls of whipped cream.*

### Dessert suggestion
*Line a mould or tin with fingers of Genoise Cake\* followed by a layer of Rhubarb Ice Cream (page 111) to which some cochineal has been added to colour it a light red. Fill the centre with the sorbet. Decorate the turned-out dessert with whipped cream tinged a delicate pink with very little cochineal, and small Meringues\*.*

**Additional recipe using grapefruit:** Grapefruit Crunch Sandwich (page 139).

---

**To reduce your sugar intake**
Replace the sugar with half the quantity of **fructose** or with an **artificial sweetener**, provided the recipe does not call for a sugar syrup. Normally, 3–4 artificial sweeteners are the equivalent of 1 ounce (25 g) sugar but always check that you have the right degree of sweetness. Artificial sweeteners must be added to custard-based ice creams after the custard has cooled.

# Hazelnut

Hazelnuts can be used plain, chopped or ground and are especially flavoursome when they are toasted. Just heat them in a 350°F (180°C, gas mark 4) oven for 10–15 minutes or put them under a moderate grill until the skin dries out and becomes flaky and easily removed when the nuts are rubbed in a tea-towel. To grind hazelnuts, whizz them to a very fine paste in a coffee grinder or blender, or pound them in a mortar. A food processor does not produce the right consistency.

**Simple Hazelnut Ice Cream**
Add 3 ounces (75 g) lightly toasted, chopped hazelnuts to any of the Basic Recipes* or to a good-quality bought vanilla ice cream.

## Hazelnut Ice Cream (with curd cheese)

*12 ounces (350 g) curd cheese, sieved*
*4 ounces (100 g) icing sugar*
*Few drops of vanilla essence*
*4 tablespoons (4 × 15 ml spoons) single cream*
*2 ounces (50 g) hazelnuts, chopped*
*1 tablespoon (15 ml spoon) sweet madeira or sherry*
*1 egg white*
*Small Chocolate Leaves* or other shapes, for decoration*

Put the cheese, sugar, vanilla essence and cream in a bowl and beat together until smooth and light. Fold in the nuts and madeira or sherry. In another bowl, whisk the egg white until stiff but not dry and fold into the ice cream mixture. Pour the mixture into a container. Cover and freeze until firm.

About 30 minutes before serving, transfer the ice cream to the refrigerator. Decorate each portion with the small chocolate leaves or other shapes.

Serves 4

***Serving suggestion***
*Serve as a sundae with sliced peaches and small Meringues*. Top with Bitter Chocolate Sauce*.*

## Rich Hazelnut Ice Cream

*6 ounces (175 g) sugar*
*5 egg yolks*
*¾ pint (450 ml) cream, whipped*
*Few drops of vanilla essence*
*3 ounces (75 g) hazelnuts, lightly toasted and ground*

Melt the sugar in a heavy-based saucepan then cook to a light amber colour. Immediately, but carefully, stir in 4 fluid ounces (100 ml) boiling water and continue stirring until the caramel has dissolved.

Whisk the egg yolks in a bowl until very thick and pale. Pour in the caramel in a slow, steady stream, whisking continuously, until the mixture is cool.

Fold in the cream, vanilla essence and hazelnuts. Pour the mixture into a container. Cover and freeze until firm.

About 30 minutes before serving, transfer the ice cream to the refrigerator.

Serves 6

***Serving suggestion***
*Serve in individual dishes and accompany with Gingersnaps*.*

***Dessert suggestion***
*Make a bombe or freeze in a cake or loaf tin with an outer layer of Orange Ice Cream (page 85) and Butterscotch Parfait (page 38) in the centre.*

## Smooth Hazelnut Ice Cream

*4 ounces (100 g) hazelnuts, lightly toasted*
*12 fluid ounces (350 ml) milk*
*2 egg yolks*
*2 ounces (50 g) sugar*
*Chocolate or coffee dragées, for decoration*

Grind the hazelnuts in a coffee grinder or a blender, or pound them in a mortar.

Heat the milk in a heavy-based saucepan over moderate heat to just below simmering point. Remove from the heat, stir in the hazelnut paste, cover and leave to cool completely. Strain the mixture through a sieve lined with a double thickness of muslin or cheesecloth, pressing it firmly to extract as much liquid as possible. Tie the ends of the muslin or cheesecloth over the hazelnut milk, compressing it tightly, and hang it over the sieve to drip. When it has finished dripping give it a final squeeze to press the last drop through. Return the hazelnut milk to the saucepan and bring to simmering point.

Whisk the egg yolks and sugar together in a bowl until light and thick, then whisk in the milk. Return the mixture to the rinsed pan and cook over low heat, stirring constantly, until it thickens. Leave to cool, stirring occasionally. Pour into a container, cover and chill for 30 minutes. Then freeze until firm, beating twice at hourly intervals.

About 40 minutes before serving, transfer the ice cream to the refrigerator. Scatter 2 or 3 chocolate or coffee dragées over each portion.

Serves 3–4

***Dessert suggestion***
*Layer with chocolate chip cookies. Decorate the turned-out dessert with whipped cream, Chocolate Curls* and chopped Caramelized* hazelnuts.*

**Additional recipes using hazelnut:** Coffee and Hazelnut Ice Cream (page 52), Honey and Hazelnut Ice Cream (page 72), Pear and Hazelnut Yogurt Ice (page 92), Apricot and Hazelnut Meringue Cake (page 140), Chocolate Truffle and Hazelnut Ring (page 142).

# Herbs, Flowers, Leaves

Some of the most unusual ices can be made with ingredients from your garden. Herbs impart a deliciously clean, fresh taste, while an infusion of leaves (including tea leaves) or flower petals adds a delicate, yet discernible, nuance of flavour and tantalizing perfume.

## Geranium Leaf Sorbet

*3 ounces (75 g) sugar*
*4 scented geranium leaves*
*Juice of 1 large lemon*
*1 egg white*
*Small geranium leaves and flowers, for decoration*

In a heavy-based saucepan, dissolve the sugar in ½ pint (300 ml) water. Bring to the boil and boil for 3 minutes. Remove from the heat, stir in the geranium leaves, cover and leave for 35 minutes.

Stir the lemon juice into the syrup. Strain the syrup into a container. Cover and chill for 1 hour. Then freeze to the slushy stage. Beat well in a bowl.

Whisk the egg white in a small bowl until stiff but not dry. Fold the egg white into the frozen syrup. Return to the container, cover and freeze until firm.

About 35 minutes before serving, transfer the sorbet to the refrigerator. Serve each portion decorated with small geranium leaves and flowers.

Serves 4

**Serving suggestion**
*Serve in Coupelles\* decorated with small, sweet geranium leaves and flowers.*

## Mint Ice Cream

*4 ounces (100 g) sugar*
*Juice of ½ lemon*
*2 ounces (50 g) fresh mint leaves, finely chopped*
*¼ pint (150 ml) soured cream*
*5 ounces (150 g) soft cheese*
*Mint sprigs, for decoration*

In a heavy-based saucepan, dissolve the sugar in ¼ pint (150 ml) water. Bring to the boil and boil for 5 minutes. Stir in the lemon juice and mint leaves and leave to infuse off the heat for about 30 minutes.

Beat the cream and cheese together in a bowl until evenly blended and smooth. Strain the syrup and gradually beat it into the cream mixture.

Pour the mixture into a container. Cover and freeze until firm, beating twice at hourly intervals.

About 20 minutes before serving, transfer the ice cream to the refrigerator. Serve with the mint sprigs.

Serves 4

**Dessert suggestion**
*Layer with chocolate chip cookies. Decorate the turned-out dessert with whipped cream and Chocolate Curls\*.*

## Thyme Sorbet

*9 ounces (250 g) sugar*
*1 bunch fresh thyme*
*1 egg white*

In a heavy-based saucepan, dissolve the sugar in 18 fluid ounces (500 ml) water. Bring to the boil and boil for about 1 minute. Remove from the heat, stir in the thyme, cover and leave to infuse for 15 minutes. Remove the thyme, cool then chill the syrup. When very cold pour the syrup into a container. Cover and freeze until becoming slushy. Beat well in a bowl.

Whisk the egg white in a small bowl until stiff but not dry. Fold into the frozen syrup. Return to the container, cover and freeze until firm.

About 30 minutes before serving, transfer the sorbet to the refrigerator.

Serves 8

**Serving suggestion**
*Scoop into Meringue Baskets\* and serve with Sponge Fingers\*.*

**Flavour variation**
*Use 8 fresh bay leaves instead of the thyme.*

## Rose Petal Sorbet

*6 ounces (175 g) granulated sugar*
*Juice of 1 small lime or lemon*
*4 ounces (100 g) rose petals*
*Pink colouring*
*Rose water, to taste*
*2 egg whites*
*Rose petals, for decoration*

In a heavy-based saucepan, dissolve the sugar in ¾ pint (450 ml) water. Add the lime juice and bring to the boil then simmer for about 10 minutes. Pour the hot syrup over the petals and leave to cool completely.

Put the rose petals and syrup in a blender and process. Then pass through a coarse strainer. Add a few drops of colouring and rose water to taste.

Pour the mixture into a container, cover and freeze to the slushy stage. Beat well in a bowl.

Whisk the egg whites in a bowl until stiff but not dry. Fold into the sorbet. Return to the container, cover and freeze until firm.

About 15 minutes before serving, transfer the sorbet to the refrigerator. Serve each portion decorated with a few rose petals.

Serves 6

**Serving suggestion**
*Serve in Ice Cream Cones\* arranged on a plate strewn with rose petals. Decorate with whipped cream, crystallized rose petals and small green leaves.*

# Blackcurrant Leaf Water Ice

*3 large lemons*
*7 ounces (200 g) sugar*
*4 large handfuls of blackcurrant leaves, washed and well dried*
*2–3 drops green colouring*
*1 egg white*
*4 bunches blackcurrants, for decoration*

Carefully remove the rind from the lemons in long strips. Squeeze the juice from the fruit.

In a heavy-based saucepan, dissolve the sugar in the lemon juice and 1½ pints (850 ml) water. Bring to the boil and boil for 4 minutes. Reserve a few blackcurrant leaves for decoration and add the remainder to the syrup, stirring them so they are well coated. Cover the pan and leave to infuse for 45 minutes.

Strain the syrup, pressing the leaves to extract as much flavour as possible. Add the colouring and pour into a container. Cover and chill. Freeze to the slushy stage. Beat well in a bowl.

Whisk the egg white in a small bowl until it stands in soft peaks then gradually whisk into the water ice. Return to the container, cover and freeze until firm.

About 45 minutes before serving, transfer the water ice to the refrigerator. Decorate each portion with blackcurrant leaves and a bunch of blackcurrants.

Serves 4

**Serving suggestion**
*Pile small scoops into frosted wine glasses, trickle a little crème de cassis over and decorate with Frosted\* blackcurrants. Serve with Sponge Fingers\*.*

*Arrange scoops on plates, decorate with frosted blackcurrants and surround with blackcurrant leaves. Serve with Langues de Chat\*.*

# Tea Ice Cream

*¼ pint (150 ml) very strong Earl Grey tea*
*¼ pint (150 ml) milk*
*¼ pint (150 ml) single cream*
*Long strip of lemon peel*
*3 egg yolks*
*4 ounces (100 g) caster sugar*
*¼ pint (150 ml) cream, whipped*

Put the tea, milk and single cream with the lemon peel into a heavy-based saucepan and bring to just below simmering point.

Whisk the egg yolks and sugar together in a bowl until thick and light then whisk in the hot liquid. Remove the lemon peel. Return the mixture to the rinsed pan and cook over a low heat, stirring constantly, until the custard thickens. Return the lemon peel to the pan and leave to cool, stirring occasionally.

Remove the lemon peel. Pour the mixture into a container. Cover and freeze until just becoming firm. Turn into a bowl, beat, then fold in the whipped cream. Return the mixture to the container, cover and freeze until firm.

About 30 minutes before serving, transfer the ice cream to the refrigerator.

Serves 6

**Serving suggestion**
*Place in Coupelles\* containing finely chopped almonds, and sprinkle with shapes cut from orange peel or fine twisted strands of orange peel. Serve with Burnt Honey Sauce\* or Orange Flower Sauce\*.*

# Mint Sorbet

*1 pound (450 g) sugar*
*20 mint leaves*
*Juice of 1 lemon*
*6 tablespoons (6 × 15 ml spoons) crème de methe*
*2 large egg whites*
*8 small mint sprigs, for decoration*

In a heavy-based saucepan, dissolve the sugar in 2 pints (1.1 litres) water over a gentle heat. Bring to the boil and boil rapidly for 8 minutes. Add the mint leaves and boil for a further 2 minutes. Remove from the heat, stir in the lemon juice and leave to infuse for 30 minutes.

Strain the syrup into a container. Cover and freeze to the slushy stage. In a bowl whisk the frozen mixture vigorously with a wire whisk to break down any ice particles. Whisk in the crème de menthe until evenly blended. Whisk the egg whites in a bowl until stiff but not dry. Whisk them into the sorbet. Return the sorbet to the container, cover and freeze until firm.

About 30 minutes before serving, transfer the sorbet to the refrigerator. Serve in cold, frosted glasses and decorate with the mint sprigs.

Serves 8

**Dessert suggestion**
*Form Grapefruit Ice Cream (page 67) into 4 balls with a tablespoon (15 ml spoon) of the sorbet in the centre of each one. Serve in Coupelles\*. Surround with grapefruit segments, pith and membrane removed, sprinkled with crème de menthe.*

**Additional recipes using herbs, flowers and leaves:** Apple and Elderflower Ice Cream (page 20), Blackberry Rose Ice Cream (page 30), Gooseberry and Geranium Leaf Yogurt Ice (page 62), Orange and Rosemary Sorbet (page 85), Raspberry Rose Water Ice (page 104), Strawberry and Elderflower Ice Cream (page 119), Strawberry Rose Ice (page 119), Elderberry Water Ice (page 135), Quince Ice Cream (page 134), Crystallized Violet Ice Cream (page 134), Crab-Apple Ice Cream (page 134), Blackcurrant, Rose Petal and Champagne Roll (page 136).

Honey comes in a whole range of blends and flavours. For more sophisticated ices, use a variety flavoured with a single herb or flower, or make your own as in the 'Provençal' version below. Either thick or clear honey can be used, unless one or the other is specifically called for in a recipe.

**Simple Honey Ice Cream**
Ripple any of the Basic Recipes* with 2 ounces (50 g) clear honey.

## Honey and Hazelnut Ice Cream

*2 ounces (50 g) butter*
*4 ounces (100 g) thick honey*
*¾ pint (450 ml) milk*
*4 ounces (100 g) hazelnuts, lightly toasted and
  ground*
*3 eggs yolks*
*2 ounces (50 g) demerara sugar*
*1 tablespoon (15 ml spoon) gelatine*
*½ pint (300 ml) cream, whipped*
*3 tablespoons (3 × 15 ml spoons) brandy*

*For decoration*
*Whipped cream*
*Chocolate-coated hazelnuts*
*Fresh peaches, apricots or orange segments, for serving*

In a heavy-based saucepan, melt the butter and honey in the milk. Bring to the boil, add the nuts, cover and leave to cool for 10 minutes.

Beat the egg yolks with the sugar in a bowl. Gradually stir in the flavoured milk. Return to the rinsed pan and cook over a gentle heat, stirring constantly, until the custard thickens, but do not allow it to boil.

Dissolve the gelatine in 3 tablespoons (45 ml) water in a small bowl set over a pan of hot water. Stir the gelatine into the custard. Leave until cool but not completely cold then fold in the cream and brandy. Cover and freeze in a 2½ pint (1.4 litre) fluted ring mould until firm.

About 45 minutes before serving, turn the ice cream out on to a chilled plate and transfer to the refrigerator. Just before serving, decorate with whipped cream and chocolate-coated hazelnuts and fill the centre with fresh fruits.

Serves 6

**Dessert suggestion**
*Freeze in a mould lined with Sponge Fingers*.
Decorate the turned-out dessert with whipped cream,
Chocolate Shapes* and shapes cut from orange peel.*

**Flavour variation**
*Add 2 tablespoons (2 × 15 ml spoons) good-quality
instant coffee granules to the milk.*

## Provençal Honey Ice Cream

*5 ounces (150 g) honey*
*1 large fresh rosemary or thyme sprig*
*6 egg yolks*
*½ pint (300 ml) milk or single cream*
*¼ pint (150 ml) crème fraîche, double or whipping
  cream*

Heat the honey and rosemary or thyme in a saucepan to just below boiling point. Remove from the heat, cover and leave to infuse for 30 minutes.

Whisk the egg yolks in a bowl until light. Uncover the honey and reheat to just below boiling point, remove the herbs and gradually pour the honey on to the egg yolks, whisking continuously.

In a heavy-based saucepan, bring the milk or cream to just below boiling point then whisk into the egg yolk mixture. Return the mixture to the rinsed pan and cook over a low heat, stirring, until the mixture thickens, but do not allow it to boil. Leave to cool.

Whisk the crème fraîche or cream until soft peaks form. Fold the cream into the honey custard. Pour into a container, cover and freeze until firm, beating once, when the mixture is just becoming firm.

About 15 minutes before serving, transfer the ice cream to the refrigerator.

Serves 6

**Serving suggestion**
*Intermingle scoops of the ice cream with scoops of
Passion Fruit Sorbet (page 128) and serve with
Almond Tuiles*.*

## Honey Ice Cream

*8 ounces (225 g) clear honey*
*5 egg yolks*
*¾ pint (450 ml) cream, whipped*
*Lemon juice, to taste*

In a heavy-based saucepan, heat the honey with 4 tablespoons (60 ml) water to just below boiling point. Whisk the egg yolks in a bowl until thick and light then whisk in the hot honey. Return the mixture to the rinsed pan and cook gently over low heat, whisking until the mixture thickens. Remove from the heat and continue to whisk until the mixture is cold.

Fold the cream into the honey mixture and add lemon juice to taste. Pour into a container, cover and freeze until firm. About 20 minutes before serving, transfer to the refrigerator.

Serves 5

**Serving suggestion**
*Make into a sundae with layers of whipped cream and
Bitter Chocolate Sauce*. Finish with a scoop of ice
cream decorated with a glacé cherry.*

# Honey and Fig Sorbet

*1³/₄ pound (800 g) can of green figs in syrup*
*5 ounces (150 g) clear honey*
*4 tablespoons (4 × 15 ml spoons) lemon juice*
*White rum, for serving*
*Whipped cream, for decoration*

Drain the figs and reserve the syrup and 4 of the figs. Purée the remaining figs with the reserved syrup, honey and lemon juice.

Pour the mixture into a container. Cover and freeze until firm, beating twice at hourly intervals.

About 30 minutes before serving, transfer the sorbet to the refrigerator. Pour a teaspoon of white rum over each portion and decorate with a swirl of cream and the reserved figs.

Serves 4

**Serving suggestion**
*Serve on a plate surrounded by sliced figs.*

# Honey and Soya Ice Cream

*³/₄ pint (425 ml) unsweetened soya milk*
*2 ounces (50 g) honey*
*Few drops of vanilla essence*
*3 tablespoons (3 × 15 ml spoons) oil*

Blend all the ingredients together until smooth. Pour into a container, cover and freeze until firm, beating twice at 45-minute intervals. About 30 minutes before serving transfer to the refrigerator.

Serves 4

**Additional recipe using honey:** Banana and Honey Ice Cream (page 29).

*KIRSCH:    see WINES, LIQUEURS*
*KIWI FRUIT:    see WARM CLIMATE*
*FRUITS*
*KUMQUAT:    see ORANGE, ETC*

# Lemon, Lime

Juicy, thin-skinned lemons make the best ices. To soften one that feels hard, and to improve its yield of juice, steep the whole lemon in boiling water before squeezing it. When sugar lumps are rubbed over the skin they absorb its essential oils and impart an extra-tangy lemon flavour to the iced mixture.

Limes may look like green lemons, but have a sweeter, more subtle flavour and character of their own – which is in no way reproduced in bottled lime cordial. If fresh lime juice is not available, use bottled unsweetened lime juice instead.

## Lemon Sorbet

*5 large sugar lumps*
*3 large thin-skinned lemons*
*4 ounces (100 g) icing sugar*

Rub the sugar lumps over the lemon skins until they are soaked with oil. Put the sugar lumps with the icing sugar into a bowl with 5 tablespoons (75 ml) water. Squeeze the lemons and strain the juice into the bowl. Stir to make sure the sugar has dissolved.

Pour the mixture into a container. Cover and freeze until firm, beating twice at 45-minute intervals.

About 20 minutes before serving, transfer the sorbet to the refrigerator.

Serves 2–3

### Serving suggestion
*Pile small scoops into tall, thin-stemmed wine glasses and decorate with strips of lime peel.*

## Lime Sorbet

*7 ounces (200 g) sugar*
*Zest and juice of 3 large or 4 small limes*
*½ ounce (15 g) gelatine*
*½ an egg white*
*White rum to serve*

In a saucepan, dissolve the sugar in 1½ pints (700 ml) water with the lime zest. Bring to the boil and simmer for 5 minutes. Remove from the heat, add the lime juice, cover and leave to cool.

Strain the syrup. Dissolve the gelatine in a little of the strained syrup then stir it into the rest of the syrup.

Pour the mixture into a container. Cover and freeze until just becoming slushy. Beat well.

Whisk the egg white in a small bowl until stiff but not dry and fold into the lime mixture. Cover and freeze until firm.

About 40 minutes before serving, transfer the sorbet to the refrigerator. Spoon a little white rum over each portion.

Serves 4–6

### Dessert suggestion
*Ripple with Avocado Ice Cream (page 27) and serve with Cigars Russe\*.*

## Lime Cream Ice

*Grated zest and juice of 3 large juicy limes*
*6 ounces (175 g) sugar*
*1 egg white*
*2 tablespoons (2 × 15 ml spoons) double cream*

Put the lime zest and juice, sugar and 1 pint (600 ml) water in a saucepan and heat gently until the sugar has dissolved. Bring to the boil and simmer gently for 12 minutes. Remove from the heat, cover and leave to cool.

Pour the mixture into a container. Cover and refrigerate for about an hour. Freeze until just becoming firm.

Remove from the freezer and gradually whisk in the egg white followed by the cream. Freeze until firm.

About 40 minutes before serving, transfer the ice to the refrigerator.

Serves 6

### Serving suggestion
*Intermingle scoops of the cream ice with scoops of Ginger Wine Sorbet (page 60). Top with whisky-flavoured whipped cream sprinkled with chopped cashew nuts.*

### Dessert suggestion
*Freeze in a mould or cake tin lined with Mince Meat Ice Cream (page 141). Decorate the turned-out dessert with whipped cream and shapes cut from lime peel. Serve with Langues de Chat\*.*

## Lemon-Lime Ice Cream

*3 large eggs, separated*
*4 ounces (100 g) caster sugar*
*Grated zest of 1 lemon*
*Grated zest of 1 lime*
*3 tablespoons (3 × 15 ml spoons) lime juice*
*¼ pint (150 ml) cream, whipped*
*Thin strips lemon and lime peel, to decorate*

Whisk the egg yolks and half the sugar in a bowl until thick and light. Stir in the lemon and lime zests and juice. Fold in the cream. In another bowl, whisk the egg whites until stiff but not dry. Fold the egg whites into the lemon-lime cream.

Pour the mixture into a container. Cover and freeze until firm.

About 30 minutes before serving, transfer the ice cream to the refrigerator. Serve decorated with knots of lemon and lime peel.

Serves 6

### Serving suggestion
*Serve as a sundae with Apple Cream Ice (page 21), bananas tossed in lime juice, and walnuts. Top with Butterscotch Sauce\* or Burnt Honey Sauce\*.*

# Sweet Lime Ice Cream

*4 eggs, separated*
*¹/₄ pint (150 ml) whipping cream*
*¹/₄ pint (150 ml) soured cream*
*8 fluid ounces (225 ml) lime curd*
*1 ounce (25 g) icing sugar*

*For decoration*
*Lime slices*
*Mint leaves*

Whisk the egg yolks in a bowl until thick and light.
Whip the creams together until soft peaks are formed.
Whip the creams into the egg yolks followed by the
lime curd.

In another bowl, whisk the egg whites until stiff but
not dry. Gradually whisk in the sugar. Fold the egg
whites into the lime curd mixture and spoon into a
container. Cover and freeze until firm.

About 20 minutes before serving, transfer the ice
cream to the refrigerator. Serve decorated with lime
slices and mint leaves.

Serves 6

**Dessert suggestion**
*Layer with Lemon Sorbet (page 74) or White Peach
Sorbet (page 88), merging the layers into each other.
Serve in a coconut-flavoured Meringue Basket\*.
Decorate with lime-slice cones containing whipped
cream, and long strands of desiccated coconut.*

# Lime and Avocado Ice Cream

*2 avocados*
*Juice of 2 large limes*
*1 ounce (25 g) icing sugar*
*¹/₄ pint (150 ml) double cream, whipped*

Remove the flesh from the avocados and purée with
the lime juice and sugar into a bowl. Fold in the cream.

Spoon the mixture into a container. Cover and
freeze until firm, beating once after an hour.

About 20 minutes before serving, transfer the ice
cream to the refrigerator.

Serves 4

**Serving suggestion**
*Serve with Sponge Fingers\*.*

**Dessert suggestion**
*Freeze in large lime shells with scalloped edges,
mounding the ice cream slightly to form a dome.
Decorate with pieces of lemon segments, pith and
membrane removed, and shapes cut from lime peel.*

# Lemon Frost

*¹/₄ pint (150 ml) lemon juice*
*3 ounces (75 g clear honey, preferably clover or a
    flower type*
*¹/₂ pint (300 ml) plain yogurt, chilled*
*2 egg whites*

*For decoration*
*Toasted almond slivers*
*Frosted\* short strips of lemon peel*

Put the lemon juice, honey and yogurt in a bowl and
beat until smooth. Pour the mixture into a container,
cover and freeze to the slushy stage. Turn into a bowl
and beat well. Whisk the egg whites until stiff but not
dry, then fold the egg whites into the yogurt mixture.

Spoon the mixture back into the container. Cover
and freeze until firm.

About 45 minutes before serving, transfer the lemon
frost to the refrigerator. Serve decorated with the
almond slivers and strips of lemon peel.

Serves 3–4

**Serving suggestion**
*Freeze in lemon shells with scalloped edges. Decorate
with lightly toasted flaked almonds and 'corkscrews' of
fine lemon peel.*

**Low calorie version**
*Use fructose, or a low calorie or artificial sweetener
instead of honey.*

# Lime Ice Cream

*3 eggs, separated*
*4 ounces (100 g) caster sugar*
*Grated zest and juice of 3 limes*
*¹/₄ pint (150 ml) soured cream, beaten*
*¹/₂ pint (300 ml) cream, whipped*
*Twisted lime slices, for decoration*

Put the egg yolks, sugar and lime juice in a bowl and
whisk until very thick and light. Whisk in the soured
cream. Fold in the whipped cream and lime zest.

In another bowl, whisk the egg whites until stiff but
not dry. Fold the egg whites into the lime mixture.

Pour the mixture into a container. Cover and freeze
until firm.

About 30 minutes before serving, transfer the ice
cream to the refrigerator. Serve each portion
decorated with a twisted lime slice.

Serves 4–6

**Dessert suggestion**
*Form into 4–6 balls and coat in plain Chocolate\*.*

# Soft Lemon Ice Cream

*Approximately 14 ounce (400 g) can evaporated milk, chilled*
*3 ounces (75 g) icing sugar*
*4 ounces (100 g) full fat soft cheese, softened*
*Finely grated zest and juice of 2 lemons*

*For decoration*
*Lemon slices*
*Fresh mint sprigs*

Put the evaporated milk into a bowl and whisk until very light. Whisk in the sugar. Fold in the cheese followed by the lemon zest and juice. Spoon into a container. Cover and freeze until firm.

About 20 minutes before serving, transfer the ice cream to the refrigerator. Serve decorated with lemon slices and mint sprigs.

Serves 4–6

**Dessert suggestion**
*Ripple with Clove Sorbet (page 115).*

# Sweet Lemon Ice Cream

*4 eggs, separated*
*8 fluid ounces (225 ml) lemon curd*
*½ pint (300 ml) double cream, whipped*
*2 ounces (50 g) icing sugar*
*Frosted\* mint leaves, for decoration*

Put the egg yolks in a bowl and whisk until pale and thick. Whisk in the lemon curd. Fold in the whipped cream.

In another bowl, whisk the egg whites until stiff but not dry then gradually whisk in the sugar. Carefully fold into the lemon cream until evenly mixed. Pour the mixture into a container. Cover and freeze until firm.

About 15 minutes before serving, transfer the ice cream to the refrigerator. Decorate with mint.

Serves 6

# Iced Lemon Mousse

*1¾ pints (1 litre) plain yogurt*
*7 ounces (200 g) caster sugar*
*Juice and finely grated zest of 2 lemons*
*2 egg whites*
*4 fluid ounces (100 ml) cream, whipped*

*For decoration*
*Crystallized lemon slices*
*Pistachio nuts*

Put the yogurt into a bowl and whisk in 4 ounces (100 g) of the sugar. Stir in the lemon zest and juice.

In another bowl, whisk the egg whites until soft peaks form. Gradually whisk in the remaining sugar and continue whisking until the mixture is very stiff. Fold the egg whites into the yogurt mixture followed by the cream.

Tie greaseproof paper collars around freezer-proof ramekins or similar small dishes. Spoon the ice cream mixture into the dishes – it should come well above the level of the dishes. Put the dishes into a polythene bag taking care that it does not touch the tops, secure and freeze until firm.

About 30 minutes before serving, transfer the mousse to the refrigerator. Take out of the polythene bag and remove the collars. Serve decorated with lemon slices and pistachio nuts.

Serves 6–8

**Serving suggestion**
*Serve as a sundae with Banana and Honey Ice Cream (page 29) and chopped hazelnuts, with Hot Fudge Sauce\* poured over.*

**Additional recipes using lemon and lime:**
Coconut and Lime Ice Cream (page 49), Ginger and Lime Granita (page 61), Melon-Lime Ice (page 83), Iced Lemon Soufflé Surprise (page 143), Lemon Icicle (page 142).

LIQUEURS:   see WINES, LIQUEURS
LOGANBERRY:   see BLACKBERRY,
                              LOGANBERRY
LYCHEE:   see WARM CLIMATE FRUITS
MANDARIN:   see ORANGE, ETC

# Mango

Mangoes can make some of the most delicious of ices – but they must be fully ripe. The skin of a ripe mango will yield under slight pressure – any signs of hardness indicate that the fruit is not at its glorious best. To separate the flesh from the skin and stone, first peel the mango with a sharp knife. Then cut the flesh away from the stone, slicing down one side then the other. Finally, trim off any remaining flesh. Canned mangoes can be used. Always sieve both fresh and canned fruit after puréeing to remove any fibres that might mar the texture of the ice.

### Simple Mango Ice Cream
Add ½ pint (300 ml) sieved mango purée to any of the Basic Recipes. Use 1 large or 2 small fresh mangoes, or a 14 ounce (400 g) can of mangoes (drained). Sweeten with icing sugar if necessary.

## Fresh Mango Ice Cream

*3 fluid ounces (75 ml) thick plain yogurt*
*3 fluid ounces (75 ml) soured cream*
*1 large or 2 small very ripe mangoes, peeled and*
  *stoned*
*2 egg whites*
*2 ounces (50 g) caster sugar*
*4 teaspoons (4 × 5 ml spoons) lime or orange juice*

Put the yogurt and soured cream in a bowl and beat together.

Purée the mango flesh and pass through a nylon sieve to remove any shreds. Beat the purée into the yogurt/cream mixture. Spoon into a container, cover and freeze to the slushy stage. Turn into a bowl and beat well.

In another bowl, whisk the egg whites until very stiff. Gradually whisk in the sugar and continue whisking until stiff again. Fold into the mango mixture with the lime or orange juice.

Spoon the mixture back into the container. Cover and freeze until firm.

About 30 minutes before serving, transfer the ice cream to the refrigerator.

Serves 4

### Serving suggestion
*Serve in Ice Cream Cones\* or Gingersnap Cones\* or on a bed of mango slices. Accompany with cream, delicately flavoured with orange liqueur.*

*Place chopped mango in the base of hollowed-out brioche, spoon in the ice cream, trickle orange-liqueur-flavoured cream over and replace the brioche tops.*

## Mango Sorbet

*4 ounces (100 g) sugar*
*9 fluid ounces (250 ml) ripe mango flesh, puréed and*
  *sieved*
*Juice of 1 lime*

Put the sugar and 2 fluid ounces (50 ml) water in a saucepan and stir over low heat to dissolve. Bring to the boil, remove from the heat and leave to cool.

Blend the syrup into the mango flesh with the strained lime juice.

Pour the mixture into a container. Cover and freeze until firm, beating 3 times at 45-minute intervals.

About 30 minutes before serving, transfer the sorbet to the refrigerator.

Serves 4

### Serving suggestion
*Serve small scoops in mango shells. Decorate with small rosettes of whipped cream and fine strips of orange peel.*

### Dessert suggestion
*Freeze in a can and coat in Crystallized Fruit Ice Cream (page 57). Decorate with Chocolate Shapes\**

## Mango Yogurt Ice

*4 ounces (100 g) sugar*
*1 large mango, puréed and sieved*
*2 tablespoons (2 × 15 ml spoons) orange juice*
*¼ pint (150 ml) thick plain yogurt*
*2 egg whites*

In a heavy-based saucepan, dissolve the sugar in ½ pint (300 ml) water over low heat. Bring to the boil and boil until the temperature reaches 230°–234°F (110°–112°C). Set aside to cool.

Whisk the mango purée, orange juice and yogurt into the syrup. Pour the mixture into a container, cover and freeze to the slushy stage. Turn into a bowl and beat well. Whisk the egg whites in a bowl until stiff but not dry and fold into the mango mixture.

Spoon the mixture back into the container. Cover and freeze until firm.

About 30 minutes before serving, transfer the ice to the refrigerator.

Serves 4

### Serving suggestion
*Serve with fresh mango slices and Low Calorie Topping\*.*

### Low calorie version
*Use fructose or a low calorie or artificial sweetener instead of sugar.*

# Iced Mango Mousse

3 egg yolks
3 ounces (75 g) icing sugar
1 very large ripe mango or 2 smaller ones, peeled and
    stoned
Lemon juice
¼ pint (150 ml) soured cream, beaten

Whisk the egg yolks and icing sugar in a bowl set over
a pan of hot water until thick, light and lukewarm.
Remove the bowl from the hot water and continue
whisking until the mixture is cold.

Sieve the mango flesh into a bowl. Sharpen it with a
little lemon juice then beat in the soured cream. Fold
into the egg yolk mixture.

Pour the mixture into a container. Cover and freeze
until firm.

About 30 minutes before serving, transfer the
mousse to the refrigerator.

Serves 5–6

**Serving suggestion**
*Use lime juice instead of lemon juice and spoon into
large lime shells with scalloped edges. Decorate with
rosettes of whipped cream delicately flavoured with
melon liqueur or brandy and a scattering of mint
leaves.*

# Quick Mango Ice Cream

Approximately 14 ounce (400 g) can mangoes,
    drained
½ pint (300 ml) double cream, whipped
Approximately 2 tablespoons (2 × 15 ml spoons)
    lemon juice

Purée the mango flesh then sieve, if necessary, to
remove any fibres. Gradually whip the purée into the
cream and add lemon juice to taste.

Pour the mixture into a container. Cover and freeze
until firm, beating well once after 1 hour.

About 30 minutes before serving, transfer the ice
cream to the refrigerator.

Serves 4

**Serving suggestion**
*Form into 4 balls, make an indentation in the top of
each and fill with Southern Comfort. Serve with
Langues de Chat\*.*

# Mango Sherbet

6 ounces (175 g) sugar
1 tablespoon (15 ml spoon) lemon juice
2 large mangoes, puréed and sieved
1 large egg white
3 tablespoons (3 × 15 ml spoons) cream, whipped

Put the sugar and ½ pint (300 ml) water in a heavy-
based saucepan and stir to dissolve. Bring to the boil
and boil for 5 minutes. Remove from the heat, stir in
the lemon juice and leave to cool.

Stir the mango purée into the syrup and pour into a
shallow metal container. Chill the mixture for 30
minutes then cover and freeze to the slushy stage.

Turn the semi-frozen mixture into a bowl and beat
well. Return the mixture to the container, cover and
freeze until just becoming slushy again. Turn out into
the bowl and beat well.

In a separate bowl, whisk the egg white until stiff but
not dry. Fold the cream and then the egg into the
mango mixture, spoon back into the container, cover
and freeze until firm.

About 30 minutes before serving, transfer the
sherbet to the refrigerator.

Serves 4–6

# Mango and Coconut
# Ice Cream

2 eggs, separated
3 ounces (75 g) caster sugar
2 fluid ounces (50 ml) single cream
2 medium, ripe mangoes, peeled and stoned
3 tablespoons (3 × 15 ml spoons) coconut liqueur
8 fluid ounces (225 ml) cream, whipped
2 ounces (50 g) coconut flakes

In a bowl, whisk the egg yolks, sugar and single cream
together. Place the bowl over a pan of hot water and
cook, stirring constantly, until the sauce thickens.
Remove from the heat and leave to cool.

Purée the flesh from the mangoes and pass through
a sieve. Blend the purée with the liqueur and fold it
into the egg yolk mixture. Put the egg whites in a bowl
and beat until stiff but not dry. Fold the egg whites,
cream and coconut flakes into the mixture. Spoon into
a shallow container, cover and freeze until firm.

About 30 minutes before serving, transfer the ice
cream to the refrigerator.

Serves 6

# Maple

Rich and sweet, with a distinctive taste, maple syrup is high in the league of popular ice cream flavours. Always check the contents on the label to make sure you get the true maple flavour – some maple syrups are blended with other ingredients like corn syrup, and taste rather bland as a result.

**Simple Maple Syrup Ice Cream**
Ripple 4 ounces (100 g) maple syrup through any of the Basic Recipes* or through a good-quality bought vanilla ice cream.

## Maple and Walnut Ice Cream

*4½ ounces (115 g) granulated sugar*
*4½ ounces (115 g) walnut halves*
*4 ounces (100 g) maple syrup*
*18 fluid ounces (500 ml) milk*
*5 ounces (150 g) caster sugar*
*4 egg yolks*
*9 fluid ounces (250 ml) cream, whipped*

To make the praline, heat the granulated sugar in a heavy-based saucepan with just enough water to moisten. Boil the syrup to 248°F (120°C). Add the nuts, remove from the heat and stir until the nuts are coated in the syrup. Return to the heat, stirring constantly, until the sugar caramelizes. Turn on to a lightly oiled cold surface and leave to cool. Reserve half of the praline for decoration and reduce the remainder to a powder in a blender or food processor.

In a heavy-based saucepan, bring the maple syrup and milk to just simmering point. Beat the sugar and egg yolks together in a bowl and stir in the flavoured milk. Pour into the rinsed pan and cook gently, stirring constantly, until the mixture thickens. Do not allow to boil. Remove from the heat and leave to cool. Pour into a container, cover and freeze until just becoming firm. Turn into a bowl and beat well. Fold in the cream and praline powder. Spoon the mixture back into the container, cover and freeze until firm.

About 30 minutes before serving, transfer the ice cream to the refrigerator. Serve decorated with the reserved walnut praline.

Serves 6

**Dessert suggestion**
*Layer with split chocolate brownies. Spoon Coffee Sauce\* over the turned-out dessert.*

# Maple Mousse

*1 egg white*
*6 ounces (175 g) maple syrup, heated*
*8 fluid ounces (225 ml) cream, whipped*
*8–12 pecan or walnut halves*

Whisk the egg white in a bowl until stiff but not dry. Slowly pour in the hot maple syrup, whisking constantly, and continue to whisk until a thick meringue is formed. Carefully fold in the whipped cream and chill.

Pour the mixture into a freezer-proof dish. Cover and freeze until the top is just beginning to harden. Arrange the nuts over the surface, cover and freeze the mousse until firm.

About 40 minutes before serving, transfer the mousse to the refrigerator.

Serves 4–6

**Serving suggestion**
*Freeze in individual dishes and decorate with the walnut halves just before serving.*

**Dessert suggestion**
*Ripple with Apricot Yogurt Ice (page 24).*

# Maple Granola Ice Cream

*2 ounces (50 g) flaked almonds, toasted*
*1½ ounces (40 g) shredded coconut, toasted*
*4 ounces (100 g) rolled oats, toasted*
*4 ounces (100 g) maple syrup*
*1 fluid ounce (25 ml) oil*
*3 ounces (75 g) each raisins, chopped dates and*
*    prunes*
*1 ounce (25 g) chopped dried apricots*
*1 pint (600 ml) cream, whipped*

Mix the almonds, coconut and oats together in a bowl. Heat the maple syrup and oil together in a small saucepan and pour over the oat mixture. Toss well to coat it evenly. Spread the mixture out on a grill and place under a medium hot grill for about 10–15 minutes, turning frequently, until well toasted. Tip into a bowl and mix in the dried fruits. Leave to cool.

Stir the granola mixture into the cream. Pour into a container, cover and freeze until firm. About 15 minutes before serving, transfer cream to the refrigerator.

Serves 5–6

**Serving suggestions**
*Serve with orange segments, pith and membrane removed, sliced bananas sprinkled with lime juice (or Drambuie, Benedictine or Galliano) or poached apple slices. Spoon over 3 tablespoons (3 × 15 ml spoons) plain yogurt beaten into 4 ounces (100 g) soft cheese and lightly sweetened with icing sugar. Decorate with fine strips of orange peel.*

# Maple and Nut Ice Cream

*2 ounces (50 g) raisins*
*2 fluid ounces (50 ml) whisky or water*
*3 eggs, separated*
*6 ounces (175 g) maple syrup*
*8 fluid ounces (225 ml) soured cream*
*3 tablespoons (3 × 15 ml spoons) melted butter*
*1½ ounces (40 g) each almonds and hazelnuts,*
*    coarsely ground*
*1 egg white*

Put the raisins and whisky or water in a small saucepan and bring to simmering point. Remove from the heat and leave to cool.

Whisk the egg yolks in a bowl until thick. Beat in the maple syrup, cream, butter and nuts.

In another bowl, whisk all the egg whites until stiff but not dry. Carefully fold the egg whites into the maple mixture with the raisins and their soaking liquor. Pour the mixture into a container. Cover and freeze until firm.

About 20 minutes before serving, transfer the ice cream to the refrigerator.

Serves 6

**Dessert suggestion**
*Layer with Sponge Fingers\*. Press finely chopped walnuts over the turned-out dessert.*

# Maple Ice Cream

*6 ounces (175 g) maple syrup*
*3 eggs, separated*
*½ pint (300 ml) cream, whipped*
*Few drops of vanilla essence*

Heat the maple syrup in a heavy-based saucepan to just below boiling point. Whisk the egg yolks in a bowl until thick then whisk in about 4 tablespoons of the maple syrup. Stir this mixture into the hot syrup and cook gently, stirring constantly, until the mixture thickens. Leave to cool, stirring occasionally. Fold the cream and vanilla into the custard. Pour the mixture into a container, cover and freeze until just becoming firm. Turn into a bowl and beat well.

Whisk the egg whites until stiff but not dry. Fold into the custard. Spoon the mixture back into the container. Cover and freeze until firm.

About 30 minutes before serving, transfer the ice cream to the refrigerator.

Serves 6–8

**Serving suggestion**
*Spoon on to hot waffles and trickle over Hot Chocolate Sauce\* or Bitter Chocolate Sauce\*. Serve with fresh apricots.*

---

*MARSALA:   see WINES, LIQUEURS*

# Melon

At their best and ripest, melons are wonderfully fragrant with a deliciously aromatic flavour. Charentais, Ogen and Gallia melons are especially suitable for ices, but Cantaloups and other musk melons are almost as good. Watermelons have a distinctive sweetness and texture.

## Melon Sorbet

1 large ripe Ogen or Charentais melon weighing about 1½ pounds (700 g)
3 tablespoons (3 × 15 ml spoons) lemon juice
4 ounces (100 g) caster or icing sugar

Peel the melon, discard the seeds and reduce the flesh to a purée with the lemon juice and sugar.

Pour the mixture into a container. Cover and freeze until firm, beating 3 times at 45-minute intervals.

About 30 minutes before serving, transfer the sorbet to the refrigerator.

Serves 4

**Serving suggestion**
*Scoop into small balls and serve in a chilled melon shell intermingled with small wild strawberries or sliced strawberries.*

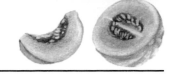

# Melon Ice Cream

2 ripe Charentais melon
Juice of 1/2 lemon
4 ounces (100 g) caster sugar
1/2 pint (300 ml) whipping or double cream
1 tablespoon (15 ml spoon) Drambuie or Benedictine

Cut the melons in half, discard the seeds and scoop out the flesh taking care not to damage the shells. Put the shells in the freezer.

Purée the melon flesh with the lemon juice and 3 ounces (75 g) of the sugar. Put the cream in a bowl and whip with the remaining sugar and the liqueur until soft peaks form. Fold the cream into the purée.

Pour the mixture into a container. Cover and freeze until firm, beating twice at hourly intervals.

About 30 minutes before serving, scoop the ice cream into the shells and refrigerate until required.

Serves 4–6

**Serving suggestion**
*Freeze in halved melon shells, then cut the shells into wedges. Decorate with Chocolate Shapes\* and long, twisted strips of orange peel. Serve with Cigars Russe\*.*

# Melon Ice Cream (with crème fraîche)

1/2 pint (300 ml) crème fraîche
4 egg yolks
4 ounces (100 g) sugar
2 small ripe Ogen, Charentais or Gallia melon to yield about 1 pound (450 g) flesh
Squeeze of orange juice

In a heavy-based saucepan, bring the crème fraîche to just below boiling point. Whisk the egg yolks with the sugar in a bowl then whisk in the hot crème. Return the mixture to the rinsed pan and cook gently, stirring constantly, until the custard thickens. Do not allow to boil. Leave to cool, stirring occasionally.

Remove the flesh from the melons, taking care not to include any hard flesh there may be near the rind. Purée the flesh then beat it into the custard, adding orange juice to taste.

Pour the mixture into a container. Cover and freeze until firm, beating twice at hourly intervals.

About 30 minutes before serving, transfer the ice cream to the refrigerator.

Serves 4–5

**Serving suggestion**
*Serve in Coupelles\* with a little crème de menthe-flavoured whipped cream spooned over. Decorate with mint leaves and shapes cut from lime peel.*

*Form into balls and pile into a chilled melon shell, its sides lined with orange or lemon slices. Decorate with sprigs of mint.*

# Watermelon Sorbet

1 1/2 pounds (700 g) watermelon, weighed without seeds or skin
10 ounces (275 g) sugar
2 cinnamon sticks
2 tablespoons (2 × 15 ml spoons) coriander seeds, crushed
3 tablespoons (3 × 15 ml spoons) lemon juice

Reduce the watermelon flesh to a purée. In a heavy-based saucepan, dissolve the sugar in 3/4 pint (450 ml) water. Add the cinnamon sticks and coriander seeds and boil for 5 minutes. Cover and leave to infuse until cold.

Strain the syrup into the watermelon purée and stir in the lemon juice.

Pour the mixture into a container. Cover and freeze until firm, beating 3 times at 45-minute intervals.

About 30 minutes before serving, transfer the sorbet to the refrigerator.

Serves 8

# Melon-Lime Ice

5 ounces (150 g) sugar
1/4 pint (150 ml) lime cordial
1 pound (450 g) melon flesh, preferably Ogen, Charentais or Gallia, puréed
2 egg whites
Twisted fine strips of lime peel, for decoration

Put the sugar and lime cordial in a bowl and stir to dissolve the sugar. Whisk into the melon flesh. Chill for about an hour. Pour into a container, cover and freeze to the slushy stage. Beat well in a bowl.

Whisk the egg whites in a bowl until stiff but not dry. Fold the egg whites into the melon-lime mixture. Return to the container, cover and freeze until firm.

About 40 minutes before serving, transfer the ice to the refrigerator. Serve each portion decorated with twisted strips of lime peel.

Serves 6

# Orange, etc

Oranges and their near relations tangerines and mandarins (which make one of the more delicious canned fruits) make sweet yet tangy ices. This section includes a recipe for kumquats. With their very thin skins, these small, oval fruits do not have to be peeled before use.

**Simple Orange Ice Cream**
Add the chopped flesh (pith and membrane removed) of 3 oranges to any of the Basic Recipes* or to a good-quality bought vanilla ice cream.

## Orange Water Ice

12 ounces (350 g) sugar
3/4 pint (450 ml) orange juice
1/4 pint (150 ml) lemon juice
Finely grated zest of 2 oranges
Finely grated zest of 1 lemon
Thin orange slices, for decoration

Dissolve the sugar in 1½ pints (850 ml) water in a heavy-based saucepan. Bring to the boil and boil for 10 minutes. Leave to cool completely.

Stir in the fruit juice and zests and pour into a container. Cover and freeze until firm, beating 3 times at 45-minute intervals.

About 1 hour before serving, transfer the ice to the refrigerator. Decorate each portion with a thin twist of orange.

Serves 6

### Serving suggestion
*Pile small scoops into chilled orange shells. Serve with Almond Tuiles*.*

## Mandarin Cream Ice

6 ounces (175 g) full fat soft cheese
1/4 pint (150 ml) natural yogurt
Approximately 11 ounce (300 g) can mandarins, puréed
2 egg whites
1 1/2 ounces (40 g) flaked almonds, toasted
Mandarin liqueur, for serving

Put the cheese in a bowl and gradually beat in the yogurt. Beat in the mandarin purée. Spoon into a container, cover and freeze to the slushy stage. Turn into a bowl and beat well.

In another bowl, whisk the egg whites until stiff but not dry and fold into the mandarin mixture.

Spoon the mixture back into the container, sprinkle the almonds over the top, cover and freeze until firm.

About 30 minutes before serving, transfer the cream ice to the refrigerator. Pour a spoonful of mandarin liqueur over each portion as it is served.

Serves 4

## Orange Sorbet de Luxe

4 ounces (100 g) sugar
2 fluid ounces (50 ml) lemon juice
3/4 pint (450 ml) frozen concentrated orange juice, thawed but not diluted
4 ounces (100 g) chunky marmalade
2 fluid ounces (50 ml) Cointreau

Dissolve the sugar in 4 fluid ounces (100 ml) water in a saucepan. Bring to the boil and boil for 1 minute. Remove from the heat and stir in the remaining ingredients. Cool completely then chill for 30 minutes.

Pour the mixture into a container. Cover and freeze, beating twice at hourly intervals, until just softly frozen. Serve immediately.

If the sorbet is made in advance and becomes hard, transfer it to the refrigerator 45–60 minutes before serving.

Serves 6–8

### Dessert suggestion
*Encase in Muesli Ice Cream (page 37). Decorate with whipped cream and fine strips of orange. Serve with white Wine Sauce*.*

## Tangerine Ice Cream

12 tangerines
4 ounces (100 g) caster sugar
1 pint (600 ml) double cream

For decoration
Shapes cut from tangerine peel
Any small shiny leaves from the garden or fresh bay leaves

Finely grate the zest from 6 of the tangerines. Mix the zest with the sugar and half of the cream in a saucepan. Heat gently to dissolve the sugar then leave to cool.

Squeeze the juice from all the tangerines and mix with the sweetened cream. Whip the remaining cream in a bowl until soft peaks form and fold into the sweetened, flavoured cream.

Pour the mixture into a container and freeze until firm, beating twice at hourly intervals.

About 30 minutes before serving, transfer the ice cream to the refrigerator. Serve decorated with the tangerine peel shapes and the leaves.

Serves 4–5

### Dessert suggestion
*Freeze in a container lined with Coconut Cake*. Spread a thin layer of mandarin-liqueur-flavoured whipped cream over the turned-out dessert and cover with finely chopped hazelnuts. Arrange tangerine segments around the base and serve with Langues de Chat*.*

# Orange and Rosemary Sorbet

4 ounces (100 g) sugar
Large rosemary sprig
¾ pint (450 ml) fresh orange juice
Grated zest of 3 large oranges

*For decoration*
*Shapes cut from orange peel*
*Small rosemary sprigs, with flowers if possible*

In a saucepan, dissolve the sugar in 4½ fluid ounces (115 ml) water and bring to the boil. Add the rosemary, remove from the heat, cover and leave to infuse for 30 minutes. Strain the syrup and blend with the strained orange juice and the zest.

Pour the mixture into a container. Cover and freeze until firm, beating well at 45-minute intervals.

About 40 minutes before serving, transfer the sorbet to the refrigerator. Decorate each portion with orange peel shapes and rosemary sprigs.

Serves 4–5

**Serving suggestion**
*Serve in Coupelles\*. Decorate with orange segments, pith and membrane removed, and sprigs of fresh rosemary, preferably in bloom.*

# Mandarin Ice Cream

8 fluid ounces (225 ml) milk
4 ounces (100 g) caster sugar
3 egg yolks
1 teaspoon (5 ml spoon) vanilla essence
¾ pint (450 ml) cream, whipped
3½ ounces (90 g) brandy snaps, roughly crumbled
Approximately 14 ounce (400 g) can mandarins,
    drained and chopped
3 tablespoons (3 × 15 ml spoons) brandy, optional

In a heavy-based saucepan, gently heat the milk to just below boiling point. Whisk the egg yolks with the sugar in a bowl until very thick and light. Whisk in the milk. Return the mixture to the rinsed pan and cook over a low heat, stirring constantly, until thickened. Remove from the heat, stir in the vanilla essence and cool, stirring occasionally.

Fold the cream, brandy snaps, mandarins and brandy, if you are using it, into the custard.

Pour the mixture into a container. Cover and freeze until firm.

About 30 minutes before serving, transfer the ice cream to the refrigerator.

Serves 6–8

**Serving suggestion**
*Freeze in a loaf tin. Serve in slices, surrounded with Bitter Chocolate Sauce\*.*

# Orange Ice Cream

3 eggs, separated
4 ounces (100 g) caster sugar
¾ pint (450 ml) double cream, whipped
Finely grated zest and juice of 2 large oranges

Put the egg yolks in a bowl. Whisk, gradually adding the sugar, until very thick and light.

In another bowl, whisk the egg whites until stiff. Fold the cream, orange juice and zest into the egg yolks followed by the egg whites.

Pour the mixture into a container. Cover and freeze until firm.

About 20 minutes before serving, transfer the ice cream to the refrigerator.

Serves 6

**Serving suggestion**
*Spoon into small Choux\* pastry shells, pile into a pyramid and pour over Hot Chocolate Sauce\* flavoured with Grand Marnier.*

**Dessert suggestion**
*Form into 6 balls with a tablespoon (15 ml spoon) of Nougat Glace à l'Orange (page 57), in the centre of each one. Coat with very lightly toasted flaked almonds. Serve with orange segments, pith and membrane removed.*

# Iced Orange-Almond Mousse

3 eggs, separated
3 ounces (75 g) caster sugar
Finely grated zest of 1 orange
3 tablespoons (3 × 15 ml spoons) orange juice
2 ounces (50 g) ground almonds
¼ pint (150 ml) double cream, whipped
Slices of glacé or fresh orange, for decoration

Put the egg yolks, sugar, orange zest and juice in a bowl and whisk until very thick and light. Fold in the ground almonds. In another bowl, whisk the egg whites until stiff but not dry and fold into the orange-almond mixture with the cream.

Pour into a container. Cover and freeze until firm.

About 20 minutes before serving, transfer the mousse to the refrigerator. Serve decorated with the orange slices.

Serves 6

**Dessert suggestion**
*Layer with Chocolate Ice Cream (page 44). Decorate the turned-out dessert with orange-liqueur-flavoured whipped cream, flaked almonds and slices of glacé orange.*

# Seville Orange Sorbet

2¼ pounds (1 kg) Seville oranges
11 ounces (300 g) cube sugar
2 ounces (50 g) caster sugar
Juice of ½ lemon
7 fluid ounces (200 ml) orange juice

To serve
Fresh orange segments
Orange caramel sauce
Caramelized* orange strips

Rub the skins of the oranges with the sugar cubes to extract as much of the essential oil as possible. Put the sugar cubes in a saucepan with the caster sugar, 2 fluid ounces (50 ml) water and the lemon juice. Heat gently to dissolve the sugar. Squeeze the juice from the oranges and add to the pan, off the heat, with the orange juice. Cool completely.

Pour the mixture into a container. Cover and freeze until firm, beating 3 times at 45-minute intervals.

About 30 minutes before serving, transfer the sorbet to the refrigerator. Serve topped by orange segments, a little orange caramel sauce and caramalized orange strips.

Serves 8

**Serving suggestion**
*Serve in wine glasses. Pour a little crème fraîche over each serving and sprinkle with chopped preserved ginger.*

# Orange Cream Ice

3 oranges
½ pint (300 ml) milk
2½ ounces (65 g) sugar
5 egg yolks
¼ pint (150 ml) cream, whipped
Crystallized orange slices, for decoration

Peel the oranges very thinly and put the zest in a heavy-based saucepan with the milk and sugar. Stir to dissolve the sugar over low heat. Then boil for 10 minutes.

Put the egg yolks in a bowl and whisk until light. Stir in the milk and return to the rinsed pan. Cook over a low heat, stirring constantly, until the custard thickens. Do not allow to boil. Strain through a fine sieve and cool, stirring occasionally.

Squeeze the oranges and stir the juice into the custard. Fold in the cream.

Pour the mixture into a container. Cover and freeze until firm, beating twice at hourly intervals.

About 40 minutes before serving, transfer the ice to the refrigerator. Serve decorated with crystallized orange slices.

Serves 4–5

**Serving suggestion**
*Scoop into individual dishes and serve with round Langues de Chat*.*

**Dessert suggestion**
*Freeze in a flan or sandwich tin lined with crushed ginger biscuits bound with melted butter. Cover with the same mixture. Decorate the turned-out dessert with brandy-flavoured whipped cream, shapes cut from orange peel and chocolate-coated peanuts.*

# Kumquat Ice Cream

12 ounces (350 g) kumquats, thinly sliced and seeds removed
6 ounces (175 g) sugar
½ pint (300 ml) double cream, whipped
1 piece of stem ginger, finely chopped, optional
Twisted fine strips of orange peel, for decoration

Put the kumquats, 7 fluid ounces (200 ml) water and the sugar in a saucepan and simmer gently until the fruit is soft. This may take 30 minutes but check occasionally.

Purée the fruit with the liquid and leave to cool.

Fold the cream into the purée with the ginger, if used. Pour into a container, cover and freeze until firm, beating twice at hourly intervals.

About 30 minutes before serving, transfer the ice cream to the refrigerator. Serve decorated with twisted strips of orange peel.

Serves 4

**Serving suggestion**
*Serve in Coupelles*. Decorate with Caramelized* strips of orange peel.*

**Dessert suggestion**
*Freeze in small boxes made from Chocolate Squares*. Decorate the tops with small swirls of whipped cream, and pieces of candied orange slices or fine strips of orange peel twisted together.*

**Additional recipes using oranges:** Orange Sorbet in a Chocolate Case (page 143), Blackberry and Orange Layer Cake (page 139).

PAPAYA:   see WARM CLIMATE FRUITS
PASSION FRUIT:   see WARM CLIMATE
FRUITS

# Peach, Nectarine

Peaches and nectarines can be substituted for each other in recipes, but nectarines have a slightly richer, more scented yet more tangy flavour. White-fleshed varieties of both fruits are the best to use. To peel peaches and nectarines, pour boiling water over them and leave for 15 seconds if they are very ripe, a little longer if they are slightly hard. The skin should come easily away from the flesh. Never leave the fruit in the water until the skin falls away of its own accord as this will affect both taste and texture. Sieving the puréed flesh gives a smoother ice, but is not always essential.

### Simple Peach Ice Cream
Purée and sieve the flesh of 1 pound (450 g) white peaches and add to any of the Basic Recipes*.

## Peach Ice Cream

*4 large ripe peaches*
*4 ounces (100 g) sugar*
*3 egg yolks*
*¼ pint (150 ml) whipping cream, whipped*
*Squeeze of lemon juice*

Peel the peaches, remove the stones and reduce the flesh to a purée.

Put the sugar and ¼ pint (150 ml) water in a saucepan and stir to dissolve over low heat. Bring to the boil.

Meanwhile, in a bowl, whisk the egg yolks until thick. Pour the boiling syrup on to the egg yolks, whisking all the time. Set the bowl over a pan of barely simmering water and continue to whisk until the mixture thickens. Remove from the heat and continue to whisk until the mixture cools.

Whisk the peach purée into the egg yolk mixture. Fold in the cream and add lemon juice to taste.

Pour the mixture into a container. Cover and freeze until firm.

About 30 minutes before serving, transfer the ice cream to the refrigerator.

Serves 4

### Dessert suggestion
*Freeze in a pie dish or cake tin lined with a crust of ground, toasted pecans or walnuts mixed with brown sugar to taste and bound with melted butter. To serve, brush the surface of the ice cream with a glaze made from melted, sieved apricot jam flavoured with lemon juice, and decorate with peach slices and mint sprigs.*

## Peach Sorbet

*1¼ pounds (500 g) ripe peaches*
*2 ripe apricots*
*11 ounces (300 g) caster sugar*
*2 tablespoons (2 × 15 ml spoons) lemon juice*

Peel and stone the peaches and apricots and reduce to a purée. Make up the purée to 1¾ pints (1 litre) with cold water. Add the sugar and stir or blend until it has dissolved. Strain through a fine sieve. Stir in the lemon juice. Pour the mixture into a container, cover and freeze until firm, beating 3 times at 45-minute intervals.

About 30 minutes before serving, transfer the sorbet to the refrigerator.

Serves 6–8

### Serving suggestion
*Poach halved, stoned peaches in wine. Enlarge the cavities if necessary, fill with scoops of sorbet and top with a teaspoonful (5 ml spoon) of crème fraîche. Serve with Macaroons*.*

### Flavour variation
*Replace the water in the recipe with a full-bodied dry white wine.*

## White Peach Sorbet

*Approximately 15 ounce (425 g) can of white peaches*
*Juices of 2 lemons*
*1 egg white*

Purée the peaches and the juice with the lemon juice then pass through a sieve.

Pour the mixture into a container. Cover and freeze to the slushy stage. Beat well in a bowl.

Whisk the egg white in a small bowl until stiff but not dry. Fold the egg white into the peach mixture. Return to the container, cover and freeze until firm.

About 30 minutes before serving, transfer the sorbet to the refrigerator.

Serves 4

### Serving suggestion
*Serve in tall, elegant glasses with a few brandy-soaked Macaroons* in the base of each. Just before serving pour wine over the sorbets.*

### Flavour variation
*Use canned yellow peaches instead of white ones and add 2 or 3 tablespoons (2 or 3 × 15 ml spoons) of white rum to the purée.*

# Iced Peach Yogurt

*4 large ripe peaches*
*Finely grated zest and juice of 2 oranges*
*1/2 pint (300 ml) plain yogurt*
*2 tablespoons (2 × 15 ml spoons) icing sugar*
*2 egg whites, stiffly whisked*

Peel and stone the peaches. Purée the flesh with the orange zest and juice, the yogurt and icing sugar. Fold in the egg whites.

Pour the mixture into individual dishes or moulds, cover and freeze until firm.

About 20 minutes before serving, transfer the ices to the refrigerator.

Serves 4

### Serving suggestion
*Freeze in individual ring moulds. Fill the centres with diced peaches, topped with Low Calorie Topping\* and a sprinkling of chopped almonds or hazelnuts if liked.*

### Low calorie version
*Use fructose or a low calorie or artificial sweetener instead of sugar.*

# Iced Nectarine Mousse

*4 ounces (100 g) sugar*
*4 large egg whites*
*1 pound (450 g) ripe nectarines, puréed and sieved*
*Squeeze of orange, lime or lemon juice*
*1/2 pint (300 ml) cream, whipped*

In a heavy-based saucepan, dissolve the sugar in 5 tablespoons (75 ml) water over low heat. Bring to the boil and boil until a temperature of 239°F (115°C) is reached.

Meanwhile, in a bowl, whisk the egg whites until very stiff. Gradually pour on the hot syrup, whisking constantly, and continue to whisk until the meringue is very thick and cold.

Fold the nectarine purée, sharpened with a little orange, lime or lemon juice, into the meringue. Fold in the cream.

Pour the mixture into a container. Cover and freeze until firm.

About 30 minutes before serving, transfer the mousse to the refrigerator.

Serves 4

### Dessert suggestion
*Freeze in hollowed-out nectarine shells. Decorate with kirsch-flavoured whipped cream, small Chocolate Shapes\* and a fine sprinkling of chopped hazelnuts. Serve with a sauce of sieved, puréed nectarines 'lifted' with a squeeze of orange juice, and Langues de Chat\*.*

# Lightly Spiced Peach Ice Cream

*12 ounces (350 g) dried peaches, soaked overnight in 1 pint (600 ml) hot water and 1/4 pint (150 ml) white wine*
*3 egg yolks*
*3 ounces (75 g) soft light brown sugar*
*1/2 pint (300 ml) milk*
*1/4 teaspoon (1.25 ml spoon) ground cinnamon*
*Large pinch grated nutmeg*
*1/4 pint (150 ml) cream, whipped*
*Long strip lemon peel*

Drain the peaches, reserving the liquor. Put the egg yolks in a bowl with the sugar and spices and whip together until thick. In a heavy-based saucepan, bring the milk to just below boiling point. Pour the hot milk on to the egg yolks, stirring. Return the mixture to the rinsed pan and cook over a low heat, stirring until thick. Cool, stirring occasionally, then pour into a container, cover and freeze until firm. Beat well in a bowl.

Finely chop half the peaches and fold into the custard with the cream. Spoon back into the container, cover and freeze until firm.

Simmer the remaining peaches in a saucepan with the lemon peel and the reserved liquor for about 5 minutes. Cool and store, covered, in the refrigerator if necessary.

About 30 minutes before serving, transfer the ice cream to the refrigerator. Gently warm the peaches and liquor and spoon a little over each portion as it is served.

Serves 6

### Serving suggestion
*Spoon into hollowed-out brioche. Add the warmed peaches, and spoon the liquor over each portion as it is served.*

**Additional recipe using peaches:** Iced Peach Charlotte (page 140).

Recipes for cakes, sauces, etc., asterisked in the dessert and serving suggestions, are given on pages 145 to 152. For instructions on layering, lining and other techniques involved in creating desserts, see pages 152 to 155. Basic recipes are on pages 16 and 17.

# Peanut

Peanut ices can be made with ground or chopped nuts, smooth or crunchy peanut butter, peanut brittle or dry-roasted or plain unsalted nuts. It is possible to buy roasted, unsalted peanuts, but if they are not available prepare your own by heating shelled, skinned nuts in a 350°F (180°C, gas mark 4) oven for about 30–45 minutes, taking care they do not become too brown. To prevent peanuts from becoming oily when you grind them, chop the nuts by hand before processing small batches, briefly, in a coffee mill, blender or food processor.

### Simple Peanut Ice Cream
Add 4 ounces (100 g) chopped unsalted peanuts to any of the Basic Recipes* or to a good-quality bought vanilla ice cream.

## Peanut Swirl

*3 eggs, separated*
*3 ounces (75 g) demerara sugar*
*18 fluid ounces (500 ml) milk*
*Few drops of vanilla essence*
*1/2 pint (300 ml) single cream*
*6 ounces (175 g) smooth peanut butter*

Beat the egg yolks with the sugar in a bowl. In a heavy-based saucepan, heat the milk to simmering point. Whisk the hot milk into the egg yolks. Return to the rinsed pan and cook gently, stirring constantly, until slightly thickened. Remove from the heat and leave to cool, stirring frequently.

Beat the vanilla essence and 4 fluid ounces (100 ml) of the cream into the custard. Put in the refrigerator to chill.

Pour the mixture into a container. Cover and freeze until just becoming firm.

Beat the remaining cream with the peanut butter in a bowl. In another bowl, whisk the egg whites until stiff but not dry. Fold the egg whites into the ice cream and when just evenly blended fold the peanut cream through the mixture to give a swirled, marbled effect. Return to the container, cover and freeze until firm.

About 45 minutes before serving, transfer the ice cream to the refrigerator.

Serves 6

### Dessert suggestion
*Freeze in a can then coat the turned-out ice in crushed Macaroons*. Serve in slices, surrounded by a sauce of puréed orange flesh.*

---

### To reduce your calorie intake
**Tofu** can be substituted for soft cheese; beat with the other ingredients until smooth. It has no cholesterol and is low in fat.

---

## Ground Peanut Ice Cream

*18 ounces (500 g) fromage blanc or sieved cottage cheese*
*4 1/2 ounces (115 g) unsalted dry-roasted peanuts, ground*
*4 1/2 ounces (115 g) caster sugar*
*5 ounces (150 g) sultanas*
*Finely grated zest of 1 lemon*
*1/2 pint (300 ml) crème fraîche or 1/4 pint (150 ml) single cream and 1/4 pint (150 ml) soured cream, mixed together*
*Twists of lemon peel, to decorate*

Leave the fromage blanc or cottage cheese to drain for 3–4 hours through a sieve lined with muslin or cheesecloth into a bowl.

Mix the nuts and sugar together and stir into the drained cheese with the sultanas and lemon zest. Fold in the crème fraîche or single and soured creams mixed together.

Pour the mixture into a container. Cover and freeze until firm.

About 30 minutes before serving, transfer the ice cream to the refrigerator. Serve decorated with twists of lemon peel.

Serves 6

### Serving suggestion
*Form into 6 balls and arrange on a serving dish, with Gingersnaps* and piped whipped cream. Decorate with chocolate vermicelli and chocolate flakes.*

## Peanut Ice Cream

*4 tablespoons (4 × 15 ml spoons) milk or single cream*
*12 ounces (350 g) soft cheese, sieved or beaten*
*4 ounces (100 g) icing sugar*
*Few drops of vanilla essence*
*4 ounces (100 g) unsalted peanuts, chopped*
*2 egg whites*

Gradually beat the milk or cream into the soft cheese then beat in the sugar and vanilla essence. Stir in the nuts.

In another bowl, whisk the egg whites until stiff but not dry then fold into the peanut mixture. Cover and freeze in individual dishes until firm.

About 30 minutes before serving, transfer the ice cream to the refrigerator.

Serves 4

### Serving suggestion
*Freeze in a ring mould. Fill the centre with small scoops of Apricot Sorbet (page 23) or Pineapple Sorbet (page 98) and surround the turned-out dessert with apricot quarters or pineapple chunks.*

# Peanut Brittle Ice Cream

*4 ounces (100 g) unsalted dry-roasted peanuts*
*4 ounces (100 g) sugar*
*3 egg yolks*
*2 ounces (50 g) icing sugar*
*8 fluid ounces (225 ml) milk*
*4 fluid ounces (100 ml) double cream*

To make the brittle, spread the peanuts on a non-stick baking tray or one lined with foil. Dissolve the sugar in 4 tablespoons (60 ml) water in a small, heavy-based pan. Bring to the boil and boil rapidly until the syrup caramelizes and turns an even, deep golden brown. Pour the caramel immediately over the peanuts and quickly stir them around so they are evenly coated. Leave to cool. Put the brittle into a heavy polythene bag and bang it firmly with a rolling pin until it is broken into small pieces – some will be pulverized.

Whisk the egg yolks and icing sugar together in a bowl until thick and pale. Whip the milk and cream together, then whisk into the egg yolks. Chill well.

Fold the peanut brittle and the fine powdery pieces into the cream mixture.

Pour the mixture into a container. Cover and freeze until firm.

About 30 minutes before serving, transfer the ice cream to the refrigerator.

Serves 4

### Dessert suggestion
*Layer with Banana Ice Cream (page 28) and Chocolate Ice Cream (page 44), gently swirling each layer into the one below. Decorate with chocolate-coated peanuts or Chocolate Curls\* and chopped peanut brittle.*

**Additional recipe using peanuts:** Peanut Chocolate Fudge Ice Cream (page 38).

# Pear

The best-flavoured ices are made from dessert pears – juicy, sweet, melting Doyenné du Comice, sweet, musky Williams, plump, 'buttery' Beurre Hardy or really ripe, late-season Conference. Whichever type you use, make sure it is ripe but not 'sleepy', that is, soft, mushy and often discoloured. Canned pears can make good ices.

### Simple Pear Ice Cream

Drain and chop the contents of a 14 ounce (400 g) can pears and add to any of the Basic Recipes*.

# Pear and Hazelnut Yogurt Ice

*Approximately 14 ounce (400 g) can pears, in natural juice*
*2 teaspoons (2 × 5 ml spoons) honey*
*1 tablespoon (15 ml spoon) lemon juice*
*½ pint (300 ml) hazelnut yogurt*
*Lemon balm leaves, for decoration*

Drain and chop the pears finely and set aside. Pour the juice into a saucepan. Add the honey and lemon juice and heat gently, stirring until evenly mixed. Cool. Whisk in the yogurt and chill for about 30 minutes.

Pour the mixture into a container. Cover and freeze until slushy. Beat well in a bowl. Fold the chopped pears into the yogurt mixture. Return to the container, cover and freeze until firm.

About 1 hour before serving, transfer the ice to the refrigerator. Serve decorated with lemon balm leaves.

Serves 4

### Low calorie version
*Add fructose or a low calorie or artificial sweetener instead of honey with the yogurt. Freeze in individual containers. Serve with Low Calorie Topping*.*

# Pear and Red Wine Sorbet

*4 medium-sized ripe dessert pears, peeled and cored*
*½ bottle (35 cl) of medium-quality red wine*
*¼ of an orange*
*¼ of a lemon*
*½ a cinnamon stick*
*4½ ounces (115 g) sugar*
*1½ fluid ounces (40 ml) Poire Williams, optional*

In a saucepan, poach the pears in the wine with the orange, lemon, cinnamon, sugar and 2½ fluid ounces (65 ml) water until tender. Remove the pears and put in a bowl. Strain the liquor over the pears and leave to cool. Purée the pears and liquor, adding the Poire Williams, if using.

Pour the mixture into a container. Cover and freeze until firm, beating well 3 times at 45-minute intervals.

About 30 minutes before serving, transfer the sorbet to the refrigerator.

Serves 4–5

### Serving suggestion
*Serve with poached pears and cinnamon-flavoured Cigars Russe*.*

### Dessert suggestion
*Encase in Pear Ice Cream (below) and surround with Langues de Chat*. Decorate with whipped cream and finely chopped hazelnuts.*

# Pear Ice Cream

*1 pound (450 g) dessert pears, peeled, cored and chopped*
*2 ounces (50 g) unsalted butter*
*1 ounce (25 g) sugar*
*1 tablespoon (15 ml spoon) orange flower water, or to taste*
*Strip of lemon peel*
*2 egg yolks*
*½ pint (300 ml) crème fraîche or 50/50 blend double and soured creams*
*Crystallized violets, for decoration*

Gently poach the pears with the butter, sugar, orange flower water, lemon peel, and 4 tablespoons (60 ml) water in an uncovered saucepan, until very soft. Remove the peel and purée the fruit and the liquor (this should have reduced by about half).

Return the purée to the pan and beat in the egg yolks. Cook over a low heat, stirring constantly, until the mixture thickens, but do not allow it to boil. Leave to cool, stirring occasionally. Pour the mixture into a container, cover and freeze until just becoming firm. Turn into a bowl and beat well.

Whip the crème fraîche or creams in a bowl until soft peaks form. Fold into the pear mixture.

Spoon the mixture back into the container. Cover and freeze until firm.

About 30 minutes before serving, transfer the ice cream to the refrigerator. Serve each portion decorated with crystallized violets.

Serves 4

### Serving suggestion
*Serve in lightly spiced Coupelles* or Gingersnap Baskets*. Arrange small thin slices of poached pears over the mounds of ice cream and sprinkle them with Poire Williams or kirsch. Decorate each serving with long fine strips of orange peel.*

### Dessert suggestion
*Make a bombe or freeze in a loaf or cake tin with the ice cream encased in a layer of Raspberry Ice Cream (page 104) followed by a layer of Pistachio Ice Cream (page 101). Surround the turned-out dessert with poached, sliced pears strewn with long, fine strips of orange peel.*

## Pear Sorbet

*3 large, ripe dessert pears, preferably Williams*
*¼ pint (150 ml) good-quality riesling wine*
*3 ounces (75 g) sugar*
*Long strip of lemon peel*

*For decoration*
*Poached pear slices*
*Maraschino cherries*

Peel, core and slice the pears. Poach the pears with the wine, sugar and lemon peel for about 5 minutes until the slices are tender. Remove the pan from the heat and leave to cool. Remove the lemon peel and purée the cold mixture.

Pour the mixture into a container. Cover and freeze until firm, beating well at 45-minute intervals.

About 15 minutes before serving transfer the sorbet to the refrigerator. Serve decorated with poached pear slices and maraschino cherries.

Serves 4

### Dessert suggestion
*Make into a bombe with a centre of Ginger Crush (page 61).*

## Pear Ice Cream (with kirsch)

*2 large ripe dessert pears*
*3 tablespoons (3 × 15 ml spoons) lemon juice*
*3½ ounces (90 g) sugar*
*2 egg whites*
*4 fluid ounces (100 ml) double cream*
*1 ounce (25 g) icing sugar*
*2 fluid ounces (50 ml) Poire Williams, eau-de-vie or*
*    good-quality kirsch*

Peel and core the pears then purée with the lemon juice. Chill. Dissolve the sugar in 1½ fluid ounces (40 ml) water in a small heavy-based saucepan. Bring to the boil and boil for 2 minutes until the syrup runs off the spoon in a slightly sticky stream.

In a bowl, whisk the egg whites, preferably using an electric whisk, until soft peaks form. Pour in the boiling syrup in a steady stream, whisking constantly for 2–3 minutes until the mixture is stiff, shiny and cool. Chill.

In another bowl, whip the cream with the icing sugar and Poire Williams or kirsch until soft peaks form. Carefully fold in the pear purée then the meringue.

Spoon the mixture into a container. Cover and freeze until firm.

About 20 minutes before serving, transfer the ice cream to the refrigerator.

Serves 4

### Serving suggestion
*Serve in scooped-out pear shells or chocolate-coated Meringue Baskets\*. Decorate with small rosettes of whipped cream, and crystallized violets or roses. Serve with Langues de Chat\*.*

## Pear Ice Cream (with soft cheese)

*1¼ pounds (550 g) ripe pears, cored*
*3 fluid ounces (75 ml) apple juice*
*3½ ounces (90 g) light brown sugar*
*¼ teaspoon (1.25 ml spoon) ground cinnamon*
*2 eggs, separated*
*5 ounces (150 g) full-fat soft cheese, beaten*

Gently poach the pears in the apple juice with the sugar and cinnamon in a covered pan until tender. Purée the pears with the cooking liquid then pass through a fine sieve. Return the mixture to the rinsed pan, stir in the egg yolks and heat gently until slightly thickened. Set aside to cool.

Beat the cheese into the pear mixture. Pour into a container, cover and freeze until just becoming firm. Turn into a bowl and beat well. Whisk the egg whites in a bowl until stiff but not dry then fold into the cold mixture.

Spoon the mixture back into the container. Cover and freeze until firm.

About 30 minutes before serving, transfer the ice cream to the refrigerator.

Serves 4

### Serving suggestion
*Serve with Mars Bar Sauce\* or Hot Chocolate Sauce\* and Langues de Chat\*.*

### Dessert suggestion
*Layer with crushed Macaroons\*. Decorate the turned-out dessert with slices of crystallized orange and grated chocolate. Serve with white Wine Sauce\*.*

---

**To reduce your calorie intake**
**Tofu** can be substituted for soft cheese; beat with the other ingredients until smooth. It has no cholesterol and is low in fat.

---

*PECAN: see WALNUT, PECAN*
*PEPPER (RED): see SAVOURY*

# Peppermint

Ices can be flavoured with the fresh, clean taste of peppermint in a number of ways – with oil or essence, with crushed peppermint or mint sweets, or with crème de menthe for an extra 'kick'. Peppermint is well known for the beneficial effect it has on the digestion, and a peppermint ice must surely be the most enjoyable way to ward off, or cure, an attack of indigestion.

### Simple Peppermint Ice Cream

Add 4 ounces (100 g) crushed peppermint rock to any of the Basic Recipes* or to a good-quality bought vanilla ice cream.

## Peppermint Ice Cream

*4 ounces (100 g) sugar*
*Juice of ½ lemon*
*3–4 drops peppermint essence*
*1 tablespoon (15 ml spoon) finely chopped fresh mint*
*½ pint (300 ml) cream, whipped*

*For decoration*
*Créme de menthe*
*Mint leaves*
*Bitter Chocolate Sauce*, for serving*

In a saucepan, dissolve the sugar in ¼ pint (150 ml) water. Bring to the boil and remove from the heat. Strain in the lemon juice and leave to cool.

Mix the peppermint essence into the syrup. Fold the syrup and then the chopped mint into the cream.

Pour the mixture into a container. Cover and freeze until firm, beating well after 1 hour.

About 30 minutes before serving, transfer the ice cream to the refrigerator. Spoon a little crème de menthe over each portion and decorate with mint leaves. Serve with bitter chocolate sauce.

Serves 4

### Serving suggestion
*Freeze in small Chocolate Cases* and serve as petits fours.*

### Dessert suggestion
*Layer with Blackcurrant Ice Cream (page 32).*

### Flavour variation
*Use crème de menthe instead of peppermint essence.*

Recipes for cakes, sauces, etc., asterisked in the dessert and serving suggestions, are given on pages 145 to 152. For instructions on layering, lining and other techniques involved in creating desserts, see pages 152 to 155. Basic recipes are on pages 16 and 17.

## Mint and Chocolate Ice Cream

*2 ounces (50 g) sugar*
*3 large egg yolks*
*½ pint (300 ml) single cream*
*½ pint (300 ml) double cream*
*6 tablespoons (6 × 15 ml spoons) crème de menthe*
*4 ounces (100 g) bitter chocolate, coarsely chopped*

In a heavy-based saucepan, dissolve the sugar in 4 fluid ounces (100 ml) water. Bring to the boil and boil until a temperature of 215°F (101°C) is reached.

Whisk the egg yolks in a bowl. Slowly pour in the syrup, whisking constantly. Continue whisking until the mixture becomes thick and light.

In another bowl, whip the creams together until soft peaks form. Fold the cream into the egg yolks with the crème de menthe and chocolate.

Pour the mixture into a container, cover and freeze until firm.

About 30 minutes before serving, transfer the ice cream to the refrigerator.

Serves 6

### Dessert suggestion
*Freeze in a 'box' of Genoise Cake* or use to fill a Swiss Roll*. Decorate the outside lavishly with crème de menthe-flavoured whipped cream, Frosted* mint leaves and Chocolate Shapes*.*

## Peppermint Rock Ice Cream

*Approximately 14 ounce (400 g) can sweetened condensed milk*
*1 tablespoon (15 ml spoon) vanilla essence*
*4½ ounces (115 g) peppermint rock, crushed*
*¾ pint (450 ml) cream, whipped*
*Crumbled chocolate flake, to decorate*

Put the condensed milk, 8 fluid ounces (225 ml) water and the vanilla essence in a bowl and whisk until thick and light. Fold in the peppermint rock and the cream.

Pour the mixture into a container. Cover and freeze until firm.

About 20 minutes before serving, transfer the ice cream to the refrigerator. Serve decorated with crumbled chocolate flake.

Serves 6–8

### Dessert suggestion
*Use to fill a Chocolate Roll*. Sprinkle the outside with sifted icing sugar, or decorate with piped cream and finely crushed chocolate-mint matchsticks.*

*PERSIMMON: see WARM CLIMATE FRUITS*

# Pineapple

Although it is fashionable to serve pineapple with all manner of savoury ingredients, it is probably most enjoyable as a dessert. Ices can be made with canned, crushed pineapple as well as the fresh fruit. There is no need to waste the shell with its crown of leaves – it makes a marvellous, natural container for iced mixtures. However, the hard core that runs down the centre of the fruit cannot be used. Even puréeing and sieving will not render it edible.

**Simple Pineapple Ice Cream**
Add 8 fluid ounces (225 g) well-drained crushed pineapple to any of the Basic Recipes* or to a good-quality bought vanilla ice cream.

## Pineapple Ice Cream (with yogurt)

*½ pint (300 ml) milk*
*2 whole eggs*
*2 egg yolks*
*4 ounces (100 g) caster sugar*
*½ pint (300 ml) plain yogurt*
*10 ounces (275 g) pineapple flesh, puréed*

In a heavy-based saucepan bring the milk to boiling point. Whisk the eggs and egg yolks together in a bowl then whisk in the boiling milk. Return the mixture to the rinsed pan and cook slowly, stirring constantly, until the custard thickens. Do not allow to boil. Remove from the heat, stir in the sugar and leave to cool, stirring occasionally to prevent a skin forming.

Blend the yogurt and pineapple together then stir into the cold custard. Pour into a container. Cover and freeze, beating twice at hourly intervals.

About 30 minutes before serving, transfer the ice cream to the refrigerator.

Serves 6

**Serving suggestion**
*Pile into chilled pineapple shells and decorate with glacé cherries. Serve with wafer biscuits.*

**Dessert suggestion**
*Form into 6 balls and roll in grated chocolate or desiccated coconut. Serve with a sauce of sieved puréed pineapple flesh.*

## Pineapple and Cardamom Ice Cream

*Seeds from 6 cardamom pods, finely crushed*
*¼ pint (150 ml) milk*
*6 ounces (175 g) sugar*
*5 ounces (150 g) pineapple flesh, finely chopped*
*3 egg yolks*
*¼ pint (150 ml) double cream*

Put the cardamom seeds, milk and 1 ounce (25 g) of the sugar in a small saucepan and bring just to simmering point. Remove from the heat, cover and leave for 5–8 minutes.

Put the pineapple with the remaining sugar and ¼ pint (150 ml) water in another saucepan and simmer until soft and slightly translucent. Leave to cool.

Meanwhile, in a bowl whisk the egg yolks until thick. Whisk in the flavoured milk and the cream. Pour back into the rinsed pan and cook over a low heat, stirring constantly, until the mixture thickens. Do not allow to boil. Leave to cool, stirring occasionally.

Blend in the pineapple and pour into a container. Cover and freeze until firm.

About 20 minutes before serving, transfer the ice cream to the refrigerator.

Serves 4–5

**Dessert suggestion**
*Use to line a 'box' of Genoise Cake*, with a centre of Apple Cream Ice (page 21) or Pear Ice Cream (page 92). Serve with red or white Wine Sauce* or Coffee Sauce*.*

## Pineapple Mallow Ice Cream

*8 ounces (225 g) marshmallows, cut into pieces*
*4 fluid ounces (100 ml) medium dry white wine or cider or unsweetened apple juice*
*Approximately 13 ounce (375 g) can crushed pineapple, thoroughly drained, syrup reserved*
*½ pint (300 ml) cream, whipped*
*2 ounces (50 g) drained maraschino cherries, roughly chopped*

*For decoration*
*Pineapple cubes*
*Maraschino cherries, halved*
*Frosted* mint leaves*

Put the marshmallows, wine, cider or apple juice and pineapple syrup in a saucepan over low heat, stirring constantly, until the marshmallows have dissolved. Leave to cool.

Fold the cream into the cooled marshmallow mixture. Pour into a container, cover and freeze to the slushy stage. Beat well in a bowl.

Fold the crushed pineapple and cherries into the frozen mixture. Return to the container, cover and freeze until firm.

About 20 minutes before serving, transfer the ice cream to the refrigerator. Decorate each portion with pineapple cubes, maraschino cherry halves and frosted mint leaves.

Serves 4–6

**Serving suggestion**
*Serve in individual pâte sucrée cases, accompanied by Bitter Chocolate Sauce*.*

**Dessert suggestions**
*Ripple with Toasted Oat and Nut Ice Cream (page 36).*

*Freeze in individual Chocolate Cases*. Just before serving, decorate with fine pineapple pieces and maraschino cherries.*

## Pineapple Buttermilk Sorbet

¾ pint (450 ml) buttermilk
4 ounces (100 g) sugar
1 teaspoon (5 ml spoon) grated lemon zest
½ pint (300 ml) well-drained canned crushed
   pineapple
1 egg white
1 teaspoon (5 ml spoon) vanilla essence
Fresh mint sprigs, for decoration

Mix the buttermilk, sugar, lemon zest and pineapple together in a bowl and leave until the sugar has dissolved.

Pour the mixture into a container. Cover and freeze until just becoming firm. Beat well in a bowl.

Lightly whisk the egg white and the vanilla in a bowl. Whisk into the pineapple mixture until light and fluffy. Return to the container, cover and freeze until firm.

About 30 minutes before serving, transfer the sorbet to the refrigerator. Serve decorated with mint sprigs.

Serves 6

### Serving suggestion
*Freeze in individual ring moulds and fill the centres with chopped pineapple or scoops of Simple Chestnut Ice Cream (page 42).*

## Pineapple Sorbet

1 large ripe pineapple
Juice of 1 lemon
4 ounces (100 g) icing sugar

Cut the top, including the leaves, from the pineapple. Using a sharp knife, remove all the flesh from the pineapple, taking care not to pierce the shell and leaving a border of about ½ inch (1.25 cm). Put the pineapple shell and top into the freezer.

Cut away the core and chop the pineapple flesh then reduce to a purée. Stir in the lemon juice and sugar. Pour the mixture into a container. Cover and freeze until firm, beating 3 times at 45-minute intervals.

About 20 minutes before serving, use a spoon dipped in hot water to spoon the sorbet into the pineapple shell then place the top back in position.

Serves 4

### Serving suggestions
*Alternate the spoonfuls of sorbet with scoops of Banana Ice Cream (page 28) flavoured with brandy instead of orange juice, and halved strawberries and grapes.*

*Serve the sorbet on pineapple rings decorated with small rosettes of whipped cream and Chocolate Shapes\*.*

## Pina Colada Ice Cream

1 very large ripe pineapple
3 ounces (75 g) creamed coconut
5 ounces (150 g) icing sugar
2 fluid ounces (50 ml) white rum
½ pint (300 ml) double cream, whipped

For decoration
Cocktail cherries
Pineapple cubes
Toasted coconut strands

Remove the flesh from the pineapple and purée with all but 4 tablespoons (60 ml) of the juice that will run out when you peel the fruit. Put the reserved juice in a small saucepan. Add the creamed coconut and dissolve over low heat.

Blend in the pineapple purée, icing sugar and rum. Fold in the cream.

Pour the mixture into a container. Cover and freeze until firm.

About 35 minutes before serving, transfer the ice cream to the refrigerator. Serve in glasses with frosted rims and decorate each portion with cocktail cherries and pineapple cubes on cocktail sticks and sprinkle the coconut around the edge.

Serves 6

### Serving suggestion
*Spoon into Gingersnap Cones\* and serve surrounded by cocktail cherries and pineapple chunks.*

## Rich Pineapple Ice Cream (with soft cheese)

3 eggs, separated
2 ounces (50 g) caster sugar
8 ounces (225 g) cottage cheese, sieved
4 ounces (100 g) full fat soft cheese
¼ pint (150 ml) soured cream
Finely grated zest and juice of 1 large lemon
1¼ pounds (550 g) canned crushed pineapple, well-
   drained

Whisk the egg yolks with the sugar in a bowl until very thick and light.

Mix the cottage cheese, soft cheese, soured cream and lemon zest and juice together in a blender. Whisk the mixture into the egg yolks.

In another bowl, whisk the egg whites until stiff but not dry. Fold into the egg yolks with the pineapple.

Pour the mixture into a container. Cover and freeze until firm.

About 30 minutes before serving, transfer the ice cream to the refrigerator.

Serves 6

**Serving suggestion**
*Serve small scoops in Coupelles\*, intermingled with
small scoops of Mince Meat Ice Cream (page 141).*

**Flavour variation**
*Add 3 ounces (75 g) chopped preserved ginger when
you fold in the pineapple and egg whites.*

# Pineapple Ice Cream

*1 ripe pineapple
Juice of ½ a lemon
4 eggs, separated
4 ounces (100 g) caster sugar
1 ounce (25 g) icing sugar
¼ pint (150 ml) double cream, whipped*

Cut the pineapple in half lengthways and cut out the
central hard core. Carefully scoop out the pineapple
flesh, taking care not to pierce the shells. Put the shells
in the freezer. Purée the pineapple flesh with the
lemon juice.

Whisk the egg yolks with the caster sugar in a bowl
until thick and light. Whisk the egg whites in another
bowl until stiff. Whisk in the icing sugar and continue
whisking until stiff again. Fold the cream into the egg
yolks with the pineapple purée. Fold in the egg whites.

Pour the mixture into a container. Cover and freeze
until firm.

About 5 minutes before serving, scoop the ice cream
into the shells, using a spoon dipped briefly in hot
water, and refrigerate until required.

Serves 6–8

**Serving suggestion**
*Add glacé or candied fruits steeped in a liqueur to the
ice cream in the shells. Cover with Meringue\* and flash
under a hot grill just long enough to brown the
outside of the meringue. Serve immediately, with
Sponge Fingers\*.*

# Caribbean Sorbet

*4 ounces (100 g) caster sugar
¾ pint (450 ml) pineapple juice
Finely grated zest and juice of 1 lime
2 ounces (50 g) creamed coconut
2 egg whites*

*For decoration
Long, thin strips of lime peel
Pineapple cubes
Cocktail cherries*

In a heavy-based saucepan, dissolve the sugar in the
pineapple juice with the lime zest and juice. Bring to
the boil and boil the syrup until the temperature
reaches 230°F (110°C) (soft ball stage). Stir in the
creamed coconut and leave to cool.

Pour the mixture into a container. Cover and freeze
until slushy. Beat well in a bowl.

Whisk the egg whites in a bowl until stiff but not dry.
Fold into the pineapple mixture. Return to the
container, cover and freeze until firm.

About 20 minutes before serving, transfer the sorbet
to the refrigerator. Serve scoops of the sorbet in
chilled glasses decorated with strips of lime peel
hanging from the rim and with pineapple cubes and
cocktail cherries.

Serves 4–6

# Pineapple Crush Ice Cream

*6 ounce (175 g) can evaporated milk, chilled
2 ounces (50 g) icing sugar, sifted
2 bananas
Juice of 2 lemons
Approximately 13 ounce (375 g) can crushed
    pineapple
6 ounce (175 g) jar maraschino cherries, drained and
    halved with 2 tablespoons (2 × 15 ml spoons) syrup
    reserved*

Put the milk in a bowl and whisk until thick and frothy.
Whisk in the icing sugar.

Mash the bananas with the lemon juice. Stir them
into the milk with the pineapple and its syrup.

Reserve a few cherries for decoration and stir the
remainder into the milk with the reserved syrup.

Pour the mixture into a container. Cover and freeze
until firm, beating well after 1½ hours.

About 30 minutes before serving, transfer the ice to
the refrigerator. Serve in scoops decorated with the
reserved cherries.

Serves 4–6

**Dessert suggestion**
*Freeze in a flan tin or sandwich tin lined with crushed
amaretti biscuits. Decorate the turned-out dessert with
swirls of kirsch-flavoured whipped cream and the
reserved cherries.*

**Additional recipe using pineapple:** Pineapple and
Coconut Macaroon Cake (page 137).

# Pistachio

The pale green pistachio has a delicate yet discernible flavour. Nuts for cooking are normally available as unsalted kernels. If you do have to skin them, simply soak them in boiling water for a few minutes, then cool quickly in cold water and rub off the skins.

### Simple Pistachio Ice Cream

Add 4 ounces (100 g) chopped pistachio nuts to any of the Basic Recipes* or to a good-quality bought vanilla ice cream.

## Iced Pistachio Nougat

*1¼ pints (700 ml) single cream*
*5 egg yolks*
*8 ounces (225 g) honey*
*2 tablespoons (2 × 15 ml spoons) orange flower water*
*12 fluid ounces (350 ml) cream, whipped*
*3 egg whites*
*4 ounces (100 g) pistachio nuts*
*3 ounces (75 g) split almonds*

In a heavy-based saucepan, gently heat the cream to just below simmering point.

Beat the egg yolks in a bowl. Pour the hot cream on to the egg yolks in a slow steady stream beating continually. Return to the rinsed pan and cook over a low heat, stirring constantly, until the custard thickens. Stir in the honey. Add half the orange flower water and leave to cool, stirring occasionally. Pour into a container, cover and freeze until just becoming firm. Turn into a bowl and beat well. Fold in the cream. Whisk the egg whites in a bowl until stiff but not dry. Fold into the mixture with the nuts.

Spoon the mixture back into the container. Cover and freeze until firm.

About 30 minutes before serving, transfer the iced nougat to the refrigerator.

Serves 6–8

### Serving suggestion

*Freeze in a loaf or cake tin and decorate the turned-out dessert with candied fruits. Serve with Orange Flower Sauce\*.*

## Smooth Pistachio Ice Cream

*5 ounces (150 g) pistachio nuts*
*¾ pint (450 ml) milk*
*4 egg yolks*
*4½ ounces (115 g) sugar*
*Few drops of green food colouring, optional*
*8 ounces (225 g) drained fromage frais or low fat soft cheese, beaten*

Put the nuts in a bowl. Pour in boiling water and blanch for 1 minute. Drain and peel the nuts. Pound the nuts in a mortar or put them in a food processor with 2 tablespoons (30 ml) of the milk and process to a smooth paste.

Blend the paste with the remaining milk in a heavy-based saucepan and bring to simmering point. Remove from the heat, cover and leave for 20 minutes.

Beat the egg yolks with the sugar in a bowl until thick. Heat the flavoured milk to boiling point again and pour on to the egg yolks, stirring. Return the mixture to the rinsed pan and cook gently, stirring constantly, until thickened, but do not allow the mixture to boil. Stir in the colouring, if you are using it, and leave to cool. Beat the fromage frais or cheese into the custard and leave to become completely cold.

Pour the mixture into a container. Cover and freeze until firm, beating twice at hourly intervals.

About 30 minutes before serving, transfer the ice cream to the refrigerator.

Serves 5–6

**Serving suggestion**
*For each serving, swirl Bitter Chocolate Sauce\* around the base of a wine glass, then fill with scoops of ice cream. Top with a wafer biscuit.*

## Rich Pistachio Ice Cream

*5 ounces (150 g) caster sugar*
*1 pint (600 ml) whipping, double or 50/50 double/single cream*
*5 ounces (150 g) pistachio nuts, chopped*

Put the sugar and ¼ pint (150 ml) of the cream in a saucepan. Stir over low heat to dissolve the sugar. Remove from the heat and leave to cool. Fold in the nuts. Put the sweetened cream in a bowl with the rest of the cream and whip until soft peaks form.

Pour the mixture into a container, cover and freeze until firm, beating well after 1½ hours.

About 20 minutes before serving, transfer the ice cream to the refrigerator.

Serves 4

**Serving suggestion**
*Scoop into small Choux\* balls, form these into a pyramid and pour over Bitter Chocolate Sauce\*.*

## Pistachio and Green Chartreuse Ice Cream

*4 egg yolks*
*4 ounces (100 g) sugar*
*6 ounces (175 g) pistachio nuts, finely chopped*
*1 pint (600 ml) cream, whipped*
*2–3 tablespoons (2–3 × 15 ml spoons) Green Chartreuse*
*Green colouring, optional*

Whisk the egg yolks in a bowl until very thick and light. In a heavy-based saucepan dissolve the sugar in 5 tablespoons (75 ml) water. Bring to the boil and while it is still bubbling trickle it on to the egg yolks, whisking constantly. Continue to whisk until thickened and cold. Fold in the nuts, whipped cream, Green Chartreuse and colouring, if using.

Pour the mixture into a container, cover and freeze until firm. About 20 minutes before serving, transfer the ice cream to the refrigerator.

Serves 6

## Pistachio Ice Cream

*1 vanilla pod*
*¾ pint (450 ml) milk*
*3 eggs, separated*
*4 ounces (100 g) caster sugar*
*¼ pint (150 ml) cream, whipped*
*2 ounces (50 g) pistachio nuts, chopped*

In a heavy-based saucepan, gently heat the vanilla pod in the milk and bring to boiling point. Remove from the heat, cover and leave for 20 minutes. Remove the vanilla pod and bring the milk to boiling point again.

Meanwhile, whisk the egg yolks with the sugar in a bowl until thick and light. Whisk in the hot milk. Return the mixture to the rinsed pan and cook over a low heat, stirring constantly, until the custard thickens. Do not allow to boil. Allow to cool, stirring frequently. Pour into a container, cover and freeze until just becoming firm. Turn into a bowl and beat well.

Fold the cream and nuts into the custard. Whisk the egg whites in a bowl until stiff but not dry. Fold into the mixture and spoon back into the container. Cover and freeze until firm. About 30 minutes before serving, transfer to the refrigerator.

Serves 4–5

**Dessert suggestion**
*To make a Baked Alaska, place a large circle of Swiss Roll\* on a baking tin, sprinkle with Poire Williams or brandy and cover with the ice cream. Enclose with Meringue\* and flash under a hot grill until browned. Serve immediately.*

**Additional recipe using pistachio:** Cranberry and Pistachio Ripple (page 55).

# Plum, Prune

Plums come in many hues – rich purple, glowing golden, ruby, crimson – plus the yellow-green of greengages and the intense blue of damsons. However, the flavour of an ice is more important than its colour, so use only dessert varieties (except in the case of damsons) and taste the mixture to make sure it is sweet enough. Recipes for prunes – dried plums – are included in this section. Pie filling can be used for easy-to-make ices.

**Simple Plum Ice Cream**

Add the contents of a 7 ounce (200 g) can of plum pie filling to any of the Basic Recipes* or to a good-quality bought vanilla ice cream.

## Plum Ice Cream (with pie filling)

8 ounces (225 g) soft cheese
1/4 pint (150 ml) cream
Approximately 7 ounce (200 g) can plum pie filling
Lemon juice, to taste

Put the cheese in a bowl and beat until soft. Gradually beat in the cream taking care to keep the mixture smooth. Fold in the pie filling and add lemon juice to taste. Spoon the mixture into a container. Cover and freeze until firm, beating well after 1½ hours.

About 20–30 minutes before serving, transfer the ice cream to the refrigerator.

Serves 4

**Serving suggestion**
*Serve in individual Meringue Baskets*. Top with a spoonful of crème fraîche or yogurt and a sprinkling of flaked almonds.*

## Damson Ice Cream

1¼ pounds (550 g) damsons
6 ounces (175 g) sugar
2 large egg whites
Juice and finely grated zest of 1 small orange
1/2 pint (300 ml) cream, whipped

Wash the damsons and put them, still wet, in a heavy-based saucepan with 2 ounces (50 g) of the sugar. Cover the pan and cook gently until very soft. Pass the fruit through a sieve and remove the stones.

Dissolve the remaining sugar in 1/4 pint (150 ml) water in another saucepan. Bring to the boil and boil for 5 minutes.

Meanwhile, whisk the egg whites until stiff. Pour the boiling syrup in a slow steady stream on to the egg whites, whisking constantly, until the meringue is very stiff.

Stir the orange juice and zest into the damson purée. Fold the mixture into the cream. Gently fold the flavoured cream into the meringue.

Spoon the mixture into a container. Cover and freeze until firm.

About 30 minutes before serving, transfer the ice cream to the refrigerator.

Serves 6

**Dessert suggestion**
*Freeze between individual Meringues* flavoured with orange flower water. To serve, surround each portion with a sauce of puréed, sieved damsons. Accompany with Langues de Chat*.*

## Plum Ice Cream (with red wine)

2¼ pounds (1 kg) ripe plums, preferably Victorias
1/4 pint (150 ml) red wine
3 ounces (75 g) caster sugar
4 egg yolks
3/4 pint (450 ml) single cream
Few drops of red food colouring, optional
2 tablespoons (2 × 15 ml spoons) lemon juice
Large pinch of ground mace
Flaked almonds, for decoration

In a saucepan, poach the plums in the wine with 2 ounces (50 g) of the sugar for about 10 minutes until tender. Strain and reserve 13 fluid ounces (375 ml) of the liquor. Remove the stones from the plums and purée the flesh then pass through a sieve.

Whisk the egg yolks and remaining sugar in a bowl until thick and light. In a heavy-based saucepan, bring the cream to simmering point. Pour the hot cream on to the egg yolks whisking continuously. Return the mixture to the rinsed pan and cook over low heat until thickened, stirring constantly and taking care not to let the custard boil. Leave to cool slightly then stir in the colouring, if you are using it, the lemon juice and mace. Blend with the plum purée. Leave to cool completely.

Pour the mixture into a container. Cover and freeze until firm, beating twice at hourly intervals.

Put the reserved juice into a saucepan and boil until reduced to 6–8 fluid ounces (175–225 ml). Leave to cool.

About 45 minutes before serving, turn out the ice cream and transfer it to the refrigerator. Serve coated in plum sauce with a few almonds sprinkled over.

Serves 6

**Serving suggestion**
*Spoon into small Crêpes* and deep fry briefly. Sprinkle with icing sugar and pour over a little plum sauce.*

## Plum Ice Cream

1 pound (450 g) dark red plums
2 eggs, separated
4 ounces (100 g) caster sugar
8 ounces (225 g) curd cheese
1/4 pint (150 ml) double cream, whipped

Remove the stones from the plums then purée the flesh.

Whisk the egg yolks and sugar together in a bowl until thick and light then whisk in the cheese. In another bowl, whisk the egg whites until stiff. Fold the plum purée into the egg yolk mixture, then the cream followed by the egg whites.

Pour into a container. Cover and freeze until firm.

About 30 minutes before serving, transfer the ice cream to the refrigerator.

Serves 4

**Dessert suggestion**
*Layer with Smooth Coconut Ice Cream (page 49), in a loaf or cake tin lined with Langues de Chat\*. Gently swirl each layer into the one below. Decorate the turned-out dessert with slivovitz-flavoured whipped cream, long toasted strands of desiccated coconut and twists of lime.*

# Prune Sorbet

*1 pound (450 g) prunes, soaked overnight in tea*
*Grated zest and juice of 1 lemon*
*1/4 pint (150 ml) red wine*
*5 ounces (150 g) sugar*
*Long, thin strips of lemon peel twisted into loose corkscrews, for decoration*

Drain the excess liquid from the prunes and remove the stones. Mix the prunes with the lemon zest and juice, the red wine and sugar in a saucepan. Place over moderate heat and stir until the sugar has dissolved. Reduce the prunes to a pureé with the liquid and leave to cool.

Pour the mixture into a container. Cover and freeze until firm, beating 3 times at 45-minute intervals.

About 20 minutes before serving, transfer the sorbet to the refrigerator. Serve decorated with the corkscrews of lemon peel.

Serves 4–6

**Dessert suggestion**
*Encase in Sweet Mixed Spice Ice Cream (page 115). Serve with Sponge Fingers\*.*

# Prune Custard Ice

*12 ounces (350 g) prunes, soaked in hot water overnight*
*2 1/2 ounces (65 g) sugar*
*Long strip of orange peel*
*Approximately 15 ounce (425 g) canned dairy custard*
*Plain yogurt, for serving*

In a saucepan, cook the prunes in the minimum amount of water with the sugar and orange peel until tender. Remove the orange peel and the stones and purée the prunes with the cooking liquor. Set aside to cool.

Whip the prune purée into the custard. Pour the mixture into a container. Cover and freeze until firm, beating twice at hourly intervals.

About 30 minutes before serving, transfer the ice to the refrigerator. Serve each portion topped by a spoonful of yogurt.

Serves 4

**Dessert suggestion**
*Form into 4 balls, each enclosing a tablespoon (15 ml spoon) of Clove Sorbet (page 115). Serve with Coffee Sauce\*, Caramel Sauce\*, Burnt Honey Sauce\* or Hot Chocolate Sauce\*.*

# Victoria Ice Cream

*1 pound (450 g) ripe Victoria plums, halved and stoned*
*1 1/2 ounces (40 g) clear honey*
*Grated zest and juice of 1 lemon*
*3 ounces (75 g) demerara sugar*
*12 ounces (350 g) curd cheese*
*1/4 pint (150 ml) soured cream*
*2 egg whites*

Cook the plums in a saucepan with the honey, lemon zest and juice and sugar until they are soft. Reduce to a purée or pass through a nylon sieve.

Beat the cheese and cream together in a bowl then gradually beat in the plum purée. Cool completely then chill.

Pour the mixture into a container. Cover and freeze until just becoming firm. Beat well in a bowl.

In another bowl, whisk the egg whites until stiff but not dry. Fold into the frozen plum mixture. Return to the container, cover and freeze until firm.

About 45 minutes before serving, transfer the ice cream to the refrigerator.

Serves 4

**Serving suggestion**
*Halve and stone large, ripe plums and spoon the ice cream into the cavities. Arrange in groups on individual plates. Serve surrounded by a sauce of sieved, puréed plums, accompanied by large Macaroons\**

**Flavour variation**
*Fold baby Meringues\* into the plum mixture with the egg whites.*

**Additional recipes using prunes:** Prune Ice Cream with Brandy (page 116). Prune Ice Cream with Wine and Brandy (page 130).

---

*POMEGRANATE:    see WARM CLIMATE FRUITS*
*PRALINE:    see ALMOND*
*QUINCE:    see OLD-FASHIONED FAVOURITES*
*RAISIN:    see GRAPES*

# Raspberry, Mulberry

Raspberries have a rich, intense flavour that lends itself beautifully to all manner of iced mixtures: tangy, yogurt-based ones, ices rich in cream and refreshing sorbets. The berries are easily reduced to a purée, which should be sieved to remove the pips. One pound (450 g) raspberries will make about ½ pint (300 ml) purée, depending on the juiciness of the fruit. Canned raspberries can be used. Mulberries can be substituted for raspberries; always check whether the mixture is sweet enough.

## Simple Raspberry Ice Cream

Ripple any of the Basic Recipes* or a good-quality bought vanilla ice cream with ½ pint (300 ml) sieved raspberry purée, sweetened with a little icing sugar if necessary.

## Raspberry Rose Water Ice

5 ounces (150 g) sugar
¾ pint (450 ml) rosé wine
14 ounces (400 g) raspberries, puréed and sieved
2 fluid ounces (50 ml) lime juice

Dissolve the sugar in the wine in a saucepan over low heat. Leave to cool. Stir in the raspberry purée and lime juice and chill for an hour.

Pour the mixture into a container. Cover and freeze until firm, beating 3 times at 45-minute intervals.

About 40 minutes before serving, transfer to the refrigerator.

Serves 5–6

### Serving suggestion
*Scoop into individual Meringue Baskets\* flavoured with rose water and decorate with crystallized violets.*

## Raspberry Sorbet

1 pound (450 g) raspberries
4 ounces (100 g) icing sugar
Juice of 1 lemon

For decoration
Whole raspberries
Frosted* raspberry or mint leaves

Purée the raspberries and pass through a sieve into a bowl. Stir in the icing sugar (more or less, to taste) and lemon juice. Pour the mixture into a container. Cover and freeze until firm, beating 3 times at 45-minute intervals.

About 30 minutes before serving, transfer the sorbet to the refrigerator. Decorate each portion with whole raspberries and frosted raspberry or mint leaves.

Serves 4

### Serving suggestion
*Freeze in individual ring moulds and fill the centres with fresh raspberries. Trickle cream over the sorbet and decorate with Frosted\* raspberry or mint leaves.*

## Raspberry Ice Cream

1 pound (450 g) raspberries, puréed and sieved
3 ounces (75 g) icing sugar
Squeeze of lemon juice
3 ounces (75 g) sugar
3 egg yolks
½ pint (300 ml) cream, whipped

For decoration
Fresh raspberries
Lightly toasted flaked almonds

Put the raspberries in a bowl with the icing sugar and 'lift' the flavour with a squeeze of lemon juice.

In a heavy-based saucepan, dissolve the sugar in 4 fluid ounces (100 ml) water. Then bring to the boil and boil until the temperature reaches 234°F (112°C).

Whisk the egg yolks in another bowl until thick. Whisk in the boiling syrup in a slow steady stream and continue whisking until the mixture is cold and very light and thick. Fold in the raspberry purée and cream.

Spoon the mixture into a container. Cover and freeze until firm.

About 30 minutes before serving, transfer the ice cream to the refrigerator. Serve each portion decorated with raspberries and almonds.

Serves 4–6

### Serving suggestion
*Hollow out a large brioche and sprinkle with strawberry eau-de-vie fraise or gomme syrup. Alternate scoops of the ice cream with Pomegranate Sorbet (page 129) or Pear Sorbet (page 93) and a light sprinkling of finely chopped hazelnuts. Pour over a little more eau-de-vie or syrup.*

# Raspberry Ice Cream (with meringues)

*1 pound (450 g) raspberries*
*4 tablespoons (4 × 15 ml spoons) icing sugar*
*½ pint (300 ml) double cream*
*¼ pint (150 ml) single cream*
*3 ounces (75 g) Meringues\*, roughly broken*

Place the raspberries in a large bowl, sprinkle the sugar over and stir lightly to mix. Cover and leave in a cool place until the juices run. Purée the raspberries then pass through a sieve.

Whip the creams together in a bowl until soft peaks form. Fold in the meringues and the raspberry purée to give a marbled effect.

Pour into individual dishes or moulds. Cover and freeze until firm.

About 15 minutes before serving, transfer the ice cream to the refrigerator.

Serves 4

### Serving suggestion
*Serve as a sundae with a base of raspberries sprinkled with Galliano, followed by scoops of the ice cream and scoops of Liqueur Sorbet (page 131), preferably made with Grand Marnier, or Cointreau, or White Wine Sorbet (page 130).*

# Raspberry Ice Cream (with soured cream)

*¼ pint (150 ml) soured cream*
*¼ pint (150 ml) double cream*
*14 ounce (400 g) can raspberries, puréed and sieved*
*1 egg white*

Whip the creams together in a bowl until light and soft peaks form. Fold in the raspberry purée.

Pour the mixture into a container. Cover and freeze until just becoming firm. Beat well in a bowl.

Whisk the egg white in a small bowl until stiff but not dry. Fold into the raspberry cream. Return to the container, cover and freeze until firm.

About 30 minutes before serving, transfer the ice cream to the refrigerator.

Serves 4–5

# Raspberry Yogurt Ice

1 pound (450 g) raspberries, puréed and sieved
¼ pint (150 ml) plain yogurt
4–5 ounces (100–150 g) icing sugar
2 tablespoons (2 × 15 ml spoons) lemon juice
¼ pint (150 ml) cream, whipped
2 egg whites

For decoration
Whole raspberries
Mint sprigs

Mix the raspberries, yogurt, sugar and lemon juice together in a bowl. Stir until evenly blended then fold in the cream.

Pour into a container, cover and freeze until just becoming firm. Beat well in a bowl.

Whisk the egg whites in a bowl until stiff but not dry. Fold the egg whites into the raspberry ice. Return to the container, cover and freeze until firm.

About 20 minutes before serving, transfer the ice to the refrigerator. Serve decorated with whole raspberries and mint sprigs.

Serves 4

### Low calorie version
*Use fructose or a low calorie or artificial sweetener instead of sugar, and substitute the same quantity of sieved cottage or low fat soft cheese for the cream. Freeze in individual containers and decorate with fresh raspberries and mint leaves. Serve with Low Calorie Topping\*.*

# Mulberry Sorbet

1 pound (450 g) mulberries
Approximately 7 ounces (200 g) icing sugar
Squeeze of lemon juice
2 egg whites
Fresh mulberries, for decoration

Cook the mulberries very gently in a covered saucepan until the juices run. Strain through a fine sieve. Stir in the sugar and lemon juice to taste. Cool the mixture then chill for about an hour.

Pour the mixture into a container. Cover and freeze to the slushy stage. Beat well in a bowl.

Whisk the egg whites in a bowl until stiff but not dry. Fold into the mulberry mixture. Return to the container, cover and freeze until firm.

About 40 minutes before serving, transfer the sorbet to the refrigerator. Decorate each portion with fresh mulberries.

Serves 4–6

### Serving suggestion
*Serve in Coupelles\* intermingled with fresh mulberries. Accompany with a sauce of sieved, puréed mulberries.*

# Raspberry Ice Cream (with cottage cheese)

8 fluid ounces (225 ml) double cream, whipped
12 ounces (350 g) cottage cheese, sieved
3–4 ounces (75–100 g) icing sugar or to taste
Rose water
½ pint (300 ml) thick raspberry purée, sieved (see introduction)
Frosted\* whole raspberries, for decoration

Put the cream and cottage cheese in a bowl or blender together with the sugar and blend until smooth. Mix in a few drops of rose water and the raspberries. Refrigerate for about an hour.

Pour the mixture into a container. Cover and freeze until firm, beating twice at hourly intervals.

About 40 minutes before serving, transfer the ice cream to the refrigerator.

Serves 4

### Dessert suggestion
*Line a cake or loaf tin, charlotte or similar round mould with chocolate and mint matchsticks and fill with the ice cream. Decorate the turned-out dessert with scrolls of whipped cream, Chocolate Shapes\* and fresh raspberries.*

# Raspberry and Redcurrant Sorbet

1 pound (450 g) redcurrants
12 ounces (350 g) raspberries
3 ounces (75 g) sugar
Lemon juice
1 egg white
Whole redcurrants or raspberries, for decoration

Purée the fruits together and sieve. Put the sugar in a saucepan with ¼ pint (150 ml) water. Stir to dissolve over low heat. Stir the syrup into the fruit purée, adjusting the sweetness and adding lemon juice to taste.

Pour the mixture into a container. Cover and freeze until becoming firm around the edges. Beat well in a bowl.

Whisk the egg white in a small bowl until stiff but not dry. Fold into the frozen fruit mixture. Return to the container, cover and freeze until firm.

About 40 minutes before serving, transfer the sorbet to the refrigerator. Serve decorated with whole fruit.

Serves 4–6

### Dessert suggestion
*Ripple with Rhubarb Frost (page 110). Serve with Meringue\* fingers.*

# Raspberry Cream Cloud

12 ounces (350 g) fresh or frozen (without sugar)
    raspberries
4 ounces (100 g) caster sugar
³/₄ pint (450 ml) raspberry yogurt
3 tablespoons (3 × 15 ml spoons) lemon juice
¹/₄ pint (150 ml) double cream
2 egg whites

Pureé the raspberries then pass through a sieve. Purée the fruit again with the sugar, yogurt and lemon juice. Pour the mixture into a container. Cover and freeze until almost firm.

Just before removing the mixture from the freezer, whip the cream to the soft peak stage. In another bowl, whisk the egg whites until stiff but not dry.

Turn the raspberry mixture into a bowl and beat it to the consistency of snow. Fold in the cream and then the egg whites. Return to the container, cover and freeze until firm. About 1 hour before serving, transfer to the refrigerator.

Serves 5–6

### Serving suggestion
Serve in Ice Cream Cones* coated in desiccated coconut. Decorate with Frosted* mint leaves and small Chocolate Shapes* or Curls*. Serve with Bitter Chocolate Sauce*.

# Raspberry Cream Ice

3 ounces (75 g) caster or icing sugar
Squeeze of lemon juice
¹/₂ pint (300 ml) raspberry purée, sieved (see
    introduction)
4 ounces (100 g) full fat soft cheese
2 egg whites
Plain yogurt, for serving
Fresh raspberries, for decoration

Stir the sugar and lemon juice into the raspberry purée, adjusting the levels to taste. Pour the mixture into a container. Cover and freeze to the slushy stage. Beat well in a bowl.

Beat the cheese in a bowl. Whisk the egg whites in another bowl until stiff but not dry. Beat the cheese into the frozen raspberry purée then fold in the egg whites. Return to the container, cover and freeze until firm.

About 35–40 minutes before serving, transfer the ice to the refrigerator. Pour a spoonful of yogurt over each serving and top with a few fresh raspberries.

Serves 4

### Dessert suggestion
Form into 4 balls with a small scoop of Raspberry Sorbet (page 104) in the centre of each. Coat with finely chopped almonds. Serve with Sponge Fingers* and a sauce of puréed, sieved raspberries.

# Raspberry Spumoni

10 ounces (300 g) sugar
Juice of 2 lemons and 1 orange
7 fluid ounces (200 ml) raspberry purée, sieved
1 egg white
Approximately 1 fluid ounce (25 ml) raspberry eau-de-
    vie (framboise)

In a heavy-based saucepan dissolve 8 ounces (225 g) of the sugar in 8 fluid ounces (225 ml) water. Bring to the boil and boil for about a minute. Cool completely then strain in the lemon and orange juices, add the raspberry purée and put through a sieve. Pour the mixture into a container. Cover and freeze to the slushy stage. Beat well in a bowl.

Meanwhile, in a heavy-based saucepan dissolve the remaining sugar in 2½ fluid ounces (40 ml) water. Bring to the boil and boil until the temperature reaches 248°F (120°C), brushing down any sugar crystals that form on the side of the pan with a pastry brush.

Whisk the egg white in a bowl until stiff then gradually whisk in the very hot syrup in a slow, steady stream and continue whisking until the meringue is cold. Fold the eau-de-vie, and meringue equal to half the volume of the raspberry mixture, into the raspberry mixture. Return to the container, cover and freeze until just firm.

About 15 minutes before serving transfer the spumoni to the refrigerator.

Serves 6

---

### To reduce your sugar intake
Replace the sugar with half the quantity of **fructose** or with an **artificial sweetener**, provided the recipe does not call for a sugar syrup. Normally, 3–4 artificial sweeteners are the equivalent of 1 ounce (25 g) sugar but always check that you have the right degree of sweetness. Artificial sweeteners must be added to custard-based ice creams after the custard has cooled.

---

Recipes for cakes, sauces, etc., asterisked in the dessert and serving suggestions, are given on pages 145 to 152. For instructions on layering, lining and other techniques involved in creating desserts, see pages 152 to 155. Basic recipes are on pages 16 and 17.

# Redcurrant

Although redcurrants do not have the same intensity of flavour as blackcurrants, the fully ripe fruit has a refreshing, clear sweetness that blends enticingly with light, creamy mixtures. Always sieve redcurrants after puréeing to remove the seeds. The juice makes an exceptionally delicious sorbet.

## Iced Redcurrant Soufflé

*4 egg whites*
*10 ounces (275 g) caster sugar*
*1 pound (450 g) redcurrants, puréed and sieved*
*½ pint (300 ml) double cream, whipped*

Put the egg whites in a bowl and whisk until stiff. Gradually add the sugar, whisking well after each addition. Continue whisking until a stiff meringue is formed. Lightly fold in the redcurrant purée and then the cream.

Pour the mixture into a container. Cover and freeze until firm.

About 30 minutes before serving, transfer the soufflé to the refrigerator.

Serves 4–6

**Dessert suggestion**
*Make a bombe or freeze in a cake or loaf tin with an outer layer of Pear Ice Cream (page 92). Decorate the turned-out dessert with kirsch-flavoured whipped cream and whole redcurrants.*

## Redcurrant Sorbet

*8 ounces (225 g) sugar*
*1 pint (600 ml) redcurrant juice*
*Juice of 1 lemon*
*1 egg white*
*Pairs of Frosted\* redcurrants joined by their stalks, for decoration*

In a heavy-based saucepan, dissolve the sugar in the redcurrant juice. Bring to the boil and boil for 5 minutes. Leave to cool. Stir in the lemon juice.

Pour the mixture into a container. Cover and freeze until just becoming firm. Beat well in a bowl.

Whisk the egg white in a small bowl until stiff but not dry. Fold into the redcurrant mixture. Return to the container, cover and freeze until firm.

About 35 minutes before serving, transfer the sorbet to the refrigerator. Serve decorated with pairs of frosted redcurrants.

Serves 4

**Dessert suggestion**
*Form into 8 balls and surround with Lychee Ice Cream (page 127). Serve with fresh redcurrants and quartered lychees.*

## Redcurrant Ice Cream (with cheese and yogurt)

*1 pound (450 g) redcurrants*
*Juice of 1 lemon*
*4 ounces (100 g) caster sugar*
*5 ounces (150 g) full fat soft cheese*
*6 fluid ounces (175 ml) plain yogurt*

Purée the redcurrants with the lemon juice and strain through a fine sieve into a bowl. Stir in the sugar.

In another bowl, beat the soft cheese with the yogurt. Fold in the redcurrant purée.

Spoon the mixture into a container. Cover and freeze until firm, beating twice at hourly intervals.

About 40 minutes before serving, transfer the ice cream to the refrigerator.

Serves 4

**Dessert suggestion**
*Cover a Swiss Roll\* filled with Rose Petal Sorbet (page 70) with the ice cream. Decorate with fresh or crystallized rose petals and Frosted\* mint leaves.*

## Redcurrant Ice Cream

*1 pound (450 g) redcurrants*
*5 ounces (150 g) sugar*
*½ pint (300 ml) cream, whipped*
*Squeeze of lemon juice*

Purée the redcurrants and pass through a fine sieve into a bowl.

In a heavy-based saucepan, dissolve the sugar in ¼ pint (150 ml) water. Bring to the boil and boil for 3 minutes. Stir the syrup into the redcurrant purée. Set aside to cool. Fold the redcurrant purée into the cream, adding lemon juice to taste.

Pour the mixture into a container. Cover and freeze until firm, beating once, when the mixture becomes firm around the edges. About 30 minutes before serving, transfer to the refrigerator.

Serves 4

**Serving suggestion**
*Serve in wine glasses, decorated with redcurrants and redcurrant leaves threaded on to toothpicks.*

**Additional recipes using redcurrants:** Raspberry and Redcurrant Sorbet (page 106), Strawberry Cream Ice, with redcurrant juice (page 120).

Recipes for cakes, sauces, etc., asterisked in the dessert and serving suggestions, are given on pages 145 to 152. For instructions on layering, lining and other techniques involved in creating desserts, see pages 152 to 155. Basic recipes are on pages 16 and 17.

# Rhubarb

Tender, young, pink rhubarb stalks yield the best flavour and colour and almost melt when cooked. Forced rhubarb is tender but all too often lacks flavour, while thicker, older stalks can be stringy and coarse tasting. Wash the stalks well and trim if necessary before use, removing all trace of the leaves which contain poisonous oxalic acid. One pound (450 g) trimmed rhubarb will make about ½ pint (300 ml) of purée.

## Rhubarb Sorbet

*1 pound (450 g) young rhubarb*
*4 ounces (100 g) sugar*
*2 teaspoons (2 × 5 ml spoons) lemon juice*
*Pink food colouring, optional*
*2 large egg whites*

Reserve about one third of a stick of rhubarb and chop the remainder. Put the chopped rhubarb in a saucepan with 1 tablespoon (15 ml spoon) water and cook gently until soft. Then reduce to a purée.

In a heavy-based saucepan, dissolve the sugar in ½ pint (300 ml) water. Bring to the boil and boil for 10 minutes. Leave to cool.

Add the rhubarb purée to the syrup with the lemon juice, and pink colouring if you are using it.

Pour the mixture into a container. Cover and freeze until just becoming firm around the edges. Beat well in a bowl.

Whisk the egg whites in a bowl until stiff but not dry. Fold into the rhubarb mixture. Return to the container, cover and freeze until firm.

About 40 minutes before serving, transfer the sorbet to the refrigerator.

Serves 6

## Rhubarb Frost

*5 ounces (150 g1) drained fromage frais or soft cheese*
*¼ pint (150 ml) plain yogurt*
*½ pint (300 ml) thick rhubarb purée*
*3 ounces (75 g) icing sugar or to taste*
*Few drops rose or orange flower water, optional*
*½ ounce (15 g) gelatine dissolved in 4 tablespoons*
   *(4 × 15 ml spoons) hot water*
*2 egg whites, whisked*

Put the cheese into a bowl and gradually beat in the yogurt to form a smooth 'cream'. Beat in the rhubarb, icing sugar (the amount depends on the sharpness of the rhubarb) and rose or orange flower water, if you are using it. Gradually stir in the dissolved gelatine. Fold in the egg whites. Chill in the refrigerator for 1 hour.

Pour the mixture into a container. Cover and freeze until firm.

About 40 minutes before serving, transfer the frost to the refrigerator.

Serves 4

## Rhubarb Mousse

*1½ pounds (700 g) young rhubarb, sliced*
*6 ounces (175 g) sugar*
*3 fluid ounces (75 ml) red wine*
*¾ pint (450 ml) double cream*

Cook the rhubarb with the sugar and wine over gentle heat in a covered pan until soft. Cool completely then strain off as much liquid as possible. Reserve this liquid, freeze it separately and use for making rhubarb sauce. Pour the rhubarb into a container, cover and freeze to the slushy stage. Turn into a bowl and beat well.

Whip the cream until soft peaks form then fold into the rhubarb. Turn into a cold, 1¾ pint (1 litre) fluted metal mould. Cover and freeze until firm.

About 30 minutes before serving, turn out on to a cold plate and leave in the refrigerator. Serve with rhubarb sauce made by boiling down the reserved rhubarb juice.

Serves 8

**Serving suggestion**
*Serve in Gingersnap Baskets\* surrounded with the sauce. Decorate each serving with small shapes cut from orange peel.*

## Rhubarb and Ginger Wine Ice Cream

*1½ pounds (750 g) young rhubarb, chopped*
*4 ounces (100 g) sugar*
*¼ pint (150 ml) ginger wine*
*½ pint (300 ml) double cream, whipped*
*2 egg whites*

Poach the rhubarb with the sugar and 2 tablespoons (30 ml) water in a covered saucepan for about 7 minutes until just tender. Strain off the surplus juice and boil it until reduced and syrupy. Purée the rhubarb and pass through a fine sieve. Stir in the reduced juices and ginger wine and leave to cool.

Pour the mixture into a shallow container and chill for 30 minutes. Cover the container and freeze to the slushy stage.

Tip the rhubarb mixture into a bowl and beat well. Fold in the cream. Whisk the egg whites until stiff but not dry, then fold into the rhubarb cream. Spoon the mixture back into the container, cover and freeze until firm.

About 35 minutes before serving, transfer the ice cream to the refrigerator.

Serves 4–6

# Rhubarb Ice Cream

*1¼ pounds (550 g) young rhubarb, cut into 1 inch*
  *(2.5 cm) lengths*
*4 ounces (100 g) sugar*
*2 eggs, separated*
*8 ounces (225 g) cottage cheese, sieved*
*6 fluid ounces (175 ml) soured cream*

Poach the rhubarb with the sugar and 1 tablespoon
(15 ml spoon) water in a covered pan until soft.
Reduce the rhubarb to a purée. Beat in the egg yolks
and return to the heat. Cook gently, stirring constantly,
until the mixture thickens, but do not allow it to boil.
Leave to cool.

Whip the cottage cheese and soured cream together
in a bowl and fold into the rhubarb custard. Spoon
into a container, cover and freeze until just becoming
firm. Turn into a bowl and beat well. In another bowl,
whisk the egg whites until stiff but not dry. Fold into
the rhubarb.

Spoon the mixture back into the container. Cover
and freeze until firm. About 40 minutes before serving,
transfer to the refrigerator.

Serves 4

**Dessert suggestion**
*Freeze in a mould or cake or loaf tin surrounded by a
layer of Kulfi (page 18) and an outer jacket of Sponge
Fingers\*. Decorate the turned-out dessert with
pistachio nuts. Serve with red or white Wine Sauce\*.*

# Rhubarb and Strawberry Ice Cream

*12 ounces (350 g) young rhubarb*
*5 ounces (150 g) sugar*
*8 ounces (225 g) strawberries*
*½ pint (300 ml) cream, whipped*
*Few drops red food colouring, optional*

In a covered heavy-based saucepan, poach the rhubarb
with the sugar and 1 tablespoon (15 ml) water until
soft. Reduce to a purée with the strawberries, pass
through a sieve and leave to cool completely.

Fold in the cream and the colouring, if used. Spoon
the mixture into a shallow metal container, cover and
freeze until just becoming firm.

Tip the semi-frozen mixture into a bowl and beat
well. Spoon back into the container, cover and return
to the freezer. Repeat once more, then leave to freeze
until firm.

About 30 minutes before serving, transfer the ice
cream to the refrigerator.

Serves 4

**Serving suggestion**
*Serve with white Wine Sauce\* and Sponge Fingers\*.*

# Rhubarb Custard Ice

*1 pound (450 g) tender young rhubarb, cut into*
  *1 inch (2.5 cm) lengths*
*Juice of 1 orange*
*3 ounces (75 g) brown sugar*
*1 ounce (25 g) unsalted butter*
*7 fluid ounces (200 ml) single cream*
*3 egg yolks*

Put the rhubarb, orange juice, sugar and butter in a
covered pan and cook gently for about 3 minutes until
tender. Reduce to a purée.

In a heavy-based saucepan, bring the cream to just
below boiling point. Whisk the egg yolks in a bowl
until thick. Pour the hot cream over the egg yolks
whisking continuously. Return to the rinsed pan and
cook over a low heat, stirring constantly, until the
custard thickens but do not allow it to boil. Leave the
custard to cool, stirring occasionally.

Stir the rhubarb purée into the custard. When the
mixture is cold, pour into a container, cover and
refrigerate for an hour. Freeze until firm, beating twice
at hourly intervals.

About 40 minutes before serving, transfer the
custard ice to the refrigerator.

Serves 4

**Dessert suggestion**
*Freeze in individual containers or a flan or cake tin
lined with crushed ginger biscuits bound with melted
butter. Put orange segments, pith and membrane
removed, or drained mandarins, on the surface of the
frozen custard ice. Cover entirely with Meringue\* and
flash under a hot grill just long enough to brown the
meringue. Flambé with rum and serve immediately.*

---

**To reduce your calorie intake**
**Tofu** can be substituted for soft cheese; beat with
the other ingredients until smooth. It has no
cholesterol and is low in fat.

---

*ROSE PETAL:   see HERBS, FLOWERS,*
            *LEAVES*
*SAFFRON:   see SPICES*
*SALMON, SMOKED:   see SAVOURY*

# Savoury

A savoury ice is an unusual start to a meal – impressive and often surprisingly economical. Smoked Salmon Ice Cream, for example, provides a definite touch of luxury for a fraction of what it would cost to serve the fish in the traditional way.

## Cucumber Granita

*2 ounces (50 g) caster sugar*
*1 lemon*
*1 large cucumber*
*2 crisp dessert apples, peeled, cored and chopped*
*1 teaspoon (5 ml spoon) fresh dill or ½ teaspoon*
*   (2.5 ml spoon) dried dill weed*
*Salt and freshly ground black pepper*

*For garnish*
*Fresh dill, mint or borage sprigs*
*Strips of lemon peel*

In a heavy-based saucepan, dissolve the sugar in ¼ pint (150 ml) water. Remove the peel from the lemon in long strips and add to the syrup. Bring to the boil then simmer for 2 minutes. Remove from the heat and add the juice from the lemon. Leave to cool then chill for 10 minutes.

Peel half the cucumber but leave the peel on the other half for additional colour. Roughly chop the cucumber then purée with the apples and strained lemon-flavoured syrup. Add the dill and seasonings and chill for 30 minutes.

Pour into a container. Cover and freeze. As crystals begin to form around the edges draw them into the centre with a fork and continue until the mixture is a mass of small crystals. Serve immediately with fresh dill, mint or borage sprigs and strips of lemon peel.

Serves 5–6

**Serving suggestion**

*Serve in goblets with long twisted spirals of lemon peel hanging down the sides. Accompany with dill-flavoured biscuits made from rich shortcrust with chopped fresh dill added, or sprinkle dill seeds over each serving.*

# Smoked Salmon Ice Cream

2 ounces (50 g) smoked salmon
¼ pint (150 ml) soured cream
4 fluid ounces (100 ml) whipping cream, whipped
Juice and grated zest of 1 large juicy lemon
Approximately 1 tablespoon (15 ml spoon) finely
   chopped fresh chives
Ogen, Charentais or Gallia melon, for serving

Purée the salmon with the soured cream and put in a
bowl. Fold in the whipping cream with the lemon juice
and zest, and the chives.

Spoon the mixture into a container. Cover and
freeze until firm, beating 3 times at 45-minute
intervals. Serve straight from the freezer with slices of
the melon.

Serves 4

**Serving suggestion**
*Serve with chilled Ogen melon and wholewheat or
sesame seed-coated grissini for a delicious summer
starter.*

# Iced Tomato Cream

1 pound (450 g) ripe tomatoes, skinned
¼ pint (150 ml) thick mayonnaise
¼ pint (150 ml) soured cream
3 fluid ounces (75 ml) cream, whipped
2 teaspoons (2 × 5 ml spoons) onion juice (put
   through a garlic press)
2 teaspoons (2 × 5 ml spoons) finely chopped fresh
   basil
2 tablespoons (2 × 15 ml spoons) lemon juice
Salt and freshly ground black pepper

Purée the tomatoes. Put the mayonnaise and soured
cream in a bowl and whip together. Fold in the
whipped cream, tomato purée and remaining
ingredients.

Spoon the mixture into a container, cover and
freeze until firm. Turn into a bowl, beat well then
spoon back into the container or into a mould – a ring
mould is a good idea then the centre can be filled with
a salad or prawns when the cream is served. Cover and
freeze until firm.

About 20 minutes before serving, transfer the cream
to the refrigerator or turn it out first on to a cold plate.

Serves 6

**Serving suggestions**
*Spoon into hollowed-out tomato shells.*

*Accompany with sliced raw mushrooms, or courgettes
or red peppers lightly sprinkled with a lemon
vinaigrette.*

*Freeze in a ring mould. Surround the base with slices
of cucumber and decorate with piped soft cream
cheese and sprigs of parsley.*

# Iced Red Pepper Mousse

3 fluid ounces (75 ml) red wine vinegar
1 fluid ounce (25 ml) raspberry vinegar
10 ounces (300 g) red peppers, skinned and diced
1 red pimento
Salt and freshly ground white pepper
1 teaspoon (5 ml spoon) gelatine
4 fluid ounces (100 ml) whipping cream

For decoration
Fresh basil sprigs
Strips of red and yellow pepper

Put the vinegars in a saucepan and boil until reduced
by two-thirds. Add the peppers and simmer until thick.
Put into a blender with the pimento and plenty of
seasoning and process until smooth. Pour back into
the rinsed saucepan and heat gently.

Put the gelatine with a little water in a small bowl
placed over a pan of hot water and stir to dissolve.

Stir into the purée in the saucepan and leave to cool.

Whip the cream in a bowl until soft peaks form then
gently fold into the purée. Pour into a shallow
container, cover and freeze until just firm. Decorate
the mousse with sprigs of basil, the plates with strips of
red and yellow pepper.

Serves 4

**Serving suggestions**
*Pile on artichoke bottoms and garnish with fine strips
of red and yellow pepper.*

*Serve with prawns, crab or strips of smoked salmon
accompanied by blinis and soured cream or fromage
blanc.*

**Additional savoury recipes:** Savoury Avocado Ice
Cream (page 26), Bloody Mary Water Ice (page 117).

# Spices

The warm tones of cinnamon, the exotic scent of cloves and saffron with its luxurious perfume are all intriguing flavours for ice creams and sorbets. This section also includes a recipe using pumpkin, which blends wonderfully well with spices.

## Cinnamon Ice Cream

*1/4 pint (150 ml) milk*
*2 whole cinnamon sticks*
*4 eggs, separated*
*1 ounce (25 g) icing sugar*
*2 teaspoons (2 × 5 ml spoons) ground cinnamon*
*4 ounces (50 g) clear honey*
*1/4 pint (150 ml) soured cream*
*5 ounces (150 g) soft cheese*

In a heavy-based saucepan, heat the milk with the cinnamon sticks to just below boiling point, remove from the heat, cover and leave for about 4 hours.

Beat the egg yolks in a bowl. Sift the icing sugar and ground cinnamon together and beat into the yolks.

Remove the cinnamon sticks from the milk. Stir in the honey and bring to just below boiling point. Slowly pour on to the egg yolks, whisking constantly.

Beat the soured cream and cheese together and whisk into the custard. Continue whisking until cold. Whisk the egg whites in a bowl until stiff but not dry. Fold into the mixture.

Pour the mixture into a container. Cover and freeze until firm.

About 30 minutes before serving, transfer the ice cream to the refrigerator.

Serves 4–6

### Serving suggestion
*Serve in tall wine glasses, topped with a swirl of whipped cream and round Langues de Chat\*.*

## Saffron Ice Cream

*4 egg yolks*
*2 ounces (50 g) caster sugar*
*1/2 pint (300 ml) milk*
*1 heaped teaspoon (5 ml spoon) saffron strands*
*2 fluid ounces (50 ml) cream, whipped*

Whisk the egg yolks with the sugar in a bowl until thick and light. In a heavy-based saucepan, heat the milk to

just below simmering point then whisk into the egg yolks. Return to the rinsed pan and cook over a low heat, stirring constantly, until the mixture thickens. Do not allow to boil. Remove from the heat, strain and stir in the saffron. Leave to cool, stirring occasionally. Pour into a container, cover and freeze until just becoming firm. Turn into a bowl and beat well.

Fold in the cream. Spoon back into the container, cover and freeze until firm.

About 20 minutes before serving, transfer the ice cream to the refrigerator.

Serves 4

**Serving suggestion**
*Scoop into Meringue Baskets\* and serve with Sponge Fingers\*.*

# Sweet Mixed Spice Ice Cream

4 ounces (100 g) marshmallows, chopped
Approximately 14 ounce (400 g) can evaporated milk
2 teaspoons (2 × 5 ml spoons) mixed spice
4 ounces (100 g) soft dark brown sugar
1/4 pint (150 ml) cream, whipped

For decoration
Finely grated orange zest
Chopped sugar-coated almonds

Melt the marshmallows with the evaporated milk, spice and sugar in a bowl set over a pan of hot water, whisking constantly but lightly until smooth. Leave to cool, whisking occasionally.

Fold the cream into the marshmallow mixture. Pour into a container, cover and freeze until firm.

About 30 minutes before serving, transfer the ice cream to the refrigerator and serve decorated with the orange zest and nuts.

Serves 6–8

**Serving suggestion**
*Serve in Almond Tuiles\* with slices of poached pear. Spoon over a little apple sauce: substitute apple juice for wine in the Wine Sauce\*.*

**Dessert suggestion**
*Freeze around a centre of Prune Sorbet (page 103). Serve with Sponge Fingers\*.*

# Clove Sorbet

9 ounces (250 g) sugar
10–15 cloves
1 egg white

In a heavy-based saucepan, dissolve the sugar in 18 fluid ounces (500 ml) water. Bring to the boil and boil for 1 minute. Remove from the heat, add the cloves, cover the pan and leave to infuse for 10–15 minutes. Remove the cloves and cool before chilling.

Pour the syrup into a container, cover and freeze to the slushy stage. Beat well in a bowl.

Whisk the egg white lightly in a small bowl. Whisk into the frozen syrup. Return to the container, cover and freeze until firm.

About 40 minutes before serving, transfer the sorbet to the refrigerator.

Serves 6

**Serving suggestion**
*Pile small balls of the sorbet and of Rich Brown Bread Ice Cream (page 36) on thin slices of orange, peel and pith removed. Spoon over a little white Wine Sauce\*.*

**Dessert suggestion**
*Encase in Sweet Lemon Ice Cream (page 77) and serve with Langues de Chat\*.*

**Flavour variation**
*For a cinnamon sorbet substitute a 2 inch (5 cm) cinnamon stick for the cloves.*

# Spiced Pumpkin Pie Ice Cream

1/4 pint (150 ml) milk
1/4 pint (150 ml) single cream
3 eggs, separated
4 ounces (100 g) soft light brown sugar
1 1/2 teaspoons (7.5 ml spoon) ground cinnamon
1/4 teaspoon (1.25 ml spoon) ground cloves
1/2 teaspoon (2.5 ml spoon) ground ginger
12 fluid ounces (350 ml) pumpkin purée
Pumpkin seeds, for decoration

In a heavy-based saucepan, bring the milk and cream to just below boiling point. Put the egg yolks and sugar in a bowl and whisk until thick and light. Whisk on the hot milk and cream. Return to the rinsed pan and cook over a low heat, stirring constantly, until the mixture thickens. Stir in the spices and leave to cool, stirring occasionally. Stir in the pumpkin.

In another bowl, whisk the egg whites until stiff but not dry. Fold into the pumpkin custard.

Pour the mixture into a container. Cover and freeze until firm.

About 40 minutes before serving, transfer the ice cream to the refrigerator.

Serves 4

**Dessert suggestion**
*Freeze in a can. Coat the turned-out ice cream in chopped walnuts or pecans bound with melted butter. Serve with Burnt Honey Sauce\*.*

**Additional recipes using spices:** Chestnut and Cinnamon Circle (page 43), Lightly Spiced Peach Ice Cream (page 89), Pineapple and Cardamom Ice Cream (page 96).

Spirits are added to give a boost to a variety of different-flavoured iced mixtures, but there are also many recipes in which they are the primary flavouring. This section includes a recipe using pumpkin and another with prunes, both ideal bases for spirits.

## Iced Whisky Syllabub

*Finely grated zest and juice of 1 orange and 1 lemon*
*3 ounces (75 g) caster sugar*
*3½ fluid ounces (90 ml) whisky*
*½ pint (300 ml) double cream*

*For decoration*
*Finely chopped walnuts*
*Short twisted spirals of lemon peel*
*Macaroons\*, for serving*

Put all the ingredients in a bowl and whisk vigorously until thick and light. Pour the mixture into a container. Cover and freeze until firm, beating well after 1½ hours.

About 20 minutes before serving, transfer the syllabub to the refrigerator. Serve in tall glasses with frosted rims and decorate with chopped walnuts and lemon spirals. Serve with long spoons and accompany with macaroons.

Serves 4

### Serving suggestion
*For each serving, intermingle scoops of the syllabub with scoops of Kiwi Fruit Sorbet (page 127) finished with long, fine spirals of lemon peel. Serve with Cigars Russe\*.*

### Dessert suggestion
*Top with a layer of Pistachio Ice Cream (page 101), lightly swirling the layers together, and enclosing them in a jacket of Langues de Chat\*. Decorate the turned-out dessert with whisky-flavoured whipped cream, shapes cut from lemon peel and pistachio nuts.*

## Iced Daiquiri Mousse

*5 eggs, separated*
*6 ounces (175 g) caster sugar*
*2 fluid ounces (50 ml) lime juice*
*2 fluid ounces (50 ml) lemon juice*
*Grated zest of 1 lime and 1 lemon*
*1 tablespoon (15 ml spoon) gelatine*
*2 fluid ounces (50 ml) white rum*
*8 fluid ounces (225 ml) cream, whipped*

*For decoration*
*Crystallized lemon slices*
*Finely chopped pistachio nuts*
*Whipped cream*

Beat the egg yolks in a bowl until light and fluffy. Gradually beat in half the sugar and continue beating until light. Whisk in the lime and lemon juice and zests. Place the bowl over a pan of hot water and cook gently, stirring constantly, until the mixture thickens.

Soak the gelatine in the rum in a small bowl set over a pan of hot water. When the gelatine has dissolved stir it into the thickened egg mixture. Leave to cool.

Whisk the egg whites in a bowl until stiff then gradually add the remaining sugar, whisking well after each addition. Fold the egg whites and cream into the egg mixture and leave to cool completely.

Spoon the mixture into a freezer-proof dish and freeze until firm.

About 30 minutes before serving, transfer the mousse to the refrigerator. Decorate the top with crystallized lemon slices, chopped pistachio nuts and cream.

Serves 6–8

### Serving suggestion
*Scoop into chilled lime shells cut in half lengthways. Decorate with small rosettes of coconut-liqueur-flavoured whipped cream and long, fine strips of lemon and lime peel.*

### Dessert suggestion
*Make a bombe or freeze in a cake or loaf tin with a jacket of Pineapple Ice Cream (page 99). Decorate the turned-out dessert with lime-flavoured whipped cream and shapes cut from lime peel.*

## Prune Ice Cream (with brandy)

*9 ounces (250 g) good-quality prunes, stoned*
*Finely grated zest and juice of 1 orange*
*4 fluid ounces (100 ml) armagnac or brandy*
*1 Earl Grey tea bag*
*4 ounces (100 g) sugar*
*4½ ounces (115 g) fromage blanc or curd cheese*
*7 fluid ounces (200 ml) whipping or double cream*
*1 ounce (25 g) icing sugar*

Put the prunes in a bowl with the orange zest and juice, the armagnac and tea bag and enough water to cover and leave to soak overnight.

Next day, weigh off 7 ounces (200 g) of the prunes and keep the rest for decoration. Strain the soaking liquid into a saucepan. Add the sugar and dissolve over low heat. Then bring to the boil and boil until very syrupy and just beginning to caramelize around the edges. Pour the syrup into a food processor with the cheese and prunes and mix until just evenly blended. Cool. Pour into a container, cover and freeze until just becoming firm. Turn into a bowl and beat well.

Whip the cream in a bowl with the icing sugar. Fold into the prune mixture. Spoon back into the container. Cover and freeze until firm.

Freeze the reserved prunes separately, if not serving the ice cream within a day or so, otherwise, keep them, covered, in the refrigerator.

About 30 minutes before serving, transfer the ice cream to the refrigerator. Let the reserved prunes warm to room temperature if frozen – heat them slightly, if necessary. Serve each portion garnished with prunes and sprinkled with a little armagnac.

Serves 6

**Dessert suggestion**
*Freeze in a flan or sandwich tin lined with crushed hazelnut Macaroons\*. Decorate the turned-out dessert with orange-liqueur-flavoured whipped cream and shapes cut from orange peel. Serve the reserved prunes separately.*

# Bloody Mary Water Ice

*½ pint (300 ml) tomato juice*
*3 fluid ounces (74 ml) vodka*
*Juice of 2 lemons*
*4–6 drops Worcestershire sauce*
*6 ice cubes, crushed*
*½ green pepper, finely diced*
*4 celery leaves, chopped*
*Celery salt and freshly ground black pepper*

*For garnish*
*6 × 4 inch (10 cm) cucumber sticks*
*6 mint, basil, borage or watercress sprigs.*

Put the tomato juice, vodka, lemon juice, Worcestershire sauce and crushed ice together in a blender and mix at high speed. Add the green pepper, celery leaves and seasoning to taste and blend again until smooth.

Pour into a container. Cover and freeze until firm, beating 3 times at 45-minute intervals.

About 30 minutes before serving, transfer the water ice to the refrigerator. Spoon the water ice into small chilled goblets, add a cucumber stick to look like a straw and garnish with the mint, basil, borage or watercress sprigs.

Serves 6

**Dessert suggestion**
*Freeze in a mould and surround the base of the turned-out water ice with celery leaves and coronets formed from cucumber slices with mayonnaise piped into the centres, finished with a fine sprinkling of fresh fennel or dill leaves.*

Recipes for cakes, sauces, etc., asterisked in the dessert and serving suggestions, are given on pages 145 to 152. For instructions on layering, lining and other techniques involved in creating desserts, see pages 152 to 155. Basic recipes are on pages 16 and 17.

# Egg Nog Ice Cream

*Approximately 6 ounce (175 g) can condensed milk, chilled*
*3 eggs*
*4 fluid ounces (100 ml) rum*
*¼–½ teaspoon (1.25–2.5 ml spoon) freshly grated nutmeg*
*½ pint (300 ml) cream, whipped*

Put the milk, eggs, rum and nutmeg in a bowl and whisk until very light and thick. Fold in the cream.

Pour the mixture into a container. Cover and freeze until firm. About 20 minutes before serving, transfer to the refrigerator.

Serves 4–5

**Serving suggestions**
*Serve as a sundae with Atholl Brose (page 37) with Chunky Marmalade Sauce\* poured over and topped with flaked almonds.*

*Serve in individual glasses with Sponge Fingers\*.*

**Dessert suggestion**
*Freeze in a flan or sandwich tin lined with crushed ginger biscuits bound with melted butter, the top covered with more crushed ginger biscuits. Decorate the turned-out dessert with whipped cream and crystallized lemon or orange slices.*

# Pumpkin Sorbet

*3 ounces (75 g) sugar*
*1 lb (450 g) fresh, peeled pumpkin, diced*
*3 tablespoons (3 × 15 ml spoons) dark rum*
*2–3 tablespoons (2–3 × 15 ml spoons) lemon juice*
*½ teaspoon (2.5 ml spoon) ground cinnamon*
*1 large egg white*
*Sugared cranberries, for decoration*

In a heavy-based saucepan, dissolve the sugar in ½ pint (300 ml) water. Bring to the boil and boil for 5 minutes. Leave to cool until tepid. Put the syrup and pumpkin in a blender and blend until smooth. Add the rum, lemon juice and cinnamon and blend again. Pass through a sieve into a measuring jug. There should be 1½ pints (850 ml) so add some water, if necessary. Leave to cool completely.

Pour the mixture into a container. Cover and freeze until slushy. Beat well in a bowl.

Whisk the egg white in a small bowl until stiff but not dry. Whisk it into the pumpkin ice. Return to the container, cover and freeze until firm.

About 1 hour before serving, transfer the sorbet to the refrigerator. Served decorated with sugared cranberries.

Serves 8

**Additional recipes using spirits:** Atholl Brose (page 37), Ginger Ice Cream (page 61).

# Strawberry

The fresh, fragrant taste of ices made at home with fresh strawberries is totally different to the flavour of most commercial products. The berries also blend well with a number of other ingredients, such as redcurrants, orange juice and even rose water. Always remember to hull strawberries before puréeing and sieving them.

**Simple Strawberry Ice Cream**
Add ½ pint (300 ml) sieved strawberry purée to any of the Basic Recipes*.

## Strawberry Rose Ice

*1 pound (450 g) strawberries, hulled*
*4 ounces (100 g) caster sugar*
*1 teaspoon (5 ml spoon) rose water*
*¾ pint (450 ml) plain yogurt*
*1 egg white*
*Crystallized pink rose petals, for decoration*

Purée the strawberries, sugar, rose water and yogurt together. Strain through a fine sieve into a container. Cover and freeze until just becoming firm. Beat well in a bowl.

Whisk the egg white in a small bowl until stiff but not dry and fold into the frozen strawberry mixture. Return to the container, cover and freeze until firm.

About 30 minutes before serving, transfer the ice to the refrigerator. Serve decorated with crystallized rose petals.

Serves 4–5

**Serving suggestion**
*Freeze in small decorative moulds. Surround with fresh or crystallized rose petals and decorate with Low Calorie Topping*.*

**Dessert suggestion**
*Freeze in individual 'sandwiches' made from crushed digestive biscuits bound with melted butter. Decorate with whipped cream flavoured with a good-quality strawberry syrup, and small pieces of strawberry.*

**Low calorie version**
*Use fructose, or a low calorie or artificial sweetener instead of sugar.*

## Strawberry and Elderflower Ice Cream

*5 ounces (150 g) sugar*
*Finely pared zest of 2 lemons*
*2 handfuls elderflowers*
*7 ounces (200 g) full fat soft cheese, beaten*
*3 fluid ounces (75 ml) milk*
*1 pound (450 g) strawberries, puréed and sieved*
*1 egg white*
*Small elderflower sprigs, for decoration*

In a heavy-based saucepan, dissolve the sugar in 18 fluid ounces (500 ml) water. Bring to the boil, add the lemon zest and boil for 7 minutes. Remove from the heat, stir in the elderflowers, cover and leave to cool completely.

Whisk the cheese and milk together in a bowl until smooth and airy.

Strain the syrup and measure 8 fl oz (225 ml) into the strawberry purée. Stir to mix and fold into the cheese and milk mixture. Spoon into a container, cover and freeze until becoming firm. Turn into a bowl and beat well.

Whisk the egg white in a small bowl until stiff but not dry. Fold the egg white into the strawberry mixture.

Spoon back into the container, cover and freeze until firm.

About 30 minutes before serving, transfer the ice cream to the refrigerator. Decorate each portion with a small sprig of elderflowers.

Serves 4–5

### Serving suggestion
*Arrange scoops on white plates and surround with a sauce of sieved, puréed strawberries, perhaps 'lifted' with a little strawberry eau-de-vie (fraise). Decorate with sprigs of elderflowers or elderberries and serve with Sponge Fingers\*.*

---

> ### To reduce your sugar intake
> Replace the sugar with half the quantity of **fructose** or with an **artificial sweetener**, provided the recipe does not call for a sugar syrup. Normally, 3–4 artificial sweeteners are the equivalent of 1 ounce (25 g) sugar but always check that you have the right degree of sweetness. Artificial sweeteners must be added to custard-based ice creams after the custard has cooled.

---

## Iced Strawberry Mousse

*3 ounces (75 g) sugar*
*4 egg yolks*
*¼ pint (150 ml) cream, whipped*
*10 ounces (275 g) strawberries, puréed and sieved*
*2 tablespoons (2 × 15 ml spoons) orange liqueur or orange juice*

In a heavy-based saucepan, dissolve the sugar in 4 tablespoons (60 ml) water. Bring to the boil and boil until the temperature reaches 234°F (112°C).

Meanwhile, whisk the egg yolks in a bowl until very thick and light. Gradually whisk in the boiling syrup and continue whisking until well increased in volume.

Fold in the cream. Blend the strawberry purée and liqueur or orange juice together and fold into the egg yolk and cream mixture.

Pour into a container. Cover and freeze until firm.

About 20 minutes before serving, transfer the mousse to the refrigerator.

Serves 4–5

### Serving suggestions
*Pile each serving into a mound on a circle of Genoise Cake\* sprinkled with kirsch. Arrange sliced strawberries neatly over the sides. Surround with a sauce of sieved, puréed strawberries and make a cobweb pattern (like feather icing) with crème fraîche. Sprinkle a little icing sugar carefully over the strawberries.*

*For each serving, put a few strawberries in the base of a tall wine glass, then fill the glass with scoops of iced mousse. Decorate with fresh strawberry leaves.*

*For each serving, make an indentation in the base of a large Meringue\* and fill with the mousse. To serve, pour over a little Orange Flower Sauce\*, Chocolate Sauce\*, Bitter Chocolate Sauce\* or Fudge Sauce\*.*

# Iced Strawberry Soufflé

6 ounces (175 g) sugar
3 egg whites
½ pint (300 ml) cream, whipped
1¼ pounds (550 g) strawberries, puréed and sieved
Lemon juice
2 tablespoons (2 × 15 ml spoons) kummel or kirsch,
    optional

For decoration
Whipped cream
Crystallized roses or violets

In a heavy-based saucepan, dissolve the sugar in 4 fluid ounces (100 ml) water. Bring to the boil and boil for 5 minutes.

Meanwhile, whisk the egg whites in a bowl, set over warm water, until just stiff. Slowly pour the syrup on to the egg whites, whisking constantly. Remove the bowl from the warm water and continue to whisk until the meringue is cold and very thick.

Fold in the cream and strawberry purée and 'lift' the flavour with lemon juice, adding the kummel or kirsch, if using.

Pour the mixture into a container. Cover and freeze until firm.

About 20 minutes before serving, transfer the soufflé to the refrigerator. Decorate with whipped cream and crystallized roses or violets.

Serves 6

**Dessert suggestion**
*Freeze in a cake or loaf tin around a centre of Rose Petal Sorbet (page 70) or Crystallized Rose Petal Ice Cream (see Crystallized Violet Ice Cream, pages 134-5). Decorate the turned-out dessert with rose petals, fresh or crystallized, leaves and piped whipped cream. Serve with Sponge Fingers\*.*

# Strawberry Ice Cream (with strawberry yogurt)

¾ pound (350 g) strawberries, hulled
4 ounces (100 g) caster sugar
¾ pint (425 ml) strawberry yogurt
3 tablespoons (3 × 15 ml spoons) lemon juice
¼ pint (150 ml) double or whipping cream
2 egg whites
Sliced strawberries, for decoration

Put the strawberries, sugar, yogurt and lemon juice together in a blender and process until smooth. Strain the mixture through a fine sieve into a container, cover and freeze to the slushy stage. Beat well in a bowl.

Whip the cream in a bowl until soft peaks form. In another bowl whisk the egg whites until stiff but not dry. Fold the cream and then the egg whites into the frozen strawberry mixture. Return to the container, cover and freeze until firm.

About 45 minutes before serving, transfer the ice cream to the refrigerator. Serve each portion decorated with strawberry slices.

Serves 5

**Dessert suggestion**
*Layer with fine sheets of almond Meringue\*. Decorate the turned-out dessert with whipped cream, lightly toasted almonds and strawberries.*

# Iced Strawberry Crush

½ pound (225 g) strawberries, puréed and sieved
1 tablespoon (15 ml spoon) lemon juice
4 teaspoons (4 × 15 ml spoons) icing sugar
4 ounces (100 g) made Meringues\*, roughly broken
¼ pint (150 ml) double cream, whipped
1 egg, separated
1½ ounces (40 g) caster sugar

Mix the strawberry purée, lemon juice and sugar together in a bowl. Cover and leave in a cool place for 2 hours.

Fold the meringues into the cream. Whisk the egg yolk with the caster sugar in a bowl until very thick and light. In another bowl, whisk the egg white until stiff but not dry.

Fold the purée, cream and then the egg white into the egg yolk mixture. Spoon into a container, cover and freeze until firm.

About 30 minutes before serving, transfer the crush to the refrigerator.

Serves 4–5

**Dessert suggestion**
*Freeze in a Chocolate Case\*. Decorate the top with crushed peppermint or mint sweets and small Chocolate Curls\*.*

**Flavour variation**
*Make with Macaroons\* instead of meringues.*

# Strawberry Cream Ice (with redcurrant juice)

5–6 ounces (150–175 g) sugar
1 pound (450 g) strawberries, puréed and sieved
¼ pint (150 ml) redcurrant juice
1 tablespoon (15 ml spoon) lemon juice
½ pint (300 ml) cream, whipped
Frosted\* redcurrants or sliced strawberries, for
    decoration

In a heavy-based saucepan, dissolve the sugar in ¼ pint (150 ml) water. Bring to the boil and boil until the syrup reaches 234°F (112°C). Set aside to cool.

Blend the strawberry purée, redcurrant juice and lemon juice with the syrup. Gradually pour the mixture into the cream and fold lightly together.

Pour the mixture into a container. Cover and freeze until firm, beating twice at hourly intervals.

About 30 minutes before serving, transfer the cream ice to the refrigerator. Serve decorated with frosted redcurrants or sliced strawberries.

Serves 5–6

**Dessert suggestion**
*Spoon into individual Meringue Baskets\*. Decorate with redcurrants or sliced strawberries.*

# Strawberry Cream Ice

*4 ounces (100 g) sugar*
*1 pound (450 g) strawberries, puréed and sieved*
*Squeeze of lemon juice*
*1 egg white*
*¼ pint (150 ml) double cream, whipped*
*Sliced whole strawberries, for decoration*

In a heavy-based saucepan, dissolve the sugar in ½ pint (300 ml) water. Bring to the boil and boil steadily for 10 minutes. Cool then blend with the strawberry purée and lemon juice.

Pour the mixture into a container. Cover and freeze to the slushy stage. Beat well in a bowl.

Whisk the egg white in a bowl until stiff but not dry. Fold the cream and then the egg white into the frozen strawberry mixture. Return to the container, cover and freeze until firm.

About 40 minutes before serving, transfer the ice to the refrigerator. Serve each portion decorated with sliced strawberries.

Serves 4

**Serving suggestions**
*Spoon into Ice Cream Cones\* coated in desiccated coconut.*

*Serve with Marshmallow Sauce\* or Bitter Chocolate Sauce\*.*

# Strawberry Ice Cream

*1½ pounds (700 g) strawberries, hulled*
*Juice of ½ an orange*
*6 ounces (175 g) caster sugar*
*¾ pint (450 ml) double cream, whipped*

Purée the strawberries with the juice then stir in the sugar. Strain through a fine sieve. Fold the cream into the purée.

Pour the mixture into a container. Cover and freeze until firm, beating twice at hourly intervals.

About 30 minutes before serving, transfer the ice cream to the refrigerator.

Serves 6–8

**Serving suggestion**
*Freeze in individual fancy moulds and serve on a bed of sliced strawberries, lightly sprinkled with orange liqueur, if liked. Decorate with mint leaves.*

# Strawberry Tofu Ice Cream

*10 ounces (300 g) tofu*
*10 ounces (275 g) strawberries, puréed and sieved*
*½ ounce (15 g) fructose or to taste*
*Few drops of vanilla essence*

Blend all the ingredients together until smooth. Pour into a container, cover and freeze until firm, beating twice at hourly intervals.

About 30 minutes before serving, transfer the ice cream to the refrigerator.

Serves 3–4

# Strawberry Water Ice

*2 pounds (900 g) strawberries, hulled*
*2 tablespoons (2 × 15 ml spoons) kirsch*
*2 tablespoons (2 × 15 ml spoons) grenadine syrup*
*Juice of 1 lemon*

Purée then sieve the strawberries into a bowl. Mix in all the other ingredients.

Pour the mixture into a container. Cover and freeze until firm, beating 3 times at 45-minute intervals.

About 35 minutes before serving, transfer the water ice to the refrigerator.

Serves 6

**Additional recipes using strawberries:** Rhubarb and Strawberry Ice Cream (page 111), Passion Fruit and Strawberry Ice Cream (page 128).

Recipes for cakes, sauces, etc., asterisked in the dessert and serving suggestions, are given on pages 145 to 152. For instructions on layering, lining and other techniques involved in creating desserts, see pages 152 to 155. Basic recipes are on pages 16 and 17.

# Vanilla, Custard

Vanilla is *the* traditional ice cream, and a firm favourite with many people. The best ices are flavoured with a whole vanilla pod steeped in warm cream or milk. Wash and dry the pod when you remove it and keep it for further use. If you store it in a jar of sugar, the vanilla flavour will permeate the sugar, which can then be used in a variety of desserts. For a more pronounced taste, split the pod open to release the seeds (also called beans) into the ice cream. Genuine vanilla essence and extract can be used, with discretion, but try to avoid artificial flavourings. Recipes for custard ice creams, also traditional favourites, are included in this section.

## Fresh Custard Ice Cream

Use the Basic Custard Ice Cream on page 16, or a good-quality bought dairy custard. Beat the bought version before putting it into the freezer and twice during freezing, at 45-minute intervals.

## Philadelphia Ice Cream

*18 fluid ounces (500 ml) double or whipping cream*
*2½ ounces (65 g) caster or icing sugar*
*Pinch of salt*
*Approximately ½ teaspoon (2.5 ml spoon) finely grated vanilla seed or bean (found inside a split vanilla pod)*

Put all the ingredients in a bowl and whisk together until thick. Pour the mixture into a container. Cover and freeze until firm, beating twice at hourly intervals.

About 20 minutes before serving transfer the ice cream to the main refrigerator.

Serves 4–6

### Dessert suggestion
*Encase in Apricot Ice Cream (page 24). Decorate with whipped cream flavoured with apricot brandy or brandy, lightly toasted flaked almonds and chocolate dragées or Chocolate Shapes\*. Serve with Cigars Russe\*.*

# Vanilla Ice Cream

*4 eggs, separated*
*4 ounces (100 g) icing sugar, sifted*
*1 teaspoon (5 ml spoon) vanilla essence*
*½ pint (300 ml) double cream, whipped*

Whisk the egg whites until stiff in a bowl. Add the icing sugar a tablespoon (15 ml) at a time, whisking well after each addition. Whisk in the egg yolks one at a time with the vanilla essence. Carefully fold in the cream.

Pour the mixture into a large container or 8 small dishes. Cover and freeze until firm.

If frozen in a large container, transfer to the refrigerator about 15 minutes before serving.

Serves 8

**Serving suggestion**
*Make into a sundae with sliced strawberries, topped with whole berries and a sauce made from sieved, puréed ripe strawberries.*

**Dessert suggestion**
*Serve in a chequerboard with one of the following ice creams: Butterscotch Ice Cream (page 39), Caramel Ice Cream (page 39), Cherry Ice Cream (page 41), Chocolate Ice Cream (page 44), Raspberry Ice Cream (page 104), Strawberry Ice Cream (page 121), Walnut Ice Cream (page 124). Spread whipped cream, flavoured with a liqueur if liked, over the turned-out dessert. Decorate with nuts, chocolate or fruit.*

# Rich Vanilla Ice Cream

*3 ounces (75 g) sugar*
*¾ pint (450 ml) whipping cream*
*½ vanilla pod, split*
*4 egg yolks*
*2 ounces (50 g) unsalted butter, diced*

Dissolve the sugar in the cream in a heavy-based saucepan. Add the vanilla pod and bring to the boil. Remove from the heat, cover the pan and leave to infuse for 15 minutes.

Lightly whisk the egg yolks in a bowl. Strain in the cream mixture, whisking all the time, and continue to whisk until the custard is light and frothy. Pour back into the pan and cook gently, stirring constantly, until the mixture thickens slightly. Do not allow to boil. Remove from the heat and stir in the butter.

Pour the mixture into a shallow container and cool completely. Cover and freeze until firm, beating well after about 1½ hours.

About 30 minutes before serving transfer the ice cream to the refrigerator.

Serves 4

# Vanilla Yogurt Ice Cream

*1 egg*
*3 ounces (75 g) caster sugar*
*2 ounces (50 g) golden syrup*
*6 fluid ounces (175 ml) whipping or double cream*
*6 fluid ounces (175 ml) plain yogurt*
*1½ teaspoons (1½ × 5 ml spoons) vanilla essence*
*Pinch of salt*

Put all the ingredients in a bowl and thoroughly whisk together until smooth and light. Pour the mixture into a container. Cover and freeze until firm, beating twice at hourly intervals. About 30 minutes before serving, transfer the ice cream to the refrigerator.

Serves 6

# Custard Ice Cream

*1 large egg, separated*
*2 ounces (50 g) sugar*
*1 heaped tablespoon (15 ml spoon) custard powder*
*1 pint (600 ml) milk*
*Approximately 1½ ounce (40 g) packet dessert topping*

Blend the egg yolk, sugar and custard powder together in a bowl with ¼ pint (150 ml) of the milk. In a heavy-based saucepan, bring ½ pint (300 ml) of the milk to boiling point and stir into the blended mixture. Return to the rinsed pan and cook over a gentle heat, stirring constantly, until the custard has thickened. Do not allow to boil. Leave to cool, stirring occasionally to prevent a skin forming.

Make up the dessert topping with the remaining milk. Whisk the egg white until stiff but not dry. Fold the dessert and the egg white into the cooled custard.

Pour the mixture into a container. Cover and freeze until firm.

About 30 minutes before serving, transfer the ice cream to the refrigerator.

Serves 4–5

**Serving suggestion**
*For each serving, pile the ice cream in the centre of a rum baba, doughnut or waffle soaked in rum and top with Hot Fudge Sauce\*, Butterscotch Sauce\*, Hot Chocolate Sauce\*, Caramel Sauce\* or Mars Bar Sauce\*.*

**Additional recipes using custard:** Banana Custard Ice Cream (page 28), Blackberry Custard Ice (page 30), Prune Custard Ice (page 103), Rhubarb Custard Ice (page 111).

*VIOLETS, CRYSTALLIZED:   see OLD-FASHIONED FAVOURITES*
*VODKA:   see BLOODY MARY WATER ICE (page 117)*

# Walnut, Pecan

The purest-tasting walnut ices are made soon after the walnut season with fresh nuts removed from their shells just before use. Packaged nuts do not have the same quality of flavour, even when they are sealed under a vacuum. To toast walnuts, heat the peeled nuts in a 350°F (180°C, gas mark 4) oven until golden brown. Chop walnuts by hand before grinding them, briefly in small batches, in a coffee mill or food processor. Pecans have a higher fat content than walnuts, and lose their freshness even more quickly. They can be substituted for walnuts in recipes.

**Simple Walnut Ice Cream**
Add 4 ounces (100 g) chopped walnuts to any of the Basic Recipes*.

## Iced Pecan Mousse

*1½ pounds (700 g) sugar*
*4 ounces (100 g) pecans, coarsely chopped*
*4 egg whites*
*¾ pint (425 ml) cream, whipped*
*Whole strawberries or pecan halves, for decoration*

Heat half the sugar gently in a heavy-based saucepan until it melts and caramelizes. Stir in the pecans and continue to heat, stirring, until a rich golden brown. Pour immediately on to an oiled surface and leave to become cold and hard. Put the caramel in a thick polythene bag or thick cloth and hit with a rolling pin to break it into fairly coarse granules.

Dissolve the remaining sugar in ¼ pint (150 ml) water in a heavy-based saucepan. Bring to the boil and boil to 234°F (112°C). Meanwhile, whisk the egg whites in a bowl until stiff. Whisk the boiling syrup into the egg whites and continue whisking until the meringue is cool and very stiff. Fold in the crushed caramel and the cream.

Pour the mixture into a freezer-proof bowl or soufflé dish. Cover and freeze until firm.

About 15 minutes before serving, remove from the freezer. Decorate with the strawberries or pecan halves and place in the refrigerator.

Serves 6

### Serving suggestion
*Spoon into Ice Cream Cones* and surround with Bitter Chocolate Sauce*.*

### Dessert suggestion
*Form into 6 balls and coat in finely grated plain chocolate or cocoa powder. Serve with orange slices steeped in a dessert wine, and Cigars Russe*.*

## Rich Walnut Ice Cream

*4 egg yolks*
*4 ounces (100 g) caster sugar*
*½ pint (300 ml) milk*
*2 ounces (50 g) marzipan, chopped*
*4 ounces (100 g) walnuts, ground*
*¼ pint (150 ml) cream, whipped*
*Walnut halves, for decoration*

Whisk the egg yolks and sugar together in a bowl. Bring the milk to simmering point in a heavy-based saucepan. Remove from the heat and stir into the egg yolks. Stir in the marzipan and nuts. Leave to cool, stirring occasionally. Pour into a container, cover and freeze until becoming firm. Turn into a bowl and beat well. Fold in the cream.

Spoon the mixture back into the container. Cover and freeze until firm.

About 20 minutes before serving, transfer the ice cream to the refrigerator. Serve decorated with walnut halves.

Serves 5

### Dessert suggestion
*Layer with Apple Sauce Yogurt Ice (page 21). Decorate with whipped cream, chopped walnuts and short strips of orange peel.*

## Walnut Ice Cream

*2 eggs, separated*
*3 ounces (75 g) icing sugar, sifted*
*8 ounces (225 g) double cream fresh cheese*
*2 tablespoons (2 × 15 ml spoons) sweet madeira, optional*
*1½ ounces (40 g) walnuts, very lightly toasted and crushed*

Put the egg yolks and the sugar in a bowl and whisk until very light. Beat in the cheese and continue beating until the mixture is smooth.

In another bowl, whisk the egg whites until stiff but not dry. Carefully fold the egg whites into the cheese mixture with the madeira, if using, and the walnuts.

Pour the mixture into a container. Cover and freeze until firm.

About 30 minutes before serving, transfer the ice cream to the refrigerator.

Serves 4

### Dessert suggestion
*Layer with Coffee Ice Cream (page 50) and Caramel Ice Cream (page 39). Serve in slices with thickish slices of apple lightly caramelized in butter, sugar and crushed coriander seeds. Accompany with Sponge Fingers*.*

# Fresh Walnut Ice Cream

*2 ounces (50 g) shelled fresh walnuts, peeled and*
  *roughly chopped*
*18 fluid ounces (500 ml) milk*
*4 egg yolks*
*4 ounces (100 g) acacia honey*
*1 tablespoon (15 ml spoon) walnut liqueur, optional*

In a heavy-based saucepan, slowly bring the walnuts and the milk to boiling point. Remove from the heat, cover and leave to infuse for 15 minutes.

Whisk the egg yolks with the honey in a bowl until very light and thick. Whisk in the milk and walnuts. Return to the rinsed pan and cook over gentle heat until the custard thickens, but do not allow it to boil. Pour the custard into a bowl and leave to cool, stirring occasionally.

Put in the refrigerator to chill. Stir in the liqueur, if using, and pour into a container. Cover and freeze until firm, beating twice at hourly intervals.

About 30 minutes before serving, transfer the ice cream to the refrigerator.

Serves 4

**Serving suggestion**
*Serve in Coupelles\* with Orange Flower Sauce\*.*

# Walnut Mocha Ice Cream

*3 ounces (75 g) caster sugar*
*3 ounces (75 g) walnut halves*
*10 ounces (300 g) plain chocolate, chopped*
*¼ pint (150 ml) freshly made strong black coffee*
*Finely grated zest and juice of 1 orange*
*¾ pint (450 ml) cream, whipped*

*For decoration*
*Chopped walnuts lightly Caramelized\* with sugar*
*Finely grated orange zest*

In a heavy-based saucepan, melt the sugar over low heat until it begins to caramelize. Stir in the walnuts and continue to stir until the mixture is a deep golden brown. Pour on to a cold oiled surface and leave to cool. Put the praline into a thick polythene bag and break into small pieces with a rolling pin.

Melt the chocolate with the coffee and orange juice in a bowl placed over a pan of hot water. Leave to cool. Mix in the orange zest and walnut praline. Fold in the cream.

Pour the mixture into individual moulds and leave until completely cold. Cover the moulds and freeze until firm.

About 20 minutes before serving, turn out the moulds and transfer to the refrigerator. Decorate with caramelized walnuts and orange zest.

Serves 6

# Walnut Tofu Ice Cream

*3 ounces (75 g) chopped walnuts*
*3 ounces (75 g) brown sugar*
*10 ounces (300 g) tofu*
*Very large pinch of ground cinnamon*
*Large pinch of grated nutmeg*
*2 tablespoons (2 × 15 ml spoons) chopped crystallized*
  *ginger, optional*

Put the nuts and 8 fluid ounces (225 ml) water in a saucepan and simmer for 10 minutes. Purée the nuts and liquid in a blender until smooth and pass through a sieve. While still warm, mix with the sugar and then with the tofu, spices and ginger, if using.

Pour into a container. Cover and freeze until firm, beating twice at hourly intervals.

About 30 minutes before serving, transfer the ice cream to the refrigerator.

Serves 4

# Butter Pecan Ice Cream

*6 ounces (175 g) light brown sugar*
*2 eggs, beaten*
*1 ounce (25 g) unsalted butter*
*7 fluid ounces (200 ml) milk*
*Few drops of vanilla essence*
*3 tablespoons (3 × 15 ml spoons) medium sherry*
*8 fluid ounces (225 ml) whipping cream, whipped*
*4 ounces (100 g) toasted pecan nuts, chopped*

Put the sugar and 4 fluid ounces (100 ml) water in a heavy-based saucepan and stir to dissolve. Bring to the boil and boil for 2 minutes. Allow to cool slightly then slowly pour on to the eggs, whisking constantly.

Pour the mixture into a bowl placed over a pan of hot water and cook, stirring constantly, until the mixture thickens. Remove from the heat and stir in the butter. Leave to cool slightly then stir in the milk, vanilla essence and sherry and leave to cool completely.

Pour the mixture into a shallow metal container and chill for 30 minutes then cover and freeze until just becoming firm.

Tip the semi-frozen mixture into a bowl and beat well. Fold in the cream and nuts then spoon back into the container, cover and freeze until firm.

About 35 minutes before serving, transfer the ice cream to the refrigerator.

Serves 6

**Additional recipes using walnuts or pecans:**
Apple and Walnut Ice Cream (page 20), Maple and Walnut Ice Cream (page 80), Pecan Pie Ice Cream (page 135).

# Warm Climate Fruits

Exotic fruits – papaya, lychees, passion fruit and persimmon are just a few – make delicious and attractive ices that add a sense of occasion to any meal.

## Papaya Sorbet

1½ pounds (700 g) papayas
4 ounces (100 g) caster sugar
1½ tablespoons (1½ × 5 ml spoons) lemon juice
2 teaspoons (2 × 5 ml spoons) kirsch
1 small egg white

Peel the papayas, scrape out the seeds and purée the flesh. Put in a bowl and add the sugar, lemon juice and kirsch. In another bowl, whisk the egg white until stiff but not dry and fold into the papaya mixture.

Pour the mixture into a container. Cover and freeze until firm, beating 3 times at 45-minute intervals.

About 30 minutes before serving, transfer the sorbet to the refrigerator.

Serves 4

**Serving suggestion**
*Serve in wine glasses and decorate each serving with peach and kiwi fruit slices and a glacé cherry.*

## Kiwi Fruit Sorbet

2 ounces (50 g) sugar
6 kiwi fruit
2 egg whites
Cointreau or other orange liqueur

Dissolve the sugar with ¼ pint (150 ml) water in a small heavy-based saucepan. Bring to the boil and boil for 1–2 minutes. Leave to cool.

Halve the kiwi fruit and remove the skins. Then reduce the flesh to a purée and blend with the cooled syrup.

Whisk the egg whites in a bowl until stiff but not dry. Carefully fold them into the kiwi fruit mixture.

Pour the mixture into a container. Cover and freeze until firm, beating 3 times at 45-minute intervals.

About 15 minutes before serving, transfer the sorbet to the refrigerator. Pour about 1 teaspoon (5 ml) Cointreau or other orange liqueur over each serving to bring out the flavour.

Serves 6

**Dessert suggestion**
*Encase in Pistachio and Green Chartreuse Ice Cream (page 101). Decorate the turned-out dessert with brandy-flavoured whipped cream and Chocolate Shapes*.*

## Lychee Ice Cream

4 ounces (100 g) sugar
½ pint (300 ml) milk
1 pint (600 ml) double or whipping cream
1 vanilla pod, split
8 egg yolks
Approximately 14 ounce (400 g) can lychees, drained and very finely sliced
Preserved stem ginger in syrup, for serving

In a heavy-based saucepan, heat the sugar, milk, cream and vanilla pod to just below boiling point. Remove from the heat, cover and leave for 30 minutes.

Beat the egg yolks in a bowl. Strain in the milk mixture, stirring. Return to the rinsed pan and heat gently, stirring constantly, until the custard thickens. Do not allow to boil. Leave to cool, stirring occasionally. Chill for an hour.

Stir in the lychees and pour into a container. Cover and freeze until firm, beating twice at hourly intervals.

About 40 minutes before serving, transfer the ice cream to the refrigerator. Slice the ginger into fine strips and sprinkle over each portion as it is served together with a spoonful of the syrup.

Serves 6–8

**Serving suggestion**
*Serve in Gingersnap Baskets* or Cones* intermingled with sliced fresh or canned lychees.*

**Dessert suggestion**
*Encase in a layer of Blackcurrant Ice Cream (page 32) followed by a jacket made with fingers of Genoise Cake*.*

## Papaya Ice Cream

12 fluid ounces (350 ml) papaya flesh (from about 1¼ pounds/500 g papayas), puréed
Juice of 1 large juicy lemon
Juice of ½ a large juicy orange
Approximately 6 ounces (175 g) icing sugar
½ pint (300 ml) cream, whipped

In a bowl, blend the papaya flesh with the fruit juices and sweeten with the sugar. Fold in the cream. Taste and adjust the sugar level, if necessary, to make the mixture slightly oversweet.

Pour the mixture into a container. Cover and freeze until firm, beating twice at hourly intervals.

About 30 minutes before serving, transfer the ice cream to the refrigerator.

Serves 6

**Serving suggestion**
*Freeze in a ring mould. Fill the centre with Lime Ice Cream (page 75) and decorate with twisted lime slices and shapes cut from lemon peel. Serve with Almond Tuiles*.*

# Quick Lychee Sorbet

1¼ pounds (550 g) canned lychees
2 tablespoons (2 × 15 ml spoons) orange flower water
1 tablespoon (15 ml spoon) kirsch, optional
2 egg whites

Purée the lychees with their juice, the orange flower water and kirsch, if you are using it.

Pour the mixture into a container. Cover and freeze to the slushy stage. Beat well in a bowl.

Whisk the egg whites in a bowl until stiff but not dry. Fold into the sorbet. Return to the container, cover and freeze until firm.

About 10 minutes before serving, transfer the sorbet to the refrigerator.

Serves 6

### Serving suggestions
*Accompany with Chunky Marmalade Sauce\* made with lime or ginger marmalade.*

*Serve with Almond Tuiles\* flavoured with orange flower water.*

*For each serving, arrange one or two scoops on a plate with a selection of different coloured sorbets such as Apricot Sorbet (page 23), Blackberry Sorbet (page 30) and Rhubarb Sorbet (page 110).*

# Persimmon Ice Cream

3 large, sweet, very ripe persimmons
3 ounces (75 g) caster sugar
2 tablespoons (2 × 15 ml spoons) lemon juice
¾ pint (450 ml) whipping cream, whipped

Cut the persimmons in half, scoop out the flesh and pass through a nylon sieve into a bowl to remove the seeds. Stir in the sugar and lemon juice and fold in the cream.

Pour the mixture into a container. Cover and freeze until firm, beating twice at hourly intervals.

About 45 minutes before serving, transfer the ice cream to the refrigerator.

Serves 4–6

### Dessert suggestion
*Make a bombe or freeze in a cake or loaf tin enclosed in a layer of Candied Peel Ice Cream (page 59) with a jacket of Quick Brown Bread Ice Cream (page 36) flavoured with 2½ fluid ounces (65 ml) orange liqueur (added when the ingredients are stirred together). Decorate the turned-out dessert with whipped cream and pour over a sauce made from puréed orange flesh.*

# Passion Fruit Sorbet

6 ounces (175 g) sugar
Peel and juice of 1 lemon
1 pound (450 g) passion fruit pulp (from about 1½ pounds/750 g fruit), strained
1 egg white

In a heavy-based saucepan, dissolve the sugar in ¾ pint (450 ml) water. Add the lemon peel and bring to the boil. Boil for 5 minutes. Cool and strain the syrup. Stir in the passion fruit pulp and lemon juice. Chill for 30 minutes.

Pour the mixture into a container. Cover and freeze to the slushy stage. Beat well in a bowl.

Whisk the egg white in a small bowl, until stiff but not dry and fold into the passion fruit mixture. Return to the container, cover and freeze until firm, beating 3 times at 45-minute intervals.

About 40 minutes before serving, transfer to the refrigerator.

Serves 6

# Passion Fruit and Strawberry Ice Cream

3 egg yolks
2½ ounces (65 g) sugar
½ pint (300 ml) milk
Pulp and seeds of 6 passion fruit
¼ pint (150 ml) strawberry purée (from about 6 ounces/150 g hulled strawberries)
Squeeze of orange juice
¾ pint (425 ml) crème fraîche, beaten

*For decoration*
*Whipped cream*
*Strawberries*

Put the egg yolks and sugar in a bowl and whisk until thick and light. In a heavy-based saucepan, heat the milk to just below boiling point. Pour the hot milk on to the egg yolks, whisking continuously. Return the mixture to the rinsed pan and cook over a low heat, stirring constantly, until the mixture thickens. Do not boil. Remove from the heat and whisk until cool.

Mix half the custard with the pulp and seeds of the passion fruit and half with the strawberry purée. Add a squeeze of orange juice to each mixture then leave until cold.

Sieve each mixture into a separate bowl. Fold half the crème fraîche into each one. Fold the two mixtures together to give a marbled effect. Pour the mixture into a container. Cover and freeze until firm.

About 30 minutes before serving, transfer the ice cream to the refrigerator. Serve each portion decorated with a swirl of cream and a sliced strawberry.

Serves 4–5

# Passion Fruit Ice Cream

*8 ripe passion fruit*
*1 teaspoon (5 ml spoon) lemon juice*
*2 eggs, separated*
*4 ounces (100 g) caster sugar*
*½ pint (300 ml) cream, whipped*

*For decoration*
*Pulp and seeds of 1 passion fruit*
*Whipped cream*

Cut the passion fruit in half and scoop the pulp out into a sieve placed over a bowl. Press through the sieve to extract as much juice as possible. Discard the seeds. Add the lemon juice.

Whisk the egg yolks and half the sugar in a bowl until very thick and light. In another bowl, whisk the egg whites until stiff but not dry. Gradually whisk in the remaining sugar. Fold the egg yolks into the passion fruit mixture then the cream and egg whites. Freeze in a 1¾ pint (1 litre) loaf tin or mould until firm.

About 20 minutes before serving, unmould the ice cream on to a cold plate, spoon the passion fruit pulp and seeds down the centre and finish with whipped cream.

Serves 6

# Pomegranate Sorbet

*8 ounces (225 g) sugar*
*¾ pint (450 ml) pomegranate juice (from 6–8 fruit)*
*Juice of ½ lemon*

In a heavy-based saucepan, dissolve the sugar in ½ pint (300 ml) water and bring to the boil. Cool then stir in the remaining ingredients. Chill for an hour.

Pour the mixture into a container. Cover and freeze until firm, beating 3 times at 45-minute intervals.

About 30 minutes before serving, transfer the sorbet to the refrigerator.

Serves 6–8

### Dessert suggestion
*Encase in Pear Ice Cream (with kirsch) (page 93). Decorate the turned-out dessert with whipped cream, flavoured with kirsch or grenadine syrup if liked, and crystallized rose petals.*

---

*WATERMELON:    see MELON*
*WHISKY:    see SPIRITS*

# Wines, Liqueurs

At first sight ices made from wines or liqueurs may seem to be an extravagance. However, they need not be expensive. Wines can be bought in half bottles and most liqueurs are available in miniature sizes. Remember, though, that it is a false economy to use an inferior-quality product as this will mar the taste of the ice. There is also a recipe using prunes and wine (plus brandy) – a delicious combination.

**Simple Liqueur Ice Cream**
Add 3 tablespoons (3 × 15 ml spoons) of any liqueur to any of the Basic Recipes*.

## Red Wine Granita

7 ounces (200 g) sugar
1 × 26 fluid ounce bottle (75 cl) red wine, preferably
  St. Emilion or Pomerol
Juice of 1 orange
Juice of 1 lemon
Fresh mint leaves, for decoration

In a heavy-based saucepan, dissolve the sugar in 7 fluid ounces (200 ml) water. Bring to the boil and boil for 1 minute. Leave to cool completely.

Stir the wine and fruit juices into the syrup. Chill for 30 minutes then strain into a container. Cover and freeze until lightly set and a mass of small, light crystals. Stir the granita and spoon into 6 cold claret glasses, shaping it into a dome. Serve garnished with mint leaves.

Serves 6

## Prune Ice Cream (with wine and brandy)

12 ounces (350 g) best prunes, stoned
7 fluid ounces (200 ml) good sweet wine
4 tablespoons (4 × 15 ml spoons) armagnac or
  brandy
2½ ounces (65 g) sugar
3 egg yolks
1 ounce (25 g) plain flour
7 fluid ounces (200 ml) milk infused with a vanilla
  pod
¼ ounce (7 g) unsalted butter
Few drops of vanilla essence
7 fluid ounces (200 ml) double cream

Cut the prunes into 3 or 4 pieces and put in a bowl with the wine and armagnac or brandy. Cover and leave to macerate in a cool place for several hours.

Whisk the sugar, egg yolks and flour together in a bowl until very thick and pale. In a heavy stainless steel or enamel saucepan, slowly bring the milk and vanilla pod to just on boiling point. Gradually strain the milk on to the egg yolk mixture, whisking all the time (keep the vanilla pod, washed and dried, for future use). Pour the custard mixture back into the pan and bring to the boil over a moderate heat, whisking all the time.

Simmer over a low heat for 2–3 minutes to cook the flour, still whisking. Remove from the heat, beat in the butter and a few drops of vanilla essence. Pour into a bowl, cover closely with cling film and leave to cool, then refrigerate.

Pour into a container, cover and freeze until becoming firm. Turn into a bowl and beat well. Whip the cream, adding a little of the unabsorbed syrup from the prunes, until soft peaks form. Fold the cream into the custard with half the macerated prunes.

Spoon the mixture back into the container. Cover and freeze until firm. Freeze the remaining fruit and syrup separately, unless serving the ice cream within a day or so. Otherwise keep covered in the refrigerator.

About 45 minutes before serving, transfer the ice cream to the refrigerator and let the fruit and syrup warm to room temperature. Spoon some of the fruit and syrup over each portion as it is served.

Serves 4–6

**Dessert suggestion**
*Encase in Tea Ice Cream (page 71). To serve, spoon some of the reserved prunes and syrup over the top of the turned-out dessert, allowing the syrup to trickle over the surface and down the sides, and surround with the remaining prunes and syrup.*

## White Wine Sorbet

8 ounces (225 g) sugar
2 lemons
8 fluid ounces (225 ml) good-quality white wine
2 egg whites

In a heavy-based saucepan, dissolve the sugar in 6 fluid ounces (175 ml) water. Bring to the boil and boil until the temperature reaches 225°F (105°C). Remove from the heat.

Thinly pare the peel from one of the lemons and add it to the syrup. Cover and leave for a few hours.

Remove the lemon peel from the syrup and stir in the wine and juice from both lemons. Pour the mixture into a container, cover and freeze until slushy. Beat well in a bowl.

Whisk the egg whites in a bowl until stiff but not dry. Fold them into the frozen wine syrup. Return to the container, cover and freeze until firm, although it will not become really hard. Serve straight from the freezer.

Serves 5–6

**Serving suggestions**
*Intermingle small scoops of the sorbet with small scoops of Melon Ice Cream (page 83) and Quick Mango Ice Cream (page 79) in a chilled melon half.*

*Serve small scoops of the sorbet with scoops of White Peach Sorbet (page 88) piled into Almond Tuiles*.*

**Dessert suggestion**
*Freeze in a cake or loaf tin around a centre of Grape Ice Cream (page 64). Decorate the turned-out dessert with whipped cream and quartered black grapes.*

# Gewürztraminer Sorbet

1 pound (450 g) sugar
½ bottle (35 cl) gewürztraminer wine
Juice of 1 orange
Juice of 1 lemon
3 egg whites

In a heavy-based saucepan, dissolve the sugar in 1 pint (600 ml) water. Bring to the boil then simmer for 10 minutes. Set aside to cool.

Pour the wine and an equal amount of the sugar syrup into a bowl and mix in the strained fruit juices.

Pour the mixture into a container. Cover and freeze to the slushy stage. Beat well in a bowl.

Whisk the egg whites in a bowl until stiff but not dry. Fold into the wine mixture. Return to the container, cover and freeze until firm.

Serve directly from the freezer.

Serves 6–8

**Serving suggestion**
*For each serving, put sliced strawberries (wild, if possible) in the bottom of a tall, slim, frosted glass and sprinkle with strawberry eau-de-vie (fraise). Add scoops of the sorbet and top with more sliced strawberries. Sprinkle with eau-de-vie and pour over some good-quality sweet sparkling wine. Finish with a scattering of lightly toasted flaked almonds. Serve with long-handled spoons.*

# Liqueur Sorbet

6 ounces (175 g) sugar
Finely grated zest and juice of 1 lemon
6 tablespoons (6 × 15 ml spoons) liqueur, e.g. Grand Marnier, crème de cassis, apricot brandy
1 egg white
Bay leaves, for decoration

In a heavy-based saucepan, dissolve the sugar in 12½ fluid ounces (365 ml) water. Bring to the boil and boil for 5 minutes. Remove from the heat, stir in the lemon zest and juice and the liqueur. Leave to cool completely.

Strain the syrup and pour into a container. Cover and chill for 30 minutes. Place in the freezer and freeze to the slushy stage. Beat well in a bowl.

Whisk the egg white in a small bowl until stiff but not dry. Fold into the sorbet. Return to the container, cover and freeze until firm.

About 30 minutes before serving, transfer the sorbet to the refrigerator. Decorate each portion with bay leaves.

Serves 4

**Dessert suggestion**
*Encase in an appropriately flavoured and coloured ice cream. Maraschino with Vanilla Ice Cream (page 123) is a good combination.*

# Iced Kirsch Soufflé

8 ounces (225 g) caster sugar
4 egg whites
2 fluid ounces (50 ml) good-quality kirsch
½ pint (300 ml) crème fraîche or double cream, whipped
Crystallized violets, for decoration

In a heavy-based saucepan, dissolve the sugar in ¼ pint (150 ml) water. Bring to the boil and boil for 3–5 minutes or until the temperature reaches 234°F (112°C).

Whisk the egg whites in a bowl until stiff. Gradually pour in the syrup, whisking well. Whisk in the kirsch then carefully fold in the crème fraîche or double cream. Leave to cool then chill in the refrigerator.

Pour the mixture into a freezer-proof soufflé dish and freeze until firm.

About 20 minutes before serving, transfer the soufflé to the refrigerator. Decorate with crystallized violets.

Serves 6

**Serving suggestion**
*Pile scoops into the centres of pineapple rings and decorate with small Macaroons\*.*

**Dessert suggestion**
*To make a Bombe Aida encase in Strawberry Ice Cream (page 121) and decorate the turned-out dessert with whipped cream, halved black cherries and Chocolate Curls\*.*

# Iced Zabaglione

4 egg yolks
5 fluid ounces (150 ml) marsala
3 tablespoons (3 × 15 ml spoons) caster sugar
½ pint (300 ml) double cream
Macaroons\*, to serve

Whisk the egg yolks, marsala and sugar together in a bowl placed over a pan of hot water, until very thick and light. Put the bowl into a basin of iced or very cold water to prevent the mixture cooking further and whisk until it is cold.

In another bowl, whip the cream until soft peaks form. Carefully fold the cream into the marsala mixture.

Pour the mixture into a container. Cover and freeze until firm.

About 20 minutes before serving, transfer the iced zabaglione to the refrigerator. Serve with macaroons.

Serves 4

**Serving suggestion**
*Serve with Cigars Russe\* or Sponge Fingers\*.*

**Dessert suggestion**
*Freeze in a Chocolate Case\* around a centre of Seville Orange Sorbet (page 86).*

# Champagne Ice Cream

12 ounces (350 g) sugar
3 tablespoons (3 × 15 ml spoons) orange juice
2 tablespoons (2 × 15 ml spoons) brandy
14 fluid ounces (400 ml) champagne or good-quality
 dry sparkling wine
7 fluid ounces (200 ml) double cream
Strawberries marinated in slightly sweetened brandy,
 to serve

In a heavy-based saucepan, dissolve the sugar in
½ pint (300 ml) water. Bring to the boil and boil until
the temperature reaches 230–234°F (110–112°C).
Leave to cool.

Stir the orange juice, brandy and champagne into
the syrup. Pour the mixture into a container. Cover
and freeze until just becoming firm. Beat well in a
bowl.

Whip the cream in a bowl until soft peaks form. Fold
the cream into the champagne ice. Return to the
container, cover and freeze until firm.

About 30 minutes before serving, transfer the ice
cream to the refrigerator. Serve with the marinated
strawberries.

Serves 6

### Serving suggestion
*Freeze in a ring mould and fill the centre with
strawberries steeped in brandy. Sprinkle lightly with
caster sugar.*

### Dessert suggestion
*Encase in Iced Apricot Mousse (page 25). Decorate the
turned-out dessert with warmed apricot-brandy-
flavoured whipped cream and flaked almonds.*

# Liqueur Cream Ice

7 ounces (200 g) sugar
Juice of 1 lemon
3 fluid ounces (75 ml) any type of liqueur
¼ pint (150 ml) cream, whipped
Crystallized fruits soaked in cognac, to serve

In a heavy-based saucepan, dissolve the sugar in
¾ pint (450 ml) water. Bring to the boil and boil until
the temperature reaches 234°F (112°C). Set aside to
cool.

Stir the strained lemon juice into the syrup. Pour
into a container, cover and freeze to the slushy stage.

Stir the liqueur into the frozen mixture and fold in
the cream. Return to the freezer and freeze until firm.

About 40 minutes before serving, transfer the ice to
the refrigerator. Serve each portion topped by
crystallized fruits soaked in cognac.

Serves 4

### Serving suggestion
*Freeze in small Chocolate Cases* and serve as petits
fours.*

### Dessert suggestion
*Layer with a similar-flavoured ice cream or sorbet, or
one with a complementary or contrasting flavour:
Cointreau with Orange Ice Cream (page 85), crème de
cacao with Mint Sorbet (page 71), Amaretto with
Apricot Ice Cream (page 24) or Chocolate Ice Cream
(page 44).*

# Marsala and Chocolate Ice Cream

4 ounces (100 g) sugar
3 ounces (75 g) flaked almonds, toasted
5 ounces (150 g) bitter plain chocolate
3 fluid ounces (75 ml) marsala
3 egg whites
6 ounces (175 g) caster sugar
¾ pint (450 ml) cream, whipped
Few drops of almond essence

In a heavy-based saucepan, dissolve the sugar in
2 tablespoons (2 × 15 ml spoons) water. Bring to the
boil and boil until pale golden at the edges. Shake the
pan until the syrup is evenly browned then quickly stir
in the almonds and pour on to an oiled surface to cool.
When the praline is cold put it in a thick polythene bag
and hit with a rolling pin until broken into small
pieces.

Melt the chocolate in the marsala in a bowl set over
a pan of hot water. Then leave to cool slightly.

Whisk the egg whites in a bowl until stiff. Gradually
whisk in the caster sugar and continue whisking until
the meringue is stiff and glossy. Fold in the cream with
the almond essence and praline. Carefully fold in the
chocolate to give a marbled effect.

Pour the mixture into a container. Cover and freeze
until firm.

About 10 minutes before serving, transfer the
mousse to the refrigerator.

Serves 8

### Dessert suggestion
*Freeze in a cake or loaf tin lined with plain or
hazelnut Meringues* around a centre of Raspberry
Sorbet (page 104). Serve with crème fraîche.*

# Dessert Wine Granita

3½ ounces (90 g) sugar
½ bottle (35 cl) good-quality dessert wine
Juice of ½ an orange
Juice of ½ a lemon
Mint leaves, for decoration

In a heavy-based saucepan, dissolve the sugar in
3½ fluid ounces (90 ml) water. Bring to the boil and
boil for 1 minute. Leave to cool.

Stir the wine and fruit juices into the syrup. Pour the mixture into a container. Cover and freeze until just firm, occasionally forking through the mixture to form small granules. Serve straight from the freezer, decorating each portion with mint leaves.

Serves 5–6

**Additional recipes using wines and liqueurs:**
Apricot and Wine Ice Cream (page 23), 'Irish Coffee' Banana Ice Cream (page 28), Ginger Wine Sorbet (page 60), Grapefruit and Vermouth Granita (page 67), Pear Ice Cream (page 92), Pistachio and Green Chartreuse Ice Cream (page 101), Rhubarb and Ginger Wine Ice Cream (page 110), Blackcurrant, Rose Petal and Champagne Roll (page 136).

# Old-Fashioned Favourites

The ices in this section are based on old-fashioned recipes, with ingredients like elderberries and quinces. They include cassata – a traditional favourite.

## Crab-Apple Ice Cream

*2 pounds (900 g) crab-apples*
*12 ounces (350 g) sugar*
*Juice of 1 large juicy orange*
*1/2 pint (300 ml) cream, whipped*

Cut the crab-apples in half and remove the stalks. Put them in a large saucepan, just cover with water and simmer until soft, adding a little more water if necessary. Pass the crab-apples through a sieve.

In a heavy-based saucepan, dissolve the sugar in 1/4 pint (150 ml) water. Bring to the boil and boil for 3 minutes. Set aside to cool.

Add the syrup to the crab-apples with the orange juice – taste and adjust the level of sweetness and orange, if necessary.

Pour the mixture into a container. Cover and freeze to the slushy stage. Beat well in a bowl.

Fold the cream into the frozen mixture. Return to the container, cover and freeze until firm.

About 30 minutes before serving, transfer the ice cream to the refrigerator.

Serves 4–5

### Serving suggestion
*Serve in Gingersnap Baskets\*. Decorate with ginger-wine-flavoured cream and flaked almonds.*

## Quince Ice Cream

*2 pounds (900 g) quinces, peeled, cored and chopped*
*12 ounces (350 g) sugar*
*Juice of 1 orange*
*1/2 pint (300 ml) whipping or double cream*

Put the quinces, sugar and just enough water to cover in a saucepan and cook gently for about 40 minutes or until soft, adding more water if necessary. Pass the quinces through a sieve – there should be about 1 pint (600 ml) purée.

Mix in the orange juice and pour into a container. Cover and freeze to the slushy stage. Beat well in a bowl. Whip the cream in a bowl until soft peaks form. Fold into the purée. Return to the container, cover and freeze until firm.

About 30 minutes before serving, transfer the ice cream to the refrigerator.

Serves 5–6

### Dessert suggestion
*Make a bombe or freeze in a cake or loaf tin with a jacket of finely chopped walnuts Caramelized\* with sugar and orange zest, followed by a layer of the ice cream around a centre of Iced Whisky Syllabub (page 116).*

## Cider Sorbet

*7 ounces (200 g) sugar*
*3 fluid ounces (75 ml) lemon juice*
*18 fluid ounces (500 ml) apple purée*
*1/4 pint (150 ml) dry cider*
*Mint leaves, for decoration*

In a heavy-based saucepan, dissolve the sugar in 7 fluid ounces (200 ml) water. Bring to the boil and boil for about a minute or until the temperature reaches 215°F (102°C). Strain in the lemon juice and leave to cool.

Blend the apple purée and cider into the syrup. Pour the mixture into a container, cover and freeze until firm, beating well 3 times at 45-minute intervals.

About 40 minutes before serving, transfer the sorbet to the refrigerator. Decorate each portion with mint leaves.

Serves 6–8

### Serving suggestion
*Serve in Almond Tuiles\* with slices of apple poached in calvados or brandy. Decorate with fine strips of orange peel.*

### Dessert suggestion
*Encase in Apple Cream Ice (page 21). Decorate the top of the turned-out dessert with slices of red-skinned apples and surround the base with calvados-flavoured whipped cream and chopped walnuts.*

## Crystallized Violet Ice Cream

*3 ounces (75 g) caster sugar*
*4 egg yolks*
*1 ounce (25 g) crystallized violet petals*
*3/4 pint (450 ml) cream, whipped*
*1–2 tablespoons (1–2 × 15 ml spoons) strawberry eau-de-vie (fraise)*

*For decoration*
*Whipped cream*
*Crystallized violet petals*

Dissolve the sugar in 4 tablespoons (60 ml) water in a heavy-based pan. Bring to the boil and boil until the syrup reaches 230°F (110°C).

Whisk the egg yolks in a bowl until very light and thick. Gradually whisk in the hot syrup. Continue whisking until cold.

Fold in the crystallized violet petals, cream and fraise.

Pour the mixture into a container. Cover and freeze until firm.

About 20 minutes before serving transfer the ice cream to the refrigerator. Decorate with whipped cream and crystallized violets.

Serves 4

## Dessert suggestion
*Freeze in a fancy mould. Pipe whipped cream around the base and top of the turned-out dessert and decorate with fresh or crystallized violets.*

## Flavour variation
*Use 1 ounce (25 g) crystallized rose petals instead of violet petals; garnish with crystallized roses.*

# Elderberry Water Ice

*6 ounces (175 g) sugar*
*1 pound (450 g) elderberries*
*Squeeze of lemon juice*
*Sparkling sweet elderberry wine ('champagne'), for serving*

In a heavy-based saucepan, dissolve the sugar in ½ pint (300 ml) water. Bring to the boil and boil for 5 minutes. Stir in the elderberries and simmer until tender.

Purée the elderberries and pass through a fine sieve into a bowl. Strain in the lemon juice to taste. Chill for 30 minutes. Pour into a container, cover and freeze until firm, beating 3 times at 45-minute intervals.

About 30 minutes before serving, transfer the water ice to the refrigerator. Pour some sparkling sweet elderberry wine over each portion as it is served.

Serves 4–6

## Serving suggestion
*Scoop into tall, slim, frosted glasses and trickle over a little elderflower 'champagne' or wine. Serve with Meringue Fingers\*.*

## Dessert suggestion
*Ripple with Redcurrant Ice Cream (page 108) and cover the sides and top of the turned-out dessert with Sponge Fingers\*. Surround the base with decorative swirls of whipped cream and redcurrants.*

# Pecan Pie Ice Cream

*3 eggs, separated*
*3 ounces (75 g) sugar*
*2 ounces (50 g) unsalted butter, melted*
*5 fluid ounces (150 ml) milk*
*8 fluid ounces (225 ml) light corn syrup*
*5 ounces (150 g) pecan nuts, roughly chopped*
*Few drops of vanilla essence*

Put the egg yolks and sugar in a bowl and whisk together until light. Place the bowl over a pan of hot water and cook, stirring constantly, until the mixture thickens slightly. Do not allow to boil. Remove from the heat and whisk in the butter.

Heat the milk and corn syrup in a saucepan until just beginning to bubble around the edges. Pour the milk and syrup on to the egg mixture, stirring constantly. Leave the mixture to cool, stirring occasionally.

Pour the mixture into a shallow container, cover and freeze until just becoming firm around the edges.

Tip the semi-frozen mixture into a bowl and beat well. In another bowl, whisk the egg whites until stiff but not dry, then fold into the corn syrup mixture with the pecans and vanilla essence. Spoon back into the container, cover and freeze until firm.

About 30 minutes before serving, transfer the ice cream to the refrigerator.

Serves 4

# Cassata

*½ pint (300 ml) Vanilla Ice Cream (page 123), slightly softened*
*½ pint (300 ml) Strawberry Ice Cream (page 121) or Raspberry Ice Cream (page 104), slightly softened*
*1 ounce (25 g) glacé cherries, chopped*
*1 ounce (25 g) angelica, chopped*
*1 ounce (25 g) blanched almonds, chopped*
*1 ounce (25 g) candied peel, chopped*
*¾ pint (450 ml) Pistachio Ice Cream (page 101), slightly softened*
*Candied fruits, for decoration*

Chill a 2 pint (1.1 litre) mould. Spoon in the vanilla ice cream and smooth it evenly over the base and sides. Cover and freeze until firm. Then smooth the strawberry or raspberry ice cream evenly over the base and sides of the frozen lining. Cover and freeze until firm.

Fold the cherries, angelica, almonds and candied peel into the pistachio ice cream and spoon into the centre of the mould. Cover and return to the freezer for at least 6 hours.

About 35–40 minutes before serving turn the cassata out on to a chilled plate and leave in the refrigerator. Serve decorated with candied fruits.

Serves 6

# Special Occasions

Different-flavoured ices can be combined with each other, and with a variety of ingredients, to make spectacular desserts – with the added advantage that, impressive as they are, most can be prepared well ahead of time.

I have included dessert suggestions as well as serving suggestions with many of the recipes in the first part of the book. The ones that follow are rather more elaborate, and include some of my favourite set-pieces for special occasions.

# Jamaica Freezer Cake

*1 oblong moist Jamaica ginger cake*
*4 tablespoons (4 × 15 ml spoons) ginger marmalade*
*1 tablespoon (15 ml spoon) advocaat, optional*
*1/2 pint (300 ml) double cream, whipped*
*Slices of candied fruits, for decoration*

Cut the cake horizontally into 4 even slices. Fold the marmalade and advocaat, if using, into the cream then sandwich the cake back together with about half of the mixture. Place the cake on a freezer tray and spread the remaining cream mixture over the top and sides.

Freeze, then pack in a rigid container if storing for any length of time.

About 20 minutes before serving, place the cake on a cold plate. Decorate with the candied fruit to serve.

Serves 6–8

# Coffee Ice Cream Slice

*For the meringue*
*3 egg whites*
*6 ounces (175 g) caster sugar*
*1/2 teaspoon (2.5 ml spoon) ground cinnamon*

*For the ice cream*
*6 ounces (175 g) full fat cheese*
*2 1/2 ounces (90 g) caster sugar*
*2 tablespoons (2 × 15 ml spoons) coffee essence*
*1/2 pint (300 ml) milk*
*1 tablespoon (15 ml spoon) lime juice*

*For decoration*
*Marrons glacés*
*Bitter Chocolate Sauce\**

Make the meringue mixture according to the recipe on page 150, folding the cinnamon in at the end. Line baking sheets with foil or silicone paper. Spread the meringue into 3 rectangles, 9 × 4 inches (23 × 10 cm) each, on the baking sheets. Bake at 275°F (140°C, gas mark 1) for 2–3 hours until dry and crisp. Cool on a wire rack.

To make the ice cream, put the soft cheese, sugar and coffee essence in a bowl and blend until smooth. Gradually beat in the milk and lime juice. Pour the mixture into a container, cover and freeze until just becoming firm.

On a baking sheet sandwich the meringue layers together with the ice cream and return to the freezer until firm. Overwrap with foil or freezer paper, pack to protect the meringue and leave until required.

Just before required, unwrap the meringue and decorate with the marrons glacés, whole or chopped as required, and trickle a thin stream of chocolate sauce over the top.

Serves 6–8

# Pineapple and Coconut Macaroon Cake

*4 ounces (100 g) coconut cream*
*4 ounces (100 g) ground almonds*
*4 ounces (100 g) caster sugar*
*2 egg whites*
*1 medium-sized fresh pineapple*
*4 tablespoons (4 × 15 ml spoons) kirsch*
*4 ounces (100 g) caster sugar*
*2 egg whites*
*8 fluid ounces (225 ml) double cream*

*For decoration*
*Fresh pineapple*
*Whipped cream*
*Toasted flaked almonds*

To make the macaroons, whisk the coconut cream, almonds and sugar together in a bowl. Mix in the egg whites to form a stiff, sticky mixture. Line a baking sheet with rice or silicone paper. Spread the mixture into four 6 1/2 inch (16.25 cm) circles on the lined baking sheet. Put in the oven and cook at 375°F (190°C, gas mark 5) for about 12 minutes until lightly browned. Transfer the macaroons to a wine rack and leave to cool.

Peel the pineapple. Remove the core then reduce the flesh to 3/4 pint (450 ml) purée, adding a little water, if necessary. Add the kirsch and leave in a cool place to marinate for a few hours.

Dissolve the sugar in 2 fluid ounces (50 ml) water and any juice left over when the pineapple is peeled in a small heavy-based saucepan. Bring to the boil and boil for 5 minutes.

Whisk the egg whites in a bowl to a stiff white foam then gradually whisk in the hot syrup and continue whisking until cool.

In another bowl, whip the cream to a consistency similar to the meringue. Lightly fold the cream into the pineapple purée followed by the meringue.

Pour the mixture into a container. Cover and place briefly in the freezer.

Trim the 4 macaroons to fit into a loose-bottomed 6 1/2 inch (16.25 cm) cake tin. Press one into the bottom of the tin and cover with one-third of the pineapple mixture. Continue with alternate layers of macaroons and pineapple mixture then cover and freeze until firm.

About 30–45 minutes before serving, push up the bottom of the cake tin – if necessary, run a knife around the inside of the tin – and when the whole cake is released remove it from the base with a knife and place on a cold plate. Decorate with pineapple, cream and almonds and leave in the main part of the refrigerator.

Serves 8–10

# Chocolate-Coated Coffee Ice Cream Balls

*½ pint (300 ml) milk*
*2 ounces (50 g) coarse oatmeal, toasted*
*¼ pint (150 ml) soured cream*
*4 ounces (100 g) full fat soft cheese*
*4 ounces (100 g) caster sugar*
*3 egg yolks, lightly beaten*
*2 teaspoons (2 × 5 ml spoons) instant coffee granules*
*1 tablespoon (15 ml spoon) Irish cream liqueur*
*4 ounces (100 g) plain chocolate*

Put the milk and oatmeal in a saucepan and bring to the boil. Simmer gently for 4–5 minutes. Remove from the heat.

Blend the soured cream, cheese and sugar together in a bowl. Gradually stir in the oatmeal mixture. Whisk in the egg yolks, coffee granules and liqueur. Leave to cool completely.

Pour the mixture into a container. Cover and freeze until firm.

Soften the ice cream for 10–15 minutes at room temperature then scoop out small balls on to a foil-lined baking sheet. Return to the freezer for at least 4 hours or until hard.

Meanwhile, break the chocolate into a small bowl, add 5 tablespoons (75 ml) water and melt over a pan of simmering water until smooth. Leave to cool and thicken. Dip each ice cream ball into the melted chocolate, shake off any excess and return to the baking sheet. Freeze for at least 30 minutes until set.

About 10 minutes before serving, transfer to the refrigerator.

Serves 4–6

# Cranberry Snowballs

*1 egg white*
*½ pint (300 ml) crème fraîche*
*2 tablespoons (2 × 15 ml spoons) milk*
*12 ounces (350 g) bought cranberry purée or 12 fluid ounces (350 ml) thick, sweetened home-made cranberry purée*
*3 ounces (75 g) icing sugar*
*1 ounce (25 g) cranberries*
*2 teaspoons (2 × 5 ml spoons) sugar*
*4 tablespoons (4 × 15 ml spoons) brandy or whisky, warmed*
*Cigars Russe\*, for serving*

Whisk the egg white in a small bowl until stiff but not dry. In another bowl whip the crème fraîche with the milk until soft peaks form. Fold the cranberry purée and sugar into the cream followed by the egg white. Pour into a container, cover and freeze until just becoming firm.

Meanwhile, cook the cranberries in 4 tablespoons (60 ml) water by the method for Cranberry Ice Cream on page 55. After the second heating remove the cranberries from the liquid with a slotted spoon and put into a bowl with the sugar and brandy or whisky. Cover and leave to cool.

Divide the cranberry cream into 4 and roll each quarter into a smooth ball inside a piece of freezer-proof foil, enclosing a quarter of the marinated cranberries in the centre. Place in the freezer until firm.

About 30 minutes before serving, transfer the balls to the refrigerator. Carefully peel away the foil and serve with Cigars Russe\*.

Serves 4

# Blackcurrant, Rose Petal and Champagne Roll

*3 egg quantity Whisked Sponge Cake\**
*Caster sugar*
*Champagne Ice Cream (page 132)*
*Rose Petal Sorbet (page 70)*
*Blackcurrant Ice Cream (page 32)*

*For decoration*
*Whipped cream*
*Rose petals*
*Frosted\* blackcurrants*
*Frosted\* blackcurrant leaves*

Spoon the whisked sponge into a greased and lined 9 × 13 inch (23 ×33 cm) Swiss roll tin, smooth the surface and bake in an oven preheated to 375°F (190°C, gas mark 5) for about 8 minutes.

Meanwhile, place a sheet of greaseproof paper on a warmed, dampened tea towel and sprinkle it liberally with caster sugar.

Turn the cooked cake out on to the sugared paper, carefully peel away the lining paper and quickly roll up the cake leaving the sugared paper inside. Leave to cool.

Leave the champagne ice cream at room temperature for about 25 minutes, the sorbet for 10 minutes.

Unroll the cake and remove the greaseproof paper. Spread the cake with the sorbet. Spoon the champagne ice cream lengthways down the centre (if a batch is made specifically, any left over can be used in the decoration) and roll the cake up. Place the roll in the freezer for 1 hour.

Leave the blackcurrant ice cream at room temperature for 35 minutes. Spread the blackcurrant ice cream over the roll and return it to the freezer for 30 minutes.

Decorate the roll with whipped cream, any remaining champagne ice cream, rose petals or crystallized roses, and frosted blackcurrants and leaves.

Serves 6–8

# Iced Christmas Pudding

6 ounces (175 g) mixed sultanas and raisins
3 ounces (75 g) currants
2 ounces (50 g) each mixed peel and glacé cherries,
    chopped
4 tablespoons (4 × 15 ml spoons) brandy
8 ounces (225 g) full fat soft cheese
3 ounces (75 g) caster sugar
1/2 teaspoon (2.5 ml spoon) mixed spice
1/2 pint (300 ml) milk

For decoration
Whipped cream
Glacé cherries

Soak the fruits and peel in the brandy for 4 hours or
more.

Put the cheese in a bowl and beat until smooth. Beat
in the sugar and spice. Gradually beat in the milk,
taking care to keep the mixture smooth. Fold in the
fruits and brandy. Spoon the mixture into a container.
Cover and freeze until firm.

About 20 minutes before serving, transfer the ice
cream to the refrigerator.

Serves 4–5

# Grapefruit Crunch Sandwich

1/2 ounce (15 g) gelatine
1 pound (450 g) soft cheese
6 1/2 fluid ounces (184 g) concentrated frozen
    grapefruit juice, thawed
3 ounces (75 g) caster sugar
1/2 pint (300 ml) double cream, whipped
2 ounces (50 g) digestive biscuits, crushed
2 ounces (50 g) gingernut biscuits, crushed
2 ounces (50 g) butter, melted
1 ounce (25 g) demerara sugar

For decoration
Mint leaves
Knots tied with strips of grapefruit peel

Dissolve the gelatine in 3 tablespoons (45 ml) water in
a bowl placed over a pan of hot water. Set aside to
cool.

Put the cheese in a bowl and beat until smooth.
Gradually beat in the grapefruit juice and caster sugar.
Blend in the cooled gelatine. Fold the cream into the
grapefruit mixture. Spoon half the mixture into a
lightly oiled 8 inch (20 cm) cake tin, preferably a
spring-form or loose-bottomed one. Place this briefly
in the freezer.

Mix the biscuit crumbs with the melted butter and
demerara sugar and leave to cool. Press the crumbs
evenly over the top of the grapefruit mixture in the tin
and cover with the remaining grapefruit mixture.

Cover and freeze until firm.

About 30 minutes before serving turn the sandwich
out on to a cold plate and leave in the refrigerator. Just
before serving decorate with mint leaves and
grapefruit peel knots.

Serves 8

**Flavour variation**
Use frozen concentrated orange juice instead of
grapefruit juice.

# Blackberry and Orange Layer Cake

For the blackberry ice
6 ounces (175 g) caster sugar
2 tablespoons (2 × 15 ml spoons) rose water
1 pound (450 g) blackberries
1 egg white

For the orange butter
4 ounces (100 g) unsalted butter, softened
4 ounces (100 g) caster sugar
Finely grated zest of 2 oranges
Juice of 1 orange or 3 tablespoons (3 × 15 ml spoons)
    orange liqueur
4 ounces (100 g) hazelnuts, toasted and finely ground
4 fluid ounces (100 ml) double cream
Butter
Approximately 24 Sponge Fingers*
Juice of 2 oranges
2 ounces (50 g) Meringues*, roughly crushed

To make the blackberry ice, boil the sugar in 8 fluid
ounces (225 ml) water in a heavy-based saucepan for
10 minutes. Remove from the heat and stir in the rose
water. Leave to cool.

Sieve the blackberries and add the fruit to the syrup.
Pour into a container, cover and freeze until just
becoming slushy. Beat well in a bowl.

Whisk the egg white in a small bowl until stiff. Fold it
into the blackberry mixture.

Meanwhile, make the orange butter: beat the butter
and sugar in a bowl until fluffy. Beat in the orange zest,
juice or liqueur and hazelnuts. Whip the cream until it
stands in soft peaks and fold into the butter.

Thickly butter the side of a 2 pint (1.1 litre) charlotte
mould or bowl. Dip the sponge fingers in the orange
juice and arrange them around the sides and over the
bottom of the mould. Cover the base with half the
orange butter. Spoon half of the slushy blackberry ice
over the orange butter and cover with the crushed
meringues. Place in the freezer until the ice is firm.

Cover the ice with the remaining orange butter.
Place in the freezer until firm, then spoon in the
remaining blackberry ice. Cover and freeze overnight.

About 15 minutes before serving, trim the ends of
the sponge fingers, invert the mould on to a cold plate
and leave in the refrigerator.

Serves 6

# Black Forest Bombe

*For the chocolate ice cream*
*4 ounces (100 g) plain chocolate, broken into small*
  *pieces*
*6 ounces (175 g) soft cheese*
*3½ ounces (90 g) caster sugar*
*8 fluid ounces (225 ml) milk*
*¼ pint (150 ml) double cream*

*For the cherry ice cream*
*3½ ounces (90 g) soft cheese*
*1½ ounces (40 g) caster sugar*
*2 fluid ounces (50 ml) milk*
*2 fluid ounces (50 ml) double cream*
*Approximately 7 ounce (200 g) can cherry pie filling*

*For the plain ice cream*
*3½ ounces (90 g) soft cheese*
*1½ ounces (40 g) caster sugar*
*4 fluid ounces (100 ml) milk*
*2 tablespoons (2 × 15 ml spoons) double cream*

*For decoration*
*Whipped cream*
*Black cherries, stoned*
*Chocolate Curls**

To make the chocolate ice cream, melt the chocolate in a bowl set over a pan of hot water. Leave to cool. Beat the soft cheese and sugar together in a bowl until smooth then beat in the cooled chocolate. Gradually beat in the milk until evenly blended. In another bowl, whip the cream until soft peaks form then fold into the chocolate mixture. Pour into a container, cover and freeze until just becoming firm.

To make the cherry ice cream, beat the soft cheese and sugar together in a bowl until smooth. Gradually beat in the milk. In another bowl, whip the cream until soft peaks form then fold into the cheese mixture. Lastly, fold in about half of the pie filling. Spoon into a container, cover and freeze until just becoming firm.

To make the plain ice cream, beat the soft cheese and sugar together in a bowl until smooth then gradually beat in the milk. In another bowl, whip the cream until soft peaks form then fold into the cheese mixture. Pour into a container, cover and freeze until just becoming firm.

Assemble the bombe by lining a cold 6–7 inch (15–17.5 cm) loose-bottomed cake tin with the chocolate ice cream, making sure there is an even layer over the base and sides. Cover and return to the freezer until firm then line with the cherry ice cream and return to the freezer. Fill the centre with the plain ice cream swirled with the remaining pie filling. Cover and freeze until firm.

About 20–30 minutes before serving, turn the bombe out on to a cold plate and leave in the refrigerator. Decorate with the cream, cherries and chocolate curls.

Serves 8

# Iced Peach Charlotte

*4 ounces (100 g) sugar*
*5 peaches, halved and stoned*
*3 tablespoons (3 × 15 ml spoons) brandy*
*Approximately 20 Sponge Fingers**
*Sherry*
*¾ pint (450 ml) whipping or double cream*
*2 ounces (50 g) desiccated coconut*
*1 ounce (25 g) lightly toasted flaked almonds*
*Whipped cream, for decoration*

In a heavy-based saucepan, dissolve the sugar in ½ pint (300 ml) water. Add the peaches and poach until tender. Remove the peaches with a slotted spoon and set aside on a plate. Return the pan to the heat and boil the syrup until reduced by two-thirds. Remove from the heat and stir in the brandy.

Line a charlotte mould with the sponge fingers and sprinkle them with sherry.

Put the cream and the brandy syrup in a bowl and whip until soft peaks form. Peel and chop the peaches and fold into the cream with the coconut and almonds.

Spoon the mixture into the mould, cover and freeze until firm. About 15 minutes before serving, unmould the charlotte on to a cold plate. Decorate with whipped cream.

Serves 6

# Apricot and Hazelnut Meringue Cake

*For the meringue*
*4 egg whites*
*9 ounces (250 g) caster sugar*
*2–3 drops vanilla essence*
*3 ounces (75 g) hazelnuts, ground*

*For the filling*
*2 ounces (50 g) dried apricots soaked in 7 fluid*
  *ounces (200 ml) strained tea*
*Long strip lemon peel*
*2 ounces (50 g) caster sugar*
*½ pint (300 ml) crème fraîche, whipped, or whipped*
  *cream*

*For decoration*
*Whipped cream*
*Chocolate dragées or Chocolate Curls**
*Apricot Sauce**

Prepare the meringue according to the recipe on page 150, adding the nuts with the last of the sugar. Mark two 8 inch (20 cm) circles on waxed paper and place on a baking sheet. Spread the meringue over the circles. Put the baking sheet in the oven and bake at 275°F (140°C, gas mark 1) for 50 minutes.

Remove the baking sheet from the oven. Peel away the paper and leave the meringues to cool on a rack.

To make the filling, put the apricots and their soaking liquor with the lemon peel in a saucepan and cook for about 15 minutes until tender. Remove the lemon peel, and purée into a bowl. Stir in the sugar and leave to become cold. Fold the crème fraîche or cream into the apricot purée.

Place one of the meringues upside down on a freezer-proof tray or plate and spread with the apricot cream. Cover with the other meringue and place in the freezer. When firm, cover to protect the meringue from being broken and return to the freezer.

About 10 minutes before serving, decorate with the whipped cream and chocolate dragées or curls. Leave in the refrigerator. Serve the apricot sauce separately.

Serves 6

# Mincemeat Ice Cream

*8 ounces (225 g) mincemeat*
*2 fluid ounces (50 ml) brandy*
*½ pint (300 ml) cream, whipped*
*2 egg whites*

Mix the mincemeat with the brandy in a bowl and fold into the cream. In another bowl, whisk the egg whites until stiff but not dry. Carefully fold them into the mincemeat cream. Spoon the mixture into a container. Cover and freeze until firm.

About 20 minutes before serving, transfer the ice cream to the refrigerator.

Serves 4

**Serving suggestion**
*Accompany each serving with a sprig of holly.*

# Lemon Icicle

Butter
2 ounces (50 g) ginger biscuits, finely crushed
3 eggs, separated
4 ounces (100 g) caster sugar
1/2 pint (300 ml) double cream
Finely grated zest and juice of 2 lemons

For decoration
Twisted lemon slices
Whipped cream

Fairly thickly butter a 2¼ pint (1.3 litre) loaf tin and sprinkle with the ginger biscuit crumbs to coat evenly.

Whisk the egg whites in a bowl until very stiff. Gradually add the sugar, whisking well after each addition, until the mixture is very thick.

In another bowl, whisk the cream with the egg yolks until thick and light. Carefully fold the egg yolk mixture into the egg whites with the lemon zest and juice. Pour into the biscuit-lined tin, cover and freeze until firm.

About 10 minutes before serving the dessert turn out on to a cold plate and leave in the refrigerator. Decorate with twisted lemon slices and whipped cream just before serving.

Serves 6–8

# Chocolate Truffle and Hazelnut Ring

1¼ pints (700 ml) single cream
8 ounces (225 g) caster sugar
7 egg yolks, beaten
4 ounces (100 g) cocoa powder
6 fluid ounces (175 ml) whipping cream
6 ounces (175 g) good-quality plain chocolate
2 fluid ounces (50 ml) praline or other nut liqueur
1 ounce (25 g) hazelnuts, toasted and chopped
1 tablespoon (15 ml spoon) Grand Marnier

For decoration
Whipped cream
Chocolate Curls*

In a heavy-based saucepan, gently heat the single cream and sugar until the sugar has dissolved. Bring to the boil, remove from the heat and leave to cool for 5 minutes. Pour the cream on to the egg yolks whisking constantly. Return the mixture to the rinsed pan and cook over a gentle heat, stirring constantly, until the custard thickens but do not allow it to boil. Remove from the heat and whisk in the cocoa powder, leave to cool then chill well.

Pour the custard into a container. Cover and freeze until just becoming firm.

Warm the whipping cream in a saucepan. Add the chocolate and stir until it has melted. Mix in the nut liqueur, hazelnuts and Grand Marnier then cool completely.

Line the bottom of a 2 pint (1.1 litre) ring mould with three-quarters of the chocolate ice cream. With a small spoon push the ice cream up the sides of the mould leaving a deep groove in the centre. If necessary, place in the freezer for a few minutes to firm up. Pour the cream and hazelnut mixture into the groove and spread the remaining ice cream over the top. Cover and freeze until firm.

About 30 minutes before serving, turn the ice cream out on to a cold plate and leave in the refrigerator. Decorate with whipped cream and chocolate curls just before serving.

Serves 8–10

# Chestnut and Chocolate Bombe

3/4 pint (450 g) Chocolate Ice Cream (page 44), slightly softened
4 ounces (100 g) canned whole chestnuts in syrup, drained and chopped
4 ounces (100 g) canned, sweetened chestnut purée
1 tablespoon (15 ml spoon) brandy
6 fluid ounces (175 ml) double cream
1 small egg white

For decoration
Whipped cream
Candied orange or lemon peel, roughly chopped
Marrons glacés, sliced

Spoon the chocolate ice cream into a cold 1½ pint (850 ml) bombe mould or bowl, smoothing it into an even layer over the base and sides to a depth of about 3/4 inch (20 mm) using the back of a metal spoon. Cover and freeze until firm.

Press the chopped chestnuts into the base and sides of the ice cream-lined mould, cover and return to the freezer.

Mix the chestnut purée and brandy together until well blended. Whisk the cream in a bowl until it stands in soft peaks. Gently fold into the chestnut purée. Whisk the egg white in a small bowl until stiff but not dry. Carefully fold it into the chestnut cream. Spoon the chestnut cream into the mould, cover and freeze until firm.

About 30 minutes before serving turn the bombe out on to a cold serving plate and leave in the coldest part of the refrigerator. Just before serving decorate with whipped cream, candied orange or lemon peel and slices of marrons glacés.

Serves 5–6

# Iced Lemon Soufflé Surprise

*For the filling*
*2 ounces (50 g) caster sugar*
*2 fluid ounces (50 ml) lemon juice*
*1½ ounces (40 g) unsalted butter*
*2 large egg yolks*
*1 tablespoon (15 ml spoon) finely grated lemon zest*

*For the soufflé*
*5 egg yolks*
*5 ounces (150 g) caster sugar*
*3 fluid ounces (75 ml) lemon juice*
*1 tablespoon (15 ml spoon) finely grated lemon zest*
*½ pint (300 ml) double cream*

First make the filling. Put all the ingredients together in a bowl set over a pan of hot water. Whisk for about 8 minutes until the mixture is thick enough to coat the back of a spoon but do not let it boil. Leave to cool before chilling until firm.

Tie strips of double thickness greaseproof paper or foil around 6 individual freezer-proof soufflé dishes, so that they form collars over and above the tops of the dishes.

To make the soufflé, in a bowl whisk the egg yolks briefly. Put the sugar, lemon juice and 3 fluid ounces (75 ml) water in a saucepan and stir to dissolve. Add the lemon zest and bring to the boil. Whisk the hot syrup into the egg yolks. Put the bowl over a pan of hot water, whisking constantly, until the mixture is very light and thickened. Leave to cool, stirring occasionally.

Whip 8 fluid ounces (225 ml) of the cream until soft peaks form. Fold into the cold soufflé. Divide half of this mixture between the prepared dishes.

Whip the remaining cream until soft peaks form. Reserve and keep chilled 2 tablespoons (30 ml) of the lemon filling. Fold the cream into the remaining filling and divide between the soufflés. Cover with the remaining soufflé mixture, then cover and freeze until firm.

Spoon the reserved filling into a piping bag fitted with a small star nozzle (freeze the mixture if it is too runny to pipe). Pipe a star or rosette in the centre of each soufflé (if these are frozen solid leave them in the refrigerator for 15 minutes first).

Serves 6

# Orange Sorbet in a Chocolate Case

*Oil*
*8 ounces (225 g) plain chocolate, chopped*
*4 ounces (100 g) sugar*
*Finely grated zest of 1 orange*
*13 fluid ounces (375 ml) orange juice*
*4 tablespoons (4 × 15 ml spoons) lemon juice*
*1 large egg white*

*For decoration*
*Strips of orange peel*
*Whipped cream*

Liberally oil a 1½ pint (850 ml) mould and leave it upside down to drain. Put the mould in the refrigerator to chill.

Melt the chocolate in a bowl set over a pan of hot water. As soon as it has melted pour it into the mould. Tip and rotate the mould to coat the inside evenly and completely. Put the mould in a bowl of crushed ice and tip and rotate it so that it remains evenly coated until it has set. Return the mould to the refrigerator.

In a heavy-based saucepan, dissolve the sugar in ¼ pint (150 ml) water. Bring to the boil and boil for 5 minutes. Remove from the heat, stir in the orange zest and fruit juices and leave to cool.

Pour the mixture into a container. Cover and freeze until just becoming firm. Beat well in a bowl.

Lightly whisk the egg white in a small bowl. Whisk it into the frozen mixture. Spoon the sorbet into the chocolate-lined mould. Cover and freeze until firm. Just before serving turn the dessert out on to a cold plate and decorate with strips of orange peel and whipped cream.

Serves 4–6

---

**To reduce your sugar intake**
Replace the sugar with half the quantity of **fructose** or with an **artificial sweetener**, provided the recipe does not call for a sugar syrup. Normally, 3–4 artificial sweeteners are the equivalent of 1 ounce (25 g) sugar but always check that you have the right degree of sweetness. Artificial sweeteners must be added to custard-based ice creams after the custard has cooled.

# Creating Desserts

Delicious on its own, ice cream can be even more delectable if it is served with a flourish. Some serving ideas are simple – just sprinkle the ice with a topping of your choice. Others, using a specially made sauce or accompaniments like Cigars Russe* and Almond Tuiles* involve rather more preparation. And, of course, there are almost endless combinations of different-flavoured ices, with biscuits, meringues, cakes and so on, in plain or shaped containers.

This chapter includes the sauces, accompaniments and decorations called for in the serving and dessert suggestions that follow the main recipes, as well as basic recipes for meringues, crêpes, choux pastry, etc, plus a description of the techniques involved in creating iced cakes and desserts and suggestions for unusual containers.

## Coupes and Sundaes

Among the simplest of ice cream desserts, these include a number of classic dishes:

**Poire Belle Hèlene:** vanilla ice cream, pears and hot chocolate sauce.

**Pêche Melba:** vanilla ice cream, peaches and raspberry sauce.

**Pêche Cardinale:** strawberry ice cream, peaches and redcurrant jelly.

**Champagne Charlie:** champagne ice cream, macaroons with champagne poured over.

**Café Liègoise:** coffee ice cream in a tall glass topped with a large swirl of whipped cream.

Alternatively, think up your own combinations to suit the ingredients you have and the occasion.

## Simple Toppings

The following suggestions involve little or no preparation.

Chopped or flaked, plain or toasted nuts
Desiccated coconut: colour green or pink, if desired, by putting into a jar, adding some colouring and shaking vigorously, then leaving to dry before using
Chocolate toppings: grated plain chocolate; crumbled flaky bars; chopped chocolate matchsticks; drinking chocolate
Cocoa or malted drink powder
Candied or crystallized fruit, chopped or whole
Peanut brittle; peppermints or peppermint rock; butterscotch or caramel
Crushed biscuits: gingersnaps, macaroons, etc
Crushed meringues
Fresh herbs, leaves and flowers
Crystallized roses and violets
Whipped cream: flavour to taste with liqueurs, orange flower water and so on. For a peppermint flavour, add peppermint oil or crème de menthe to taste

Fruit zests and peels: grated; cut into long, fine strips; cut into shapes with aspic cutters or the point of a sharp, small knife
Marrons glâcés, chopped or sliced
Chocolate or coffee dragées, or any small, candy decorations

## Sauces

The right sauce enhances and complements the flavour and texture of an ice. Spoon it over, to trickle down the sides, or arrange it around the ice like the frame of a picture. It can be hot, cold or warm – but should never swamp the ice cream itself.

### Butterscotch Sauce

*2 ounces (50 g) unsalted butter, diced*
*2 ounces (50 g) demerara sugar*
*2 ounces (50 g) golden syrup or corn syrup*
*¼ pint (150 ml) milk*
*Squeeze of lemon juice, optional*

Heat the butter, sugar and syrup in a heavy-based saucepan over low heat, stirring, until the sugar has dissolved. Bring to the boil and boil until the temperature reaches about 240°F (116°C). Cool slightly then stir in the milk and leave to cool completely. Add a squeeze of lemon juice to taste, if liked.

Serves 4–5

**Nutty Butterscotch Sauce**

Add 1 ounce (25 g) chopped walnuts, almonds, hazelnuts or peanuts with the milk.

### Black Cherry Sauce

*4 ounces (100 g) Morello cherry jam*
*Knob of butter*
*1 tablespoon (15 ml spoon) kirsch or brandy*
*Squeeze of lemon juice*

Put the jam, butter and ½ pint (300 ml) hot water in a saucepan and heat until evenly mixed and syrupy. Remove from the heat and stir in the kirsch or brandy and a squeeze of lemon juice to taste. Serve as it is or purée in a blender or food processor for a smooth sauce.

Serves 4–6

**Alcoholic Cherry Sauce**

For a spectacular cherry sauce, warm the fruit from a 15 ounce (approximately 430 g) can of stoneless black cherries with about half of the juice, pour 2 tablespoons (2 × 15 ml spoons) brandy over and ignite. When the flames have subsided add 1 tablespoon (15 ml spoon) kirsch and serve at once.

## Bitter Chocolate Sauce

4 ounces (100 g) good-quality plain chocolate,
    chopped
1 teaspoon (5 ml spoon) caster sugar
6 tablespoons (6 × 15 ml spoons) milk
2 tablespoons (2 × 15 ml spoons) whipping cream
3/4 ounce (20 g) unsalted butter

Melt the chocolate in a bowl set over a pan of hot
water. Put the sugar, milk, cream and butter in a
saucepan and stir to dissolve. Bring to the boil and stir
it on to the melted chocolate. Pour this mixture back
into the pan and bring to the boil, stirring. Pour it back
into the bowl and leave to cool, stirring occasionally.

Serves 4–6

## Hot Chocolate Sauce

4 ounces (100 g) plain chocolate, chopped
1 ounce (25 g) icing sugar
1/2 ounce (15 g) unsalted butter, chopped

Place all the ingredients in a bowl with 2 fluid ounces
(50 ml) hot water and place over a pan of hot water.
Heat until the chocolate has melted, stir well and serve
hot or warm.

Serves 4

## Coffee Sauce

4 ounces (100 g) sugar
1/2 pint (300 ml) strong black coffee
2 tablespoons (2 × 15 ml spoons) coffee liqueur,
    optional

Dissolve the sugar in 2 tablespoons (30 ml) water in a
heavy-based saucepan. Bring to the boil and boil until
the mixture becomes a light golden brown. Stir in the
coffee to dissolve the caramel and simmer for a few
minutes until it becomes slightly syrupy. Remove from
the heat and stir in the liqueur, if using.

Serves 4

## Hot Fudge Sauce

6 fluid ounces (175 ml) whipping or double cream
2 ounces (50 g) unsalted butter, chopped
3 ounces (75 g) soft brown sugar

Heat the cream and butter in a heavy-based saucepan
over low heat until the butter has melted, stirring
constantly. Stir in the sugar and continue stirring until
the sugar has dissolved and the mixture comes to the
boil. Boil for 2 minutes until thick and glossy.

Serves 4–6

## Burnt Honey Sauce

8 ounces (225 g) sugar
4 ounces (100 g) clear honey

In a heavy-based saucepan, dissolve the sugar in 4
tablespoons (60 ml) water. Bring to the boil and boil
for 5 minutes or until it becomes a deep brown
caramel. Off the heat stir in another 4 tablespoons
(60 ml) water, taking care as the mixture will splutter.
Cook for another 1–2 minutes until the temperature
reaches 240°F (116°C). Stir in the honey and remove
from the heat. Leave to cool.

Serves 6–8

## Chunky Marmalade Sauce

3 tablespoons (3 × 15 ml spoons) chunky marmalade
1/4 pint (150 ml) orange juice
Finely grated zest of 1 orange
Squeeze of lemon juice
2 tablespoons (2 × 15 ml spoons) whisky, optional

Gently warm the marmalade, orange juice and zest and
lemon juice together in a saucepan until the
marmalade has melted. Stir in the whisky, if using.
Serve warm.

Serves 4

### Apricot Sauce

Substitute apricot jam for the marmalade. Brandy or
rum could be substituted for the whisky.

## Fresh Fruit Sauces

Purée fresh fruit and sweeten to taste with icing sugar.
Spoon over the ice cream. Sieve raspberries,
blackberries, etc., to get rid of any pips. This is
unnecessary with fruits such as apricots unless you
want a really smooth sauce. Always remember to
remove the pith and membrane from oranges before
puréeing.

For a really dramatic effect, warm a tablespoon
(15 ml spoon) of liqueur or spirit. Ignite it and pour it,
still flaming, over the sauce after it has been spooned
over the ice. The cool richness of the ice will mingle
and contrast with the fresh warmth of the fruit sauce
and the extra 'kick' of the liqueur.

### Caramel Fruit Sauce

Heat and stir Caramelized* fruit zest in orange or other
fruit juice.

## Orange Flower Sauce

*2 egg yolks*
*2 ounces (50 g) sugar*
*8 fluid ounces (225 ml) cream*
*1 tablespoon (15 ml spoon) orange flower water*

Whisk the egg yolks and sugar together in a bowl until light. In a heavy-based saucepan, heat the cream to just below simmering point then whisk into the egg yolks. Return the mixture to the rinsed pan and cook over a low heat, stirring constantly, until the mixture thickens. Remove from the heat and stir in the orange flower water. Leave to cool, whisking occasionally.

Serves 6

## Wine Sauce

*7 fluid ounces (200 ml) dry red or white wine*
*2 cloves*
*½ cinnamon stick*
*Strip of lemon peel*
*Strip of orange peel*
*2 ounces (50 g) sugar*
*1 tablespoon (15 ml spoon) cornflour*
*2 tablespoons (2 × 15 ml spoons) redcurrant jelly or port*

Put the wine, cloves, cinnamon, lemon and orange peel and sugar in a saucepan and gradually bring to just below simmering point. Cover the pan and leave over a very low heat for about 20 minutes.

Blend the cornflour with 2 tablespoons (30 ml) water in a bowl. Strain in the spiced wine, stirring. Return to the pan and cook over a low heat, stirring, until the sauce thickens. Continue to cook for 1–2 minutes then stir in the redcurrant jelly or port. Taste and adjust the sweetness, adding more sugar if necessary.

Serves 6

## Low Calorie Topping

*2 ounces (50 g) skimmed milk powder*
*2 teaspoons (2 × 5 ml spoons) lemon juice*
*Sweetener, to taste*
*Few drops of vanilla essence, optional*

Reconstitute the milk powder with ¼ pint (150 ml) very cold water and stir in the lemon juice and sweetener together with the vanilla essence, if using. Whisk until the mixture has doubled in volume and is very thick. Leave in a cool place for 30 minutes.

Serves 4

## Quick Sauces

(All serve 4)

### Sweet and Sour Treacle Sauce

*¼ pint (150 ml) soured cream*
*1 teaspoon (5 ml spoon) black treacle*
*1 teaspoon (5 ml spoon) caster sugar*

Blend all the ingredients together. To serve hot, warm in a bowl set over a pan of hot water.

### Marshmallow Sauce

*4 ounces (100 g) marshmallows, chopped*
*¼ pint (150 ml) single cream*

Whisk the marshmallows with the cream in a bowl set over a pan of hot water.

### Caramel Sauce

*4 ounces (100 g) caramel sweets*
*¼ pint (150 ml) single cream*

Melt the caramels in the cream in a bowl set over a pan of hot water then whisk until smooth.

### Mars Bar Sauce

*1 Mars Bar, chopped*

Heat the Mars Bar in a bowl set over a pan of hot water until smooth.

## Praline

*4 ounces (100 g) caster sugar*
*4 ounces (100 g) shelled, unpeeled almonds or hazelnuts*

In a heavy-based pan, dissolve the sugar in 3 fluid ounces (75 ml) water. Add the almonds and boil for about 10 minutes until golden brown. Pour on to a cold, oiled surface and leave until set. Then place in a thick polythene bag or clean cloth and hit with a rolling pin until the praline has broken into small pieces.

# Cakes, Biscuits and Decorations

This section includes biscuits and other extras to serve with ices. There are also recipes for ingredients called for in some of the dessert suggestions in the main part of the book, and instructions on how to make decorations for party spectaculars.

## Almond Tuiles

2 egg whites
1½ ounces (40 g) unsalted butter, softened
¼ teaspoon (1.25 ml spoon) finely grated orange zest
3 ounces (75 g) caster sugar
Pinch of salt
3 tablespoons (3 × 15 ml spoons) plain flour
1 tablespoon (15 ml spoon) cornflour
1 ounce (25 g) ground almonds
Few drops almond essence and vanilla essence
2 ounces (50 g) flaked almonds

Lightly grease and flour 2 baking sheets.

Put the egg whites in a bowl and beat very lightly with a fork. In another bowl, beat the butter, orange zest, sugar and salt together until fluffy and light. Gradually add the egg whites, beating well after each addition.

Sift the flours together then fold into the beaten mixture with the ground almonds and essences.

Drop spoonfuls of the mixture on to the baking sheets, adjusting the size according to the size of tuile required. Leave plenty of space between them to allow for spreading. With a damp knife spread each spoonful out to a thin disc. Sprinkle each one with flaked almonds.

Bake in an oven preheated to 425°F (220°C, gas mark 7) for 5–7 minutes until they are golden and tinged brown around the edges. Immediately they come out of the oven remove them with a palette knife and drape around a rolling pin with the almonds outermost. Leave to harden into shape then carefully transfer to a wire rack to cool completely.

Makes approximately 20

### Almond Tuiles with Orange Flower Water

Beat a few drops of orange flower water into the butter with the orange zest, sugar and salt.

## Choux Pastry

2½ ounces (65 g) plain flour
2 ounces (50 g) butter, diced
1 teaspoon (5 ml spoon) caster sugar
2 large eggs, beaten

Sift the flour on to a sheet of greaseproof paper. Put the butter, sugar and ¼ pint (150 ml) water in a saucepan over low heat. Stir to dissolve then bring to the boil rapidly. Remove from the heat and immediately shoot all the flour in at once and beat vigorously with a wooden spoon to form a stiff paste. Return the pan to the heat and cook for 30 seconds to 1 minute, beating, until the mixture forms a smooth ball. Remove from the heat and leave to cool slightly. Gradually add the eggs, beating well after each addition and making sure that it is incorporated before adding any more. Beat until the mixture is a smooth, shiny, stiff paste.

Spoon the mixture into a piping bag fitted with a plain ½ inch (1.25 cm) nozzle. Holding the bag at right angles to a greased baking sheet, pipe ½–1 inch (1.25–2.5 cm) balls, depending on the size of shell you want. Bake in an oven preheated to 425°F (220°C, gas mark 7) for 10 minutes. Remove the choux balls from the oven and lower the temperature to 325°F (170°C, gas mark 3). Pierce a small hole in the sides of the choux balls and return them to the oven for about 15 minutes to dry. Transfer to a wire rack to cool.

Makes 4–6

## Cigars Russe

2 egg whites
4 ounces (100 g) icing sugar, sifted
1½ ounces (40 g) plain flour, sifted
2½ ounces (65 g) unsalted butter, melted
Few drops of vanilla essence

Lightly grease and flour 2 baking sheets.

Put the egg whites in a bowl and whisk until stiff. Whisk in the sugar followed by the flour. Beat in the melted butter and vanilla essence. Drop 2 or 3 spoonfuls of the mixture on to a baking sheet leaving plenty of room between them. With a wetted knife spread each spoonful out and bake in an oven preheated to 400°F (200°C, gas mark 6) for 5–6 minutes until golden brown.

Meanwhile, place another 2 or 3 spoonfuls on another baking sheet in a similar way and put in the oven half-way through the baking of the first batch. When the first spoonfuls are ready, immediately remove them with a palette knife or fish slice and wrap them around the handle of an oiled wooden spoon. Leave to harden then slip off. Repeat until all the mixture is used.

Makes approximately 18

### Cinnamon-flavoured Cigars Russe

Sift ½ teaspoon (2.5 ml spoon) ground cinnamon with the flour before whisking it into the egg whites.

## Coupelles

*2 ounces (50 g) unsalted butter*
*2 egg whites*
*2½ ounces (65 g) caster sugar*
*2 ounces (50 g) plain flour*

Lightly grease a baking sheet.

Put the butter in a small saucepan and melt over gentle heat, then allow to cool. Whisk the egg whites in a bowl until frothy. Whisk in the sugar and continue to whisk for 2–3 minutes until thick. Gently fold in the flour together with the melted butter.

Drop 3 spoonfuls on to the baking sheet and spread each one out to a circle 4 inches (10 cm) in diameter. Bake in an oven preheated to 400°F (200°C, gas mark 6) for 5–7 minutes until the edges are golden brown.

Carefully but quickly remove the biscuits with a spatula or fish slice and quickly shape around the bottom of an orange or apple or small ramekin dish. When set to shape remove from the mould and leave to cool completely on a wire cooling rack.

Cook the remaining mixture, using a cool baking sheet each time and shape the biscuits as above.

Store carefully in tins or airtight containers.

Makes 8–10

### Lightly Spiced Coupelles

Sift ¼ teaspoon (1.25 ml spoon) ground mixed spice with the flour and fold into the egg whites with the melted butter.

### Almond-flavoured Coupelles

Mix 1 ounce (25 g) finely chopped flaked almonds with the flour and butter and fold into the egg whites.

## Crêpes

*1½ ounces (40 g) plain flour*
*Pinch of salt*
*1 egg, beaten*
*1 tablespoon (15 ml spoon) melted butter*
*3 fluid ounces (75 ml) milk*

Sift the flour and salt into a bowl and form a well in the centre. Pour the egg and butter into the well. Using a spoon, stir the egg, gradually drawing in the flour. Stir until smooth. Slowly stir in the milk to make a smooth batter. Leave to stand for 2 hours.

Heat a small frying pan or crêpe pan, grease it and spoon in 2–3 tablespoons (30–45 ml) of the batter, depending on the size of the pan. Tilt the pan so that the batter coats the base evenly then cook over a medium heat for 1 minute. Turn the crêpe over and cook the other side for 1 minute. Remove the crêpe and repeat until all the batter is used up. Stack the crêpes as they are made and keep them warm.

Makes 6 crêpes

### Serving suggestion

Enclose an iced mixture, and perhaps some fruit, inside a small crêpe. Fold the crêpe over and tuck in the ends. Secure with a cocktail stick and deep fry at 375°F (190°C) for 2–3 minutes. Serve at once with a sprinkling of icing sugar.

## Genoise Cake

*4 eggs*
*4 ounces (100 g) caster sugar*
*4 ounces (100 g) plain flour, sifted*
*2 ounces (50 g) clarified butter, runny but not melted*

Line two 9 inch (22 cm) sandwich tins with greased greaseproof paper.

Put the eggs and sugar in a bowl and whisk together until very thick and light. Very carefully fold in the flour. Pour in the butter and fold it into the mixture until just evenly incorporated.

Turn into the cake tin and bake in an oven preheated to 375°F (190°C, gas mark 5) for about 30–35 minutes or until the cake shrinks slightly from the sides of the tin and the top feels springy to the touch. Leave to cool slightly before turning out, removing the paper and leaving to cool on a wire rack.

### Coconut Cake

Stir 2 ounces (50 g) desiccated coconut into the flour and fold into the egg mixture.

### Moist Ginger Cake

Stir 1 teaspoon (15 ml spoon) ground ginger with the flour and fold into the egg mixture.

## Gingersnap Baskets

*2 ounces (50 g) golden syrup*
*2 ounces (50 g) butter*
*5 ounces (150 g) caster sugar*
*2 ounces (50 g) plain flour*
*1 teaspoon (5 ml spoon) ground ginger*
*½ teaspoon (2.5 ml spoon) finely grated lemon zest*
*½ teaspoon (2.5 ml spoon) lemon juice*

Lightly grease a baking sheet.

Put the syrup, butter and sugar in a saucepan and heat gently until the sugar has dissolved. Remove from the heat and fold in the remaining ingredients. Drop 3 tablespoons (3 × 15 ml spoons) on to the baking sheet, leaving room for the mixture to spread. Bake in an oven preheated to 350°F (180°C, gas mark 4) for 7–10 minutes until golden brown.

Quickly but carefully remove with a spatula or fish slice and mould around the base of an orange, apple or a small ramekin dish or bowl. When set, remove from the moulds and leave to cool on a wire rack. Bake and shape the remaining mixture in the same way.

Makes 8-10

### Gingersnaps

Drop teaspoonfuls of the mixture on to the baking sheet. Using a spatula or fish slice, quickly but carefully transfer the cooked biscuits to a cooling rack to cool.

### Gingersnap Cones

When the mixture has cooked until it is golden brown, remove from the baking sheet with a palette knife or fish slice and mould around lightly greased cream horns. Leave to cool then carefully slip off the tins.

### Gingersnaps Shaped Like Cigars Russe

Bake in batches. When the mixture has cooked until it is golden brown, remove the snaps from the baking sheet with a palette knife or fish slice and wrap them around the handle of an oiled wooden spoon. Leave to harden then slip off. Repeat until the mixture is finished.

## Ice Cream Cones

*2 egg whites*
*4 ounces (100 g) caster sugar*
*2 ounces (50 g) plain flour, sifted*
*3 tablespoons (3 × 15 ml spoons) melted unsalted*
*    butter*

Line baking sheets with silicone paper or foil.

Put the egg whites in a bowl and whisk until stiff. Fold in half the sugar and whisk again until stiff. Fold in the remaining sugar, then the flour and butter.

Drop spoonfuls of the mixture on to the baking sheets and bake in an oven preheated to 400°F (200°C, gas mark 6) for about 3–4 minutes or until a light brown around the edges. Carefully remove from the tray with a palette knife or fish slice and mould around lightly greased cream horn tins. Leave to cool then carefully slip off the tins.

Makes approximately 14

### Coated Ice Cream Cones

Brush the outside of the cones with egg white and dip in 100's and 1000's, toasted or coloured coconut, very finely chopped nuts or chocolate vermicelli. Or brush the cones with melted plain chocolate.

## Langues de Chat

*2 ounces (50 g) butter*
*2 ounces (50 g) caster sugar*
*1 egg, beaten*
*2 ounces (50 g) plain flour, sifted*
*2 ounces (50 g) plain chocolate, optional*

Lightly grease and flour a baking sheet.

Put the butter in a bowl and cream until well softened. Beat in the sugar and continue to beat until the mixture is light and fluffy. Gradually beat in the egg then carefully fold in the flour.

Spoon the mixture into a piping bag fitted with a ½ inch (1.25 cm) plain nozzle. Pipe finger lengths on to the baking sheet, leaving sufficient room in between them to allow for spreading.

Bake in an oven preheated to 425°F (220°C, gas mark 7) for 4–5 minutes until lightly browned around the edges. Carefully remove from the baking tray with a spatula or fish slice and leave on a wire tray to cool.

If using the chocolate, melt it in a bowl set over a pan of hot water and dip the ends of the langues de chat in it. Leave to set on a wire tray.

Makes about 15

### Round Biscuits

Drop teaspoonfuls of the mixture on to the baking sheet, spacing well apart. Bake for 5–7 minutes until golden brown. If the edges are too brown, cut them off with a biscuit cutter.

## Meringues

*2 large egg whites*
*4 ounces (100 g) sugar*

Line a baking tray with silicone paper.

Whisk the egg whites until very stiff. Add half the sugar a teaspoon (5 ml spoon) at a time, whisking well after each addition. Lightly fold in the remaining sugar. Spoon the meringue mixture into a piping bag fitted with a plain ½ inch (1.25 cm) nozzle and pipe 16 balls or swirled shapes on to the tray, or use 2 tablespoons (2 × 15 ml spoons) to shape shells. Bake in an oven preheated to 225°F (110°C, gas mark ¼) for 2–2½ hours. Remove and cool.

Makes 16

### Coconut Meringues

Fold in 2 ounces (50 g) desiccated coconut with the last of the sugar.

### Hazelnut or Almond Meringues

Fold in 2 ounces (50 g) ground hazelnuts or ground almonds with the last of the sugar.

### Chocolate Meringues

Fold in 2 tablespoons (2 × 15 ml spoons) cocoa powder with the last of the sugar.

### Coffee Meringues

Dissolve 2 teaspoons (2 × 5 ml spoons) good-quality instant coffee in very little water and whisk into the egg whites with the sugar.

### Meringues with Orange Flower Water

Add a few drops of orange flower water with the last of the sugar.

### Tiny Meringues

Use a ¼ inch (15 mm) nozzle or 2 teaspoons (2 × 5 ml spoons) to shape the shells. Bake for about 45 minutes at 225°F (110°C, gas mark ¼).

## Meringue Fingers

Using a plain ½ inch (1.25 cm) nozzle pipe approximately 2¼ inch (6.5 cm) lengths. Bake for 1–1½ hours at 225°F (110°C, gas mark ¼).

## Meringue Bases

Line a baking tray with silicone paper. Mark the size and shape of base you require on the paper. Fill in the shape with piped meringue or lightly spread out the meringue with a palette knife. Bake at 225°F (110°C, gas mark ¼) for about 1 hour for small shapes, 2 hours for large ones.

## Meringue Basket

Line 6 baking trays, or as many surfaces as necessary, with silicone paper. Mark six 8–9 inch (20–22.5 cm) circles on the trays. Make the base by filling in one circle with meringue, either by spreading it with a palette knife or piping with a plain ½ inch (1.25 cm) nozzle in concentric circles. Make the sides of the basket by piping a single circle of meringue on each of the remaining shapes. Bake at 225°F (110°C, gas mark ¼) for about 1½ hours. Remove the silicone paper, cool the meringues then stack the rings on the base.

## Individual Meringue Baskets

Line a baking tray with silicone paper. Mark four to six 3–4 inch (7.5–10 cm) circles on the paper. Pipe the meringue on to the lines in concentric circles to make the bases. Then pipe 2 circles, one on top of the other, around the circumference of the base. Bake at 225°F (110°C, gas mark ¼) for about 2 hours.

## Macaroons

*4 ounces (100 g) ground almonds or hazelnuts*
*5 ounces (150 g) caster sugar*
*2 egg whites*
*Few drops of vanilla essence*

Line a baking sheet with rice paper or oiled foil.

Mix the nuts and sugar together. Whisk the egg whites until stiff then carefully fold in the ground nut mixture with the vanilla essence.

Place small spoonfuls of the mixture on the baking sheet, leaving room in between them to allow for spreading. Bake in an oven preheated to 350°F (180°C, gas mark 4) for about 20 minutes until the tops are lightly browned. Cool on a wire rack.

Makes 15–25 depending on size

## Sponge Fingers

*3 eggs, separated*
*3 ounces (75 g) caster sugar*
*3½ ounces (90 g) plain flour, sifted*
*2 drops vanilla essence*
*Sifted icing sugar*

Line baking sheets with greased greaseproof paper.

Put the egg yolks and sugar in a bowl and whisk until very thick and pale. In another bowl, whisk the egg whites until stiff then fold into the egg yolk mixture with the flour and vanilla essence.

Spoon into a piping bag fitted with a plain ½ inch (1.25 cm) nozzle and pipe finger lengths on to the baking sheets.

Dust with sifted icing sugar and bake in an oven preheated to 350°F (180°C, gas mark 4) for 10–13 minutes. Carefully remove the paper and leave the fingers to cool on a wire tray.

Makes about 20

## Whisked Sponge Cake

*3 eggs, separated*
*3 ounces (75 g) caster sugar*
*3 ounces (75 g) plain flour, sifted*
*Pinch of salt*

Line two 8 inch (20 cm) sandwich tins with greaseproof paper.

Put the egg yolks and sugar in a bowl and whisk until very thick and light. Whisk the egg whites in another bowl until stiff. Fold into the egg yolk mixture with the flour and salt.

Turn into the tins and bake in an oven preheated to 350°F (180°C, gas mark 4) for 20–25 minutes or until a light golden colour, springy to the touch and slightly shrunken from the edges of the tin.

Leave to cool slightly before turning out, removing the paper and leaving to cool on a wire rack.

### Chocolate Cake

Replace ¾ ounce (20 g) flour with the same amount of cocoa powder.

### Swiss Roll

Spoon the whisked sponge into a 9 × 13 inch (23 × 33 cm) Swiss roll tin and bake in an oven preheated to 400°F (200°C, gas mark 6) for 8–10 minutes. Turn the cake out on to a sheet of greaseproof paper, sprinkled with caster sugar, resting on a warm, dampened tea towel. Peel away the lining paper and roll up the cake with the sugared paper inside and leave to cool. Unroll the cake, remove the greaseproof paper, spread with the filling and roll up again.

### Chocolate Roll

Replace 1 tablespoon (15 ml spoon) flour with the same amount of cocoa powder. Follow the instructions for making a Swiss roll.

## Chocolate Containers and Decorations

### Chocolate Squares

To make simple chocolate squares, break a bar of cooking chocolate into a small bowl and place it over a pan of hot water. Line a baking tray with silicone paper and carefully pour the melted chocolate over it. Spread the chocolate quite thickly over the paper with a palette knife and leave it to set. Using a ruler as a guide, mark out the squares and cut them out with the point of a warm sharp knife. Peel off the paper.

### Chocolate Boxes

First freeze the ice cream in a square mould. Cut chocolate squares (as explained above). Allow the ice cream to soften slightly in the refrigerator before turning out. Gently press the chocolate squares over the sides. Transfer to a foil-covered tray and return to the freezer. When hard, cover with foil.

### Chocolate Cases

Spoon melted chocolate into two thicknesses of paper case and swirl around until the sides and base are evenly coated. If the chocolate lining seems too thin, repeat the process. Turn the case upside down and set aside. When the chocolate has set, peel off the paper. Fill the chocolate cases with small scoops of ice cream. Alternatively, fill with the iced mixture after it has been beaten for the last time, transfer to a foil-covered tray and freeze. Wrap in freezer-proof foil or cling film and pack in a rigid container to protect from damage.

### Chocolate Baskets

Make a Meringue Basket* and roll the sides in melted chocolate. Leave to set.

Alternatively, use a greaseproof paper icing bag with a ¼ inch (15 mm) nozzle. Lightly oil the inside of a small bowl. Fill the bag with melted chocolate and pipe lines of chocolate over the base and a little way up the sides. Pipe another set of lines crossways, to form a basketwork pattern. Pipe a line of chocolate joining the ends together. Leave to set then slip the basket out of the bowl.

### Chocolate Curls

Draw a potato peeler along one long edge of a bar of cold chocolate.

### Chocolate Shapes

Line a tray with silicone paper. Pour melted chocolate on the paper and spread evenly with a palette knife. Leave to set. Cut out shapes using small aspic cutters.

To make triangles, first cut out squares then cut across diagonally with the point of a warm sharp knife.

To make outline shapes, draw the outline on a piece of silicone paper. Using a greaseproof paper icing bag fitted with a fine nozzle and filled with the melted chocolate, pipe out the outline. Leave to set before peeling off the paper. You can use the icing bag to draw more complicated shapes like flowers or butterflies.

### Chocolate Leaves

Brush the surface of a leaf with melted chocolate. When the chocolate has set, peel off the leaf. Carefully mark the veins on the chocolate leaf with the point of a sharp knife.

## Fruits and Herbs

### Caramelized Peels

Remove the peel from one large orange, two small or medium lemons or one grapefruit, taking care not to include any pith. Cut it into fine strips or pretty shapes with a sharp knife or aspic cutters. In a heavy-based saucepan, moisten 9 ounces (250 g) caster sugar with a little water and stir to dissolve. Cook the syrup to a mid-amber colour. Remove from the heat and stir in the peel. After a few seconds remove the peel with a pair of tweezers or small tongs.

### Frosted Decorations

To frost fresh herbs, leaves, flowers, berries and so on, brush them with egg white and dip in caster sugar. Leave to dry.

### Compotes

Fresh or dried fruits, lightly poached in a little water or white wine and sweetened to taste with honey or sugar, are a good accompaniment to iced mixtures.

Remove the stones from fruits such as peaches and plums and cut fruit in half; core and cut in half or slice apples and pears; peel oranges and lemons (removing pith) and divide them into segments or slice them into rounds.

# Techniques

Iced desserts provide the ideal opportunity for using your creative flair. The following are the main techniques involved in creating them.

## Ice Cream Balls

Scoop slightly softened ice cream into ball shapes. Place on a foil-covered tray and freeze. Conceal a surprise in the centre – a liqueur chocolate, for example – to create a real sensation.

**To add liqueurs:** remove the balls from the freezer and allow to soften slightly. Make a thimble-size indentation on top of each and fill with liqueur, allowing it to dribble down the sides as it is served.

# Chequerboard Ices

When cut, these look like Battenberg cakes. Freeze different-flavoured iced mixtures in loaf tins. Then cut lengthways into square 'fingers'. Place contrasting flavours or colours side by side and stack on top of each other to make a chequerboard pattern. Return to the freezer.

# Coating

Freeze the iced mixture in a cylindrical mould or can or form into balls (page 152). Soften slightly if necessary then roll in a coating of crushed macaroons, meringues, biscuits, finely ground nuts, desiccated coconut, chocolate vermicelli or chocolate powder. Place the coated ice cream on a foil-covered tray and return to the freezer until firm.

## Chocolate Coating

Shape the ice cream into balls (page 152), and return to the freezer to harden. Melt the chocolate in a bowl over a pan of hot water. Remove from the heat. Dip each ice cream ball briefly into the chocolate, turning it over with a metal spoon to coat. Drain off the excess chocolate and place on a foil-covered tray. Freeze the balls and cover with foil when hard.

# Layering

This technique combines any number of flavours, textures and ingredients. Use Sponge Fingers*, Langues de Chat* or biscuits such as chocolate chip cookies and brownies. Meringues* can be crushed, or make Meringue Bases* and use them to sandwich an iced mixture – or, conversely, use the ice to sandwich a meringue. Crisp breakfast cereals, crushed biscuits bound with melted butter, chopped nuts, fruit, and any of the simple toppings on page 145 are other alternatives. All these look especially attractive if the dessert is served in tall glasses. Alternate each layer with scoops of the iced mixture or spoonfuls smoothed to form even layers.

## To Layer Ice Cream

The easiest way is to stack the different layers one on top of each other as in Neapolitan ice cream, which is made from strawberry, vanilla and chocolate ice creams. Spoon the iced mixture for the first layer into a loaf or cake tin or any other suitable container. Smooth until even, cover and freeze until firm. Soften the ice for the following layer in the refrigerator for 30 minutes. When the first layer is frozen, spoon on the softened ice cream and freeze. Continue to add layers until the dessert is complete. You can also arrange layers vertically side by side.

A more advanced method is to coat an iced mixture with one of a different flavour. Freeze the main ice in a cylindrical mould or can. Soften the coating layer in the refrigerator for 30 to 45 minutes, depending on the type of mixture. (A rich or mousse-type ice cream needs less time.) Turn out the frozen roll and coat with an outer layer of the softened mixture, using a palette knife with a broad blade. Put on a foil-covered tray and return to the freezer. When frozen, cover with foil. Soften in the refrigerator for 30 minutes before serving.

# Lining a Mould

Whatever the lining, always soften the iced mixture before spooning it into the centre. Then cover the dessert and freeze until firm. Turn out on to a cold plate and leave in the refrigerator to soften for approximately 30 minutes before serving.

## Chopped Nuts, Crushed Biscuits

Line the mould with buttered greaseproof paper. Coat the base and sides evenly with crushed biscuits or finely chopped nuts, pressing them into the buttered paper. Fill with the softened iced mixture.

## Cakes, Biscuits

To line a tin with Genoise Cake*, bake the cake mixture in a Swiss roll tin and allow to cool. Cut a piece to fit the base of the tin, and cut the remaining cake into strips the length and depth of the sides of the tin. Arrange the base piece in place and fit the strips around the sides. Fill with the softened iced mixture. To make a Genoise Cake 'box', use a square tin and fit a 'lid' of cake over the ice before freezing.

To line a charlotte mould with Genoise Cake or Whisked Sponge Cake*, bake the cake mixture in a Swiss roll tin, allow it to cool and cut it in half. Cut one half into 11 even fingers, and the remaining sponge horizontally into two strips, each the depth of the mould. Trim the fingers into triangular shapes that will fit together on the base like the spokes of a wheel. Fit the side strips into position, against the sides of the mould. Each should reach halfway round – trim the strips if necessary. Fill with the iced mixture.

To line a charlotte mould with Langues de Chat* or Sponge Fingers*, place a small circle cut from one biscuit in the centre of the base. Decide how many biscuits are needed to fill the rest of the base, then trim their sides to make triangular petal shapes that will fit together around the central disc. Arrange them in place. Square off the ends of the biscuits for the sides and fit them inside the mould, cut side down and with the curved side facing inwards. Line them up with the biscuits on the base. Fill with the iced mixture and trim the biscuits so they are flush with the filling.

## Ice Cream

Place the container in the freezer and soften the iced mixture which will be used for lining in the refrigerator for 30 minutes. Spoon the ice cream into the cold container and smooth it to an even layer over the base and sides. Cover and freeze until firm.

Soften the ice cream to go in the centre and, when

the lining is frozen, spoon in the softened ice cream. Freeze again.

To make a second lining as well as the 'jacket', smooth softened ice cream to an even layer over the base and sides once the jacket has frozen, then continue as above. An ice cream lining can also be smoothed on to a jacket of sponge or biscuits.

**Encasing or enclosing:** Spread a layer of the lining ice cream over the top of the lined and filled mould.

**Bombe:** Follow the techniques described above, and encase the filling if you do not have a bombe mould.

### Ring moulds

Ices that have been frozen in ring moulds call out to be made into desserts. Turn the ice out on to a serving plate, pile fruit in the centre and serve. If you are filling the centre with another ice cream, pile or spoon the softened mixture into the centre of the turned-out ring and freeze again until firm. Serve immediately.

### Rippling

For a ripple effect, simply fold two softened ices lightly together, or lightly fold a fruit purée or sauce into a softened ice. Proportions are flexible.

### Swirling

Freeze one layer until it is still slightly soft and spoon in a second layer of softened ice cream, gently swirling the first few spoonfuls into the base layer with a spoon. Then complete the second layer, freeze until it is still slightly soft and repeat the process with the third layer.

## Shaped Containers for Freezing

A very simple way of adding an extra special touch to iced mixtures is to make them in different-shaped containers. Decorative blancmange, brioche, tube and Balmoral loaf tins are obvious candidates, but are by no means the only ones. Even a plain loaf tin, a square or round cake tin or a sandwich tin will bring a new look to an iced mixture, whether it is served whole or cut into wedges or slices.

Individual containers such as ramekin dishes, dariole moulds, rum baba tins, cream horn moulds, waxed-paper cups, barquette tins and tartlet tins, especially if they are fluted or patterned, add a personal touch, and are especially attractive when the ices are grouped together on a serving dish.

Clean cylinder-shaped food cans may come in handy to make rolls that can then be sliced into rounds; cover the open ends with freezer-proof foil. Leave dividers in ice-cube trays to make small squares that can be piled up in glasses. Double-thick paper cases can be peeled away just before an ice is served to make a change from a scoop.

A special copper mould is not necessary if you are making a bombe. Similar-shaped desserts can be produced with plastic, foil, earthenware or ceramic freezer-proof pudding basins. You can also use cake or loaf tins or charlotte moulds.

## Turning Out Shaped Ices

Mixtures should be turned out immediately after they are taken out of the freezer and before they are allowed to soften up. Put the serving plate or dish in the freezer or refrigerator well before the iced mixture is brought out. Remove the protective wrapping from the iced mixture and invert the mould on to the serving dish or plate. Then dip a cloth in hot water, wring it out and wrap it round the outside of the mould for 30 seconds if the mould is metallic, a little longer if the mould is earthenware. If the cloth cools, dip it in hot water and wring it out again.

Then hold the plate and mould firmly together, and give them a sharp shake to release the ice before carefully lifting the mould from it. If necessary, smooth any blemishes on the surface of the ice with a warm knife that has been heated in hot water and dried.

If you put the ice back in the freezer, wrap it in freezer-proof foil or cling film and pack it in a rigid container to protect it from damage.

## Serving Dishes

Small, pretty plates, bowls or glasses are especially attractive if the rims are frosted to give a suitably icy appearance. Dip the rims in lemon juice or beaten egg white then caster sugar, and chill. Try serving two or three scoops of ice cream in a tall, slim wine glass or a bright sorbet in a champagne flute – particularly effective if some sparkling wine is poured over to trickle down and collect at the base of the glass.

Edible containers for serving ices include Meringue* or Chocolate Baskets* and Chocolate Cases*, hollowed-out brioche, Choux* balls, éclairs and Coupelles*, Gingersnap Baskets* and Ice Cream Cones*. You can also fill the centres of rum babas or ring doughnuts with small scoops of ice cream.

The hollowed-out shells of oranges, lemons, grapefruit, limes, pears, pineapples, etc., make natural dishes – scallop the edges for a final flourish. Remember to chill them well before filling them with the ice cream. Smaller fruits like peaches and apricots can also be used. Remove the stones and enlarge the cavities then fill them with small scoops of ice cream. Match the flavours or combine contrasting or complementary ones.

# Index

## *Picture acknowledgements*

Photographs: Anthony Blake
Photo Library 48, 51, 122,
129; Ian O'Leary 2, 19, 22,
26-27, 31, 33, 37, 40, 54-55,
58, 62-63, 68, 76-77, 80, 82,
86-87, 91, 97, 100, 104-105,
109, 112, 114, 118-119, 126,
141, 160; Charlie Stebbings
10, 44-45, 94-95, 132-133;
Tessa Traeger 73, 144, 153;
Nedra Westwater 136

Cover photographs: Ian
O'Leary
Paintings: Nicki Kemball

*The end*